DATE DUE

FEB - - 2007			

DEMCO 38-296

BRANDED FOR LIFE

BRANDED FOR LIFE

How Americans Are Brainwashed
by the Brands We Love

Howard J. Blumenthal

emmis

books

For further information, contact the publisher at

 Emmis Books
1700 Madison Road
Cincinnati, OH 45206
books   www.emmisbooks.com

Library of Congress Cataloging-in-Publication Data

Blumenthal, Howard J.
  Branded for life : how Americans are brainwashed by the brands we love
  / by Howard J. Blumenthal.
  p. cm.
  ISBN-13: 978-1-57860-241-4
  ISBN-10: 1-57860-241-6
  1. Brand name products--United States. 2. Product management--United States. 3. Consumers--United States--Attitudes. I. Title.
HD69.B7B58 2005
658.8'343--dc22

                                        2005020878

Cover designed by Tin Box Studio

Interior designed by Donna Collingwood

Distributed by Publishers Group West

TABLE OF CONTENTS

ABOUT THIS BOOK

Branded for Life is a book for the average person who buys a Krispy Kreme doughnut once or twice a week, grabs a twelve-pack of soda cans because it fits nicely on a refrigerator shelf, and takes the kids to Disney World for fun. This book is for people who watch *Queer Eye for the Straight Guy* and don't think much about stereotyping because the performers are entertaining. It is for moms who drive an SUV because the vehicle rides high and there's plenty of room for kids and groceries, and for parents who feel secure because Merrill Lynch is managing the family fortune. It's a book for fans of the Cleveland Indians who proudly wear hats emblazoned with a grinning Indian, and for Atlanta Braves fans who celebrate their team's successes by mimicking the motion of a tomahawk. It's for the students who learn in schools named for famous people like Robert E. Lee, Christopher Columbus, and Martin Luther King. It's a book for people who sleep more soundly beneath a crucifix.

Branded for Life buys into America's love of all sorts of brands. It attempts to explain brand management in terms of business practices and human behavior. Successful brand management is now routinely applied to education, religion, politics, government, parenting, job search, personal health, and many other aspects of our lives.

Just as Kit Kat bars and Calvin Klein underwear are a part of our lives, so, too, are The Weather Channel, the Red Cross, vitamins, MasterCard, a Wharton MBA, Dr. Phil, mad cow disease, and Alcoholics Anonymous. Plugging into a peculiar combination of need, logic, and emotion, and encouraged by media attention, commercial and noncommercial brands provide a deep and fundamental influence in many aspects of our lives.

If you've read the scary stories about Vioxx, or lived through a fight to remove Coca-Cola's vending machines from your local high school, you might wonder about our misplaced trust. Is McDonald's a contributor to obesity? Does Ford knowingly sell dangerous vehicles? Do Oreo Cookies contribute to high cholesterol? How do brand-rich corporations define "acceptable risk?" Answers to these questions would not satisfy a kindergartener's definition of right and wrong.

A closer look raises deeper questions. Did you know that Wal-Mart is now a larger economic power than Belgium, and that it will likely overtake Germany in twenty years? Or that after a company goes global, there is an international body regulating its operations? Do you believe health supplements are tested before you buy them at Wal-Mart or GNC? Why is it so difficult for Americans to eat properly and stay fit? Why do Americans continue to buy 400 billion cigarettes each year despite indisputable evidence that cigarettes cause cancer and death? Why aren't American cigarette manufacturers on a timeline to shut down operations? Are we certain there is no conspiracy between the government, the tobacco industry, and the media that benefits from the tobacco advertising? In our processed world, does anybody remember how a fresh tomato tastes?

We've set the stage. In the next decade or so, school districts will sell naming rights to school buildings. Religions and universities will become branding experts. Your home will be located on a street named for a company or product. You'll save money on car insurance because your car will be wrapped in an advertisement. You'll be peeing into a sponsored public toilet. A dozen corporations will own four out of five U.S. media outlets, each eyeing one another for acquisition in the name of public service. AOL will place a logo on the next Mars probe. You'll probably know a family whose child was named for a product and whose college education is, therefore, free.

We are losing this battle, mainly because we aren't paying attention.

What's at stake? Your personal privacy; your family's health; your children's education; our public spaces; your job and career; and the way that America is perceived by an increasingly skeptical world. And, perhaps, your sense of right and wrong.

As I wrote this book, I kept reminding myself: "I make the decisions that control my life." If you're anything like me, you'll probably find yourself repeating this mantra as well.

Enjoy, stay healthy, and don't let the bullies get you down.

—HB

P.S. Thanks to the many people who answered my questions. Special thanks to those who encouraged me to write this book, especially Oliver Goodenough, Dorothy Curley, Charles Nordlander, Barb Roedler, Richard Hunt, and Stephen Blumenthal.

PRE-TEST

Just for fun, I decided to test myself, some family members, and a few neighbors. Nobody was surprised by the results of these informal tests.

None of us had any trouble explaining what the little purple pill called Nexium was for (treating acid reflux, as we had learned on the commercials). We could all name every current Honda vehicle, including the new pickup truck (the Ridgeline). We easily named a dozen brands of cigarettes and an embarrassing number of flavors sold by Ben & Jerry's.

We were dismissive about our inability to name the bones in our arm, or explain why the sky was blue. My wife knew the name of the first vice president of the United States (John Adams), but couldn't name a single astronaut who went into space during this millennium. We had no idea of how far away the moon might be.

I asked friends to name the cast members of *The West Wing*, and then, more pointedly, to name their own senators and congressmen. Most could name a legislator or two, but easily named both the regular cast members and the occasional characters on the television series. Friends and neighbors correctly identified Bill Gates as the man who ran Microsoft, but were hazy on the names of the men who led the largest corporations (and largest employers) in our local area. They knew how many scoops of raisins were in a box of Kellogg's Raisin Bran, but none could explain what "bran" might be.

We're becoming a little shaky on our hold on real life. If it's on TV, it's part of our lives, and we remember what we have been taught. If it's not part of a marketing message, well, maybe it's not so important after all.

IN BRANDS WE TRUST

L. L. Bean is one of America's most trusted brand names. It's a brand that conjures images of the authentic Maine outdoors, solid New England families, and well-built, reliable products. The story began in 1912, when Leon Leonwood Bean returned home from a camping trip with cold, damp feet. Combining all-American ingenuity and persistence, Bean hired a local cobbler to stitch together leather uppers to the bottoms of a workman's rubber boot. He mailed a flier to fellow outdoorsmen explaining, "The Maine Hunting Shoe is designed by a hunter who has tramped the Maine woods for the last eighteen years. We guarantee them to give perfect satisfaction in every way." Bean sold one hundred boots, but ninety of those boots fell apart. Rather than giving up, Bean refunded every cent, perfected his boots, improved his fliers, and built a business. By 1925, L.L. Bean was distributing a full-size catalog, and by 1934, that catalog was fifty-two pages long. Three years later, L.L. Bean was a million-dollar company.

Nearly a century later, Bean's company still follows his Golden Rule:

"Sell merchandise at a reasonable profit, treat your customers like human beings, and they'll always come back for more."

This is not a mission statement concocted in a boardroom filled with executives who rarely interact with customers. These are words written by a man who thought nothing of customers coming to call, asking questions about fishing lures at his home or business at all hours of the day and night. (Eventually, Bean opened his Freeport, Maine, store twenty-four hours a day, and removed the locks from its doors.)

L.L. Bean is the real thing. The company sells quality merchandise, much of it made in Maine, 90 percent of it marked with the company's own logo, 100 percent of it fully returnable, at any time, if it does not meet the consumer's requirements.

What's more, L.L. Bean is a good corporate citizen. At a local level, employees are encouraged to support and participate in the Freeport Fire Department and Little League. Employees care for an eighteen-mile stretch of the Appalachian Trail. On the company Web site, you will find fifty "conservation partners."

Still, as a direct marketer, L.L. Bean mails millions of printed catalogs, costly to the environment in terms of waste paper, toxic inks, pollution related to trucking, and more. As an apparel manufacturer, L.L. Bean buys from many of the same offshore suppliers as other clothing companies, but most people don't think in terms of fifteen-year-old Asian factory workers when they think about L.L. Bean. Instead, we think about canoes, backpacks for elementary school students, and Adirondack chairs.

L.L. Bean has not acquired its competitors, nor has it become part of a larger company (Lands' End sold out to Sears).

L.L. Bean is not owned or operated by a faceless conglomerate. With just five full retail stores and fifteen outlet stores, and annual sales in excess of $1.4 billion, L.L. Bean is successful, but not out of control.

Trust in Kleenex, and in Kimberly-Clark's Brand Management

L.L. Bean is named for a real person, a man who made and sold boots. Kleenex (more accurately, Kleenex® Brand Tissues) is a name that was made up in 1924 by a Wisconsin paper mill with millions of dollars in assets and a financial need to sell more paper goods.

As the story goes, Kotex was not selling well, so there was a lot of absorbent paper around. To soak up excess inventory, Kleenex tissues were invented.

At first, Kleenex was positioned as a cold cream remover and pitched by pretty screen actresses Jean Harlow and Helen Hayes. In the 1930s, Kleenex sponsored a soap opera (a tearjerker). In the 1940s, Kleenex adopted comic-strip character Little Lulu, who appeared with a box of Kleenex tissues on an enormous Times Square billboard. Today, Kleenex concentrates on Kleenex Cold Care, tissues with lotion for sensitive noses, and other product-line extensions. So completely does Kleenex dominate the tissue category that the very word "Kleenex" is a synonym for the word "tissue."

Kleenex sells tissues in various sizes (pocket packs, travel size) for various consumers (children, those with sensitive skin). Kleenex also sells wet wipes and dinner napkins. Look closely at Cottonelle's logo, and you'll see a tiny Kleenex logo directly above it. Kleenex represents quality, but a close association with toilet paper is inconsistent with the polite Kleenex image, so the Kleenex logo is understated. Kleenex's parent company, Kimberly-Clark, also sells Huggies (baby diapers), Kotex ("pads" for "feminine care"), and Depend (adult diapers), but does not associate these products with the Kleenex name.

When Kleenex tried to sell tissues to men in the 1930s, the company understood that real men did not carry dainty facial tissues: a man-sized nose demanded a handkerchief. For sixty years, Kleenex worked away at male consumers. In the 1990s, the company sold a man-sized, extra-thick tissue. These days, few men carry a handkerchief; instead, we buy Kleenex tissues.

More than 200 billion tissues are sold every year—nearly half of them by Kleenex. At most retail stores, Kleenex tissues cost about a penny a piece. With tens of billions of dollars at stake every year, changing men's habits was clearly worth sixty years of market development.

Kimberly-Clark Professional sells products for the workplace under brand names that consumers never see: Shop-Pro, WypAll, and Kimtech, for example. Kimberly-Clark's health care products are mainly sold to hospitals: medical gloves, surgical drapes and gowns, sterilization wraps, even medical devices. Kimberly-Clark's writing and printing papers are sold under the Neenah Paper brand (in 1872, Kimberly, Clark and Co. was established in Neenah, Wisconsin). What's the connection between all of these products? The company's strategy statement explains: "Our products enhance the hygiene, health and well-being of people everyday, everywhere."

Presumably, the use of the word "our" means "people who work at Kimberly-Clark," but in fact, it doesn't. Most modern corporations are legal entities with the same rights and privileges as individuals (or, superior rights and privileges). When you read the strategy statement and realize that "our" refers to the corporation itself, the sentence becomes a little creepy.

Psychology of Brands: Rational Responses

When you buy L.L. Bean's boots or Kleenex's tissues, you do so because you believe that the boots will keep you dry and that the tissue will stay together even when wet. On the basis of practicality, availability, and reliability, both products are rational purchases. When I stop to think about paying a penny per Kleenex tissue, I suspect the profit in tissues is enormous, but I cannot imagine life without tissues, and I certainly don't want to buy tissues that fall apart when I sneeze, so I rationalize their penny-a-piece pricing. Sometimes our rational responses require confirmation from a trusted friend, relative, or authority figure. I'm comfortable with my wife's confirmation: She buys from L.L. Bean regularly and only buys Kleenex tissue.

When we buy products for purely practical reasons, our brand loyalty can be measured in decades and, often, in generations.

A Brief History of Consumers

To understand a world where Kate Spade handbags, iPods, and LEGO blocks are, more or less, modern necessities, it's helpful to understand the world before television, before radio, before advertising, before big-box retail stores, before brands ...

From the time of ancient Greece, nearly everybody either grew what they needed, bought or traded for it at a local market, or indulged themselves with risky purchases from traveling merchants.

In England and several other countries, the 1700s brought a new class of people who were neither rich nor poor. The new middle class grew quickly; a steadily increasing population established itself as on the rise, cultured, and capable of spending money on finer things. This way of thinking played into the talents of a potter named Josiah Wedgwood. He sold a set of his new ceramic dinnerware to Charlotte, the Queen of England, then made the very same set available under the brand name Queensware for middle-class households that wanted to own the same dishes as the Queen. This bit of 1765 branding is one of the first modern efforts on record (in fact, Wedgwood still sells Queensware).

> When we buy products for purely practical reasons, our brand loyalty can be measured in decades and, often, in generations.

At the time, the United States was a rural society where goods were grown, made, or purchased from the local general store or from traders. Upscale households imported quality handmade goods from England, France, and even China. The Brooks brothers operated a New York City store that developed a national reputation for ready-made suits (previously, suits were custom-made, requiring weeks for delivery). This approach was exceptional; before the Civil War, making anything in a large quantity wasn't the American way.

During the spring and summer of 1861, everything changed with the start of the Civil War. Within weeks, tens of thousands of men needed food, clothing, shelter, transport, and arms. As the Union and the Confederacy procured, businessmen prospered. And they procured just about everything under the sun. For example, in an effort to keep bored soldiers (many of whom were teenaged boys) entertained (and out of mischief) during idle times, the Army bought cigarettes, books, and games. One supplier of pocket-sized games was Milton Bradley, a Massachusetts printer.[1] On a considerably larger scale, bankers provided the funds necessary to finance the war. When the war ended, these banks built railroads, mines, and, of course, larger banks, forming the foundation of modern American industry.

The Civil War allowed the United States to reinvent itself. After the war, as factories reopened and the transportation system was improved, more people moved to the cities. Before the war, about thirty million people lived in the United States and its territories, and about two million citizens lived in U.S. cities. By 1870, ten million people lived in American cities, and by 1890, a third of all Americans lived in cities, some twenty million in all. By the turn of the century, fifteen cities boasted populations of a quarter-million or more, and one in three Americans lived in cities.

Growing food was impractical; city dwellers bought food from stores, and if they had the money, ate at the occasional restaurant (an uncommon situation at the time). They had money in their pockets, and they were willing to spend it. A new type of citizen emerged, one who purchased goods and services not only because he or she *needed* them, but because he or she *wanted* them. Customers no longer knew the cobbler who made their boots or the farmer who milled their grain. Instead, the customer became loyal to a name on a box or a bottle.[2]

So much changed—and so quickly! There were immigrants everywhere—waves of people whose queer habits, foods, ways of dressing and speaking, and conflicted desire to/not to assimilate kept everyone confused, a little frightened, and often amused. There were all sorts of new inventions. Electricity was replacing gaslights. Automobiles were beginning to appear on streets intended for horses and carriages. New trains seemed to go just about everywhere—small ones for local travel, larger trains to travel from one city to another. It was possible to travel from the Atlantic to the Pacific coast of North America by train. During just ten years in the 1880s, seventy thousand miles of new track were laid[3]—almost twice the length of today's U.S. interstate highway system[4].

Along with the middle class and the Civil War, these trains enabled brands and today's consumer culture.

For the first time, it was possible to move people and goods over long distances. A shared national culture emerged. People in Indiana began to see the world in the same way as people in Massachusetts or Maryland. Trains carried traveling salesmen, whose regional product lines began to show up in general stores and dry goods stores (clothing stores, today). The way railroad man Fred Harvey figured it, those salespeople and other travelers deserved a clean place to eat, so he developed our first chain restaurants. Western travelers on the Atchison, Topeka & Santa Fe Railway were stunned to find first-class food, service, and a clean dining room. Even better, each Harvey House was staffed by pretty, efficient, unmarried Harvey Girls[5]. The railroads also made it possible for circuses and traveling shows to crisscross the country with the nation's first show-business celebrities. By the 1880s, most Americans knew all about Buffalo Bill Cody and his "celebrated shot," Miss Annie Oakley.

For those living in cities, the railroads brought all manner of goods to newly built department stores. Here, the new consumer culture became high art. Around 1865, A.T. Stewart opened a palace with eight floors, where he sold dresses, rugs, sporting goods, toys, and more. His store was the start of a Ladies Mile of fashionable shopping in New York City. R.H. Macy (whose own star tattoo remains the company's logo) got started with a neighborhood collection of specialty stores that he consolidated in 1902 as "The World's Largest Store" on Herald Square[6]. John Wanamaker opened a huge market in Philadelphia where he sold every type of merchandise. Successful men's clothier Joseph Hudson opened a huge Detroit store—the foundation of today's Target retailing empire. The Mormons opened their own department store in Salt Lake City because they did not want to be at the mercy of non-Mormons running railroads and wagon trains. ZCMI[7] became a fourteen-store chain, now known as Meier & Frank. In Denver, it was failed miner David May's store, later the basis for the May Company (Filene's, Lord & Taylor, Meier & Frank, Marshall Field's, Kaufmann's, etc.), which has recently merged with Federated (Macy's, Bloomingdale's, etc.).

In downtown districts and in many small towns, another new type of store emerged: the five-and-dime. Unlike the old-style variety stores, and like the new department stores, the new chain stores offered fixed prices (no need to haggle) and discounts. By the early 1900s, the likes of F.W. Woolworth, S.S. Kresge, J.G. McCrory, and J.J. Newberry challenged local stores. Selling goldfish, hairbrushes, toys, underwear, sheet music, gifts, magazines, and kitchen supplies, they were the Wal-Mart of their time. Chain drug stores, cigar stores, and eventually chain gasoline dealers followed.

In just one lifetime—about sixty years—everything had changed. While consumers were distracted by merchandise from the four corners of the world, businessmen worked in the background, growing rich by controlling commodities, finance, and new industries. Working in a hidden world devoid of organized media, railroad tycoons and steel magnates (steel, to build the railroads) prospered. Trusts monopolized sugar, salt, coffee, coal, oil, and other industries. By 1900, corporations and trusts were so powerful that they were able to deflect just about any government attempt related to oversight or trustbusting.

In 1860, there were almost no corporations and almost no national companies in America. There were no brands, except perhaps the deepest roots of a company that would grow decades later. Even the idea of a large retail store was considered inspired thinking, risky, perhaps not the smartest way for a merchant to invest his money. By 1900, there were hundreds of well-known brands, including Crisco, Kellogg's Corn Flakes, Post Grape-Nuts, Shredded Wheat, Ivory Soap, Coca-Cola, Dr Pepper, Dodge, Ford, Olds-mobile, Cadillac, Welch's Grape Juice, Juicy Fruit Gum, and more. By that time, progress and the consumer were solidly under the control of corporations.

By 1925, more than half of Americans lived in cities and were freely spending their money on a wide range of consumer goods at downtown department stores and neighborhood drug stores or cigar stores. They were reading magazines filled with advertisements, going to the movies weekly, and beginning to listen to commercials on the radio. It wasn't long before brands were sponsoring radio programs. By the late 1930s, millions of Americans were buying Pepsodent toothpaste because Bob Hope told them to do just that.

Social Conditioning

As much as we love and admire celebrities, most of us would like to believe that we make our decisions based upon reasonable evidence and that we're unaffected by irrational or unreasonable persuasion. We assume that we decide how to spend our money and live our lives. In fact, most of our purchase decisions are based upon social conditioning, not logic or practical need. As marketers know so well, contemporary marketing is based upon aspiration—the person the customer aspires to be.

"Name brands did more than create dominant companies. They also served to democratize America at a time when social differences were extreme."[8]

One of the most powerful aspirations in U.S. history has long been an immigrant's desire to become a "real American." As older family members struggled to hold on to traditions while establishing themselves in the new land, their children struggled to assimilate, to modernize their lives, to discard traditional family foods, hairstyles, facial hair, even their language. When Maria came home with Levi's in place of her dress, or Shlomo came home with nonkosher Chinese food, the shouting and colorful language could be heard out into the street. Parents scolded. Neighbors gossiped. The leveling influence? Coca-Cola. Family pictures taken with Kodak cameras. Weekend outings in a used Chevrolet. A backyard barbecue cooled down with Rheingold or Pabst Blue Ribbon Beer. Johnny Carson and *The Beverly Hillbillies*. The Beatles, Bob Dylan, and the jingles heard between the songs on Musicradio 77-WABC. The Vietnam War: televised violence hosted by Walter Cronkite every night on TV. *All in the Family*, *Seinfeld*, and *Friends*. For many immigrants, these were the sources of information about American life.

In fact, many of our decisions are based upon social conditioning. This peculiar phenomenon affects our choice of foods, vacations, homes, children's names, and more. With expendable income, consumers began to think of shopping and product choice as a highly personal decision that helped to tell the world who they were and who they wanted to become.

One recent example, circa 2005: Michael, then a high school senior, struggled with his college decision. He felt that the value of a familiar brand name on his resume would be worth as much as the education itself. He enrolled at the relatively unknown Keene State College, but remained so skeptical that he continued to search for better-known schools throughout his freshman year. If he transfers (still an open issue), one of the most important reasons will be the new institution's brand name.

And another: Fred, an entrepreneur whose sales training business made him rich, looked forward to the day when he would replace his Infiniti with a Jaguar. Fred told me that he had always envisioned himself as successful, wealthy enough to afford a car like a Jaguar. For Fred, ownership of a

Jaguar symbolized his arrival. Recently, Fred e-mailed, "I have since set and achieved another goal and so just bought the XJ8 Vanden Plas long wheelbase to celebrate."

Brands as Part of American Culture

One of the great adventures in social conditioning involves one of the best-selling items in every supermarket: breakfast cereal. One in two American breakfasts are poured from boxes of dried, processed grains (sprayed with sugar and nutrients). Americans buy 3.6 billion boxes of cereal every year. The only supermarket items more popular than cereal are soda and milk.

The average American eats 160 bowls of cereal each year.

Aptly, this story begins with a tummy ache. For decades in the 1800s, unimaginably horrid eating habits and lax sanitation provided many Americans with gaseous stomach cramps. Any relief was welcome. In the late 1800s, the wealthy found relief by visiting health spas. One popular spa was the Western Health Reform Institute in Battle Creek, Michigan. The spa encouraged walks in the fresh air, exercise, lower-intestinal health, multiple daily enemas, plus whole grains and bran for a more complete digestive process.

Along with many health food specialties (stewed prunes, lemon oatmeal gruel, wheat gluten mash[9]), the Institute had always made and served its own cereals.

Under the leadership of Dr. John Henry Kellogg, Battle Creek Sanitarium became one of the largest, richest, and most influential hospitals in the United States (Kellogg was a promoter of the highest order; his guests included many celebrities, including Thomas Edison, Presidents Taft and Coolidge, Eleanor Roosevelt, George Bernard Shaw, and many dignitaries from Europe and Asia.)

In the 1880s and 1890s, Dr. Kellogg and his brother Will sold healthy alternative foods to former patients by mail and to consumers in a small number of retail stores. After a happy accident taught Will how to flake grains of wheat, Will figured out how to make corn flakes. By 1906, with some sugar added, he was selling corn flakes as The Battle Creek Co. (later renamed Kellogg Company). His brother John hated the idea, and tried everything possible—including temper tantrums and legal action—to stop Will's commercial venture. Will persevered, succeeded, and was soon copied by dozens of rival corn flakes, including a company founded by a former client, C.W. Post, who established his rival cereal company in Battle Creek.

Before corn flakes, a typical American breakfast consisted of milk, bread, butter, and maybe some cheese or salt pork. In warmer weather, some fruit might have been added. Our romantic vision of a farm fresh breakfast is, mostly, fantasy. Bread was often a day or two old, milk was either fresh from the cow or sour (no refrigeration), cheese was warmish, and the salt pork was left over from the night before. In comparison with the alternative, a healthful box of slightly sugary, slightly stale grains became wildly popular.

The mystery: Why has dry cereal remained popular when fresh milk, fresh bread, fresh cheese, and other tastier alternatives are now widely available?

The answer lies in family traditions and strong social conditioning, encouraged by effective brand management and promotion.

By 1933, Kellogg's figured out how to use radio to sell cereal. The poor-selling Rice Krispies brand became a top seller with the introduction of Snap, Crackle, and Pop, first as radio voices, then as stars of the first commercial shown in movie theaters. General Mills' Wheaties was a flop until the brand sponsored a daily radio series featuring Skippy, a troubled kid (James Thurber wrote, "The kids loved 'Skippy,' and Wheaties became a household word... You could get all the paraphernalia (a code book, instructions for a secret handshake) by sending in box tops ... and a signed statement from your mother that you ate Wheaties twice a day."[10] General Mills' Cheerios became popular as sponsor of radio's *The Lone Ranger*, as "eleven million kids purchased Cheerios boxes printed with Lone Ranger masks..."[11] These radio advertisements and promotions made cereal a standard item on the American breakfast table.

And then came television. By the 1950s, sugary cereal and children's entertainment were inseparable. In 1958, Hanna-Barbera's first hit series, *The Huckleberry Hound Show*, was filled with cartoon characters pitching their favorite Kellogg's cereals. By 1963, those cartoon characters were all over Kellogg's boxes, too. Decades later, you can still buy Kellogg's Cocoa Pebbles, based on Hanna-Barbera's first prime-time series, *The Flintstones*. When Jay Ward pitched his *Rocky & His Friends* to General Mills, the company not only bought sponsorship, it bought everything associated with the show, including the characters. Take a careful look at Cap'n Crunch. He, too, is a Jay Ward character, as were two 1965 icons, Quisp and Quake (these remain popular among cereal box and memorabilia collectors).

Still, nobody does it like Disney. The beloved children's media company has been active in the sugared cereal business since 1935, when a licensing agent bought merchandising rights to the characters for a minimum of fifty thousand dollars per year—and sold over thirty-five million dollars in Disney merchandise. According to several sources, these licensing revenues kept the Disney company alive during the company's darker times. The current Disney-Kellogg's deal is represented on store shelves by Timon & Pumbaa (Mud & Bugs), *Finding Nemo*, Hunny B's (based on Winnie the Pooh), Mickey Mouse (Mickey's Magix).

Nickelodeon also sells breakfast cereal: Green Slime. Nintendo sells Pokemon cereal. Kellogg's sells Scooby-Doo Berry Bones and *Star Wars* Tiger Power.

And if the cereal companies didn't capture your attention with cartoon characters, major sports stars have either appeared on boxes or pitched Wheaties, the Breakfast of Champions (early on, sports stars were paid with cereal, not money). From Lou Gehrig to Tiger Woods, Michael Jordan to the 1998 U.S. Gold Medal Women's Hockey Olympic team, hundreds of major sports stars have endorsed Wheaties, often with their faces on Wheaties boxes.

Is Wheaties an especially healthy food? How does Wheaties compare, say, to Cap'n Crunch, or to a slice of fresh bread? A visit to the official Wheaties site is a bit evasive: there is a nutrition tab, but no specific nutritional information is provided. Instead, there's some marketing-speak about "The Power of Whole Grain," as well as "B-Vitamins—Key for Energy Metabolism" and "Fiber—For Good Health."

The "Breakfast of Champions" could replace its slogan with "Almost as Healthy as a Slice of Fresh Whole Grain Bread." This more straightforward statement would not, however, suggest that eating Wheaties would cause you to play hockey like Wayne Gretzky or cycle with the power and grace of Lance Armstrong. (You didn't believe that anyway, did you?)

What's the future of boxed, dried, heavily processed cereal sprayed with nutrients and sugar? For the answer, visit any college dining commons and you'll find just a few foods available twenty-four/seven: peanut butter, jelly, and a stack of boxes filled with Corn Flakes, Rice Krispies, Cheerios, Apple Jacks, and Froot Loops. For a generation that learned to count with the help of Cheerios board books, this makes all the sense in the world.

Buying What You Want

During the first six months of 2005, Apple Computer shipped over eleven million iPods, an astonishing statistic for a consumer product costing over $100 (and, often, over $250). If you listen closely, you'll notice the quality of the sound from even a $399 iPod is usually inferior to the sound available on a $39 portable CD player. What we want is convenience and style; sonic fidelity is secondary[12].

Similarly, women can buy a very nice handbag at a department store (or an outlet store) for less than $50. Still, a Kate Spade Nylon Clare Classic bag for $155 can be irresistible. If you doubt that you're caught up in anything but an "I want that" consumerism, count the number of pairs of shoes at the bottom of your closet.

Track your own purchases for a week or a month. The vast majority of those purchases probably aren't basic necessities. Instead, they are tangible answers to what seem to be today's most important questions:

Will the purchase make me feel better (now)?

Will the purchase be fun to own?

Will the purchase improve my life?

In today's world, emotional conditioning is the whole ball game, the fantasy of brands, the pageant of what could be, the basis of modern society (where we don't actually need much, but it's fun to buy stuff anyway). One level beyond social conditioning and two beyond rational purchasing, emotional conditioning is the secret ingredient for music and movie marketing as well as fashion, cosmetics, and diet and fitness products and services. If it's associated with contemporary culture and promoted in the media, look beneath the very thin veneer and you'll find a hive of marketers who press your buttons through emotional conditioning.

"Performance. Prestige. Passion for Innovation." Those are the words that sell five-thousand-dollar Breitling wristwatches to men who like to pretend they're aviators.

Luxury automobiles are marketed this way, as they emphasize the new life you will experience in the State of Independence (SAAB), or the Sheer Driving Pleasure (BMW) that you may experience in a machine based upon Perfection, Re-perfected (Lexus). The names of popular SUVs reflect the commercial viability of aspirational marketing. Envision yourself behind the wheel of an Escape, Excursion, Expedition, Yukon, Everest, TrailBlazer, Pathfinder, Passport, Aviator, Armada, Rendezvous, Land Cruiser, Ascender, Explorer, Navigator, or Highlander.

When a professional musician insists upon a Bösendorfer or Steinway piano, the instrument becomes part of the musician. The astonishing photographer Henri Cartier-Bresson used a Leica camera, and inspired many amateurs and professionals to do the same. (Nothing is more depressing to the owner of a $3,500 camera than a photographer who produces exquisite work with crummy, old gear.) Upscale hobbyists become deeply involved in the mythology of their brands, whether it's a Leica M-series camera ($3,295 for the camera body, plus $1,000 or more for each interchangeable lens), or Winsor & Newton Series 7 Kolinsky Sable watercolor brushes (size ten costs more than $100). In many cases, an old prejudice (a.k.a. emotional conditioning) favors old-world European craftsmanship.

While professional chefs are probably less picky, home chefs obsess about whether to invest in a Sub-Zero refrigerator or a Viking Range. Poke around on the Web and you'll find message boards comparing the virtues of French (Sabatier) vs. German (Henckels, Wüsthof) cutlery. Contributors would like to believe that professional chefs concern themselves with similar issues. In fact, fine chefs insist upon quality tools but obsess about the quality of the ingredients (not the toys).

For those without obsessive hobbies, there are practical items whose brand and physical characteristics suggest that we are buying the best in class. One example is Nalgene bottles—"Having a Nalgene bottle clipped to your backpack became a membership badge of differentiation for the eco-friendly, health-conscious youth crowd."[13] With the simple act of going into the Kate Spade shop on M Street in Georgetown, shopping becomes a form of self-expression. Visiting a Land Rover dealership, knowing you can afford to buy a $75,000 Range Rover, running your fingers along the fine leather, caressing the perfect fit and finish of a truly superior vehicle, well, that's a statement in itself.

Advertisements and friends encourage us to shop, to treat ourselves well. As a result, we spend more money on shoes, jewelry, and watches (a total of eighty billion dollars per year) than we do on higher education (sixty billion dollars).

People define themselves through shopping: how they shop, where they shop, what they buy. What's more, shopping is a source of personal power: In a world where many people feel powerless over other people's behavior and world events, shopping provides power over things. From here, it's a short conceptual leap to elaborate shopping palaces, from E.J. Stewart's fancy New York City store from a century ago to the enormous King of Prussia double-sized mall outside Philadelphia to the new eight-hundred-acre DestiNY shopping extravaganza planned for Syracuse, New York.

Our Relationships with Brands

To a great extent, our relationships with contemporary brands are emotional, based more deeply in beliefs than in logical, rational thought.

Betty Crocker was invented by a General Mills predecessor in 1926. A year later, she was hosting her own radio show, and by 1932, forty home economists were employed to answer her mail. In the 1950s, Betty Crocker authored a cookbook that has sold in the millions. Many consumer products bear her name and her personal logo. She is among the best-known names in home cooking, the model of an American homemaker, a woman whose portrait has been redrawn seven times since 1936 to better represent the contemporary woman. Betty Crocker is not a real person and never has been.

We understand that the Lucky Charms leprechaun is just a cartoon character, the work of a skilled artist, an animator, and a voice actor. At an emotional level, the little guy makes the cereal fun, so we buy. In 1975–76, when Waldo the Wizard replaced Lucky the Leprechaun, the cereal's sales plummeted. When the leprechaun returned, so did the sales.

Endowing inanimate objects with human qualities (anthromorphizing) has been common practice in nearly all societies for thousands of years. Why? To facilitate interaction with the nonmaterial world.

In advertising, characters make an emotional connection with the consumer: Chiquita Banana, Aunt Jemima, the Michelin Man, the Green Giant, Betty Crocker, Tony the Tiger, Rastus (the Black chef who appears on Cream of Wheat), Pillsbury Doughboy, Choo-Choo Charlie (Good & Plenty candy), Charlie the Tuna, and Mr. Goodwrench.

At a logical level, we know that Crayola crayons are just wax and pigment. Crayola claims to be one of the top twenty most-recognized smells in the world. Crayola also claims to be recognized by 99 percent of Americans. Our emotional, multisensory connection to Crayola runs deep—it links personal memories of our own childhood with the pleasure of watching your own child create a yellow sun, a blue sky, and green trees. Every year, hundreds of thousands of people visit Crayola's factory in Easton, Pennsylvania, to experience the brand in a more direct way.[14]

When an actor becomes popular as a television or movie character, many viewers assume that the actor and the character are one and the same. When we envision Luke Skywalker, for example, we envision Mark Hamill at age twenty-six. It's almost inconceivable that Princess Leia's alter ego, fifty-year-old actress Carrie Fisher, no longer occupies the svelte body of a twenty-two-year-old woman. Performers who appear weekly, or even daily, on popular television series are invited into our homes more often than our closest friends and relatives. Scary but true: I'm pretty sure I spent more time with Jerry Seinfeld (who was in my house more than one hundred times last year) than with my own brother (about five times). Characters deliver on their promises, so they are invited back time and again—with a caveat. Mark Hamill must always wear his Luke Skywalker garb, Carrie Fisher must always look and act like she's twenty-two, and Jerry Seinfeld must always be an unhappy single New Yorker surrounded by selfish friends. Otherwise, no sale.

> To a great extent, our relationships with contemporary brands are emotional, based more deeply in beliefs than in logical, rational thought.

Extreme Brand Relationships

From www.starbuckseverywhere.com: "Hello, my name is Winter, and since 1997 I've been trying to visit every Starbucks in the world. Why? Well, I'm not obsessed, if that's what you're thinking, though I do consider myself something of an obsessed ~~maniac~~ enthusiast. No, my reason is simply to do something completely different."

Winter has visited (and drunk coffee in) about 4,500 Starbucks stores. On average, Starbucks opens more than ten new stores per week, but that doesn't much concern Winter, who says, "I can always visit them faster than they can build them.

Why does he do it? I asked him. Here's what he told me: "Originally, it really was to do something different. Since then, some of the things that have come out of my mission help to provide additional motivation, like the love of traveling, photography, celebrity, and the opportunities the attention has gotten me."[15]

To varying degrees, we are involved in obsessive brand relationships. I am most comfortable working on an Apple computer and find myself deeply unhappy when working on a Windows computer instead. On a rational level, I know my behavior is childish because both machines do the same job, but I have now invested thousands of dollars so that my entire family can be as happy as I am; they all work on Macintosh computers as well. Since 1983, I have owned seven Apple computers: the SE, Duo 210, LC,

PowerPC, Quadra 6100, blue G3, and silver G4, and I had no trouble recalling these name and model numbers from memory.

It's the same feeling that I get when I drive a car other than a Honda. Every few years, my wife watches me go through the ritual of shopping for a car that's not a Honda. I test drive and compare prices on comparable models made by Toyota, Volvo, and, if I'm feeling wealthy, perhaps a Land Rover or a BMW. Once I get over this ritual, she comes with me to the Honda dealer and I buy an Accord. We bought our first Accord in 1979. I am now driving our fifth Accord, a V6 model that my seventeen-year-old son "likes a lot."

One brand obsession is directly related to the writing of *Branded for Life*: Moleskine notebooks. Creative people seem to adore Moleskine notebooks, but many of us have also concocted a mythology around these oilcloth-covered blank books. Apparently, similar notebooks and sketchbooks were used by Hemingway, Van Gogh, and Matisse. For me, and for others, starting to write or draw in a Moleskine carries awesome responsibility to do the job well; I kept my Moleskines empty until I had a project worthy of their heritage. Others do the same. Hoping that *Branded for Life* would sell well, and that I would do good work as an author, I kept all of my research notes in three Moleskine notebooks.

Is this obsessive behavior? Hey, I'm not filling every available kitchen cupboard with collectible Pez dispensers or Beanie Babies (tags intact), but I do feel a strong attraction to my brands. I trust them, and they have not disappointed me. I find it difficult to walk past an Apple Store without spending a few minutes inside.

While I'm pretty sure I'm within the range of normal behavior, I do recognize the occasional obsession in myself and I am sometimes concerned about the obsessions that I see in others. For high school students who regularly contribute to an Abercrombie & Fitch or Hollister blog, those brands become a lifestyle statement, a path toward self-realization. The same might be said for over-the-top sports fans who paint their faces, chests, and bellies with team colors and dye their hair to match. Or former *Wall Street Journal* reporter Steve Sansweet, who owns the largest private collection of *Star Wars* memorabilia ("outside of George [Lucas], of course," he says). To store the collection, Sansweet added two floors to his house, but after he purchased several prop vehicles used in the films, he moved it all to a five-thousand-square-foot barn. He has written a dozen books about *Star Wars*. Eventually, Sansweet left his job as an award-winning journalist to join Lucasfilm's marketing department, but, he told *The New York Times* for its May 15, 2005, profile of his obsession, "I'm out there at Midnight Madness at Toys 'R' Us and 48 Hours of the Force at Wal-Mart just like everybody else ... Buying toys!"

What, Exactly, Is a Brand?

There are hundreds of books about brands, and each one offers a confusing definition. The best one I've found came from Michael Levine, writing in *A Branded World*:

"Branding is ... the creation and development of a specific identity for a company, product, commodity group, or person. It is carefully designed to present qualities that ... will be attractive to the public, and it is meant to be developed and perpetrated for the long haul."

Many brands are products: Grey Goose vodka, MINI Cooper automobiles, AJAX laundry detergents, or Nokia cellular telephones. Some brands are services: Google.com, American Express, UPS, Merrill-Lynch. Others are media properties: Spider-Man, *Cold Case*, *The Matrix*, Comedy Central. In the 1960s, the Motown Sound was a distinctive brand and the birthplace of musical acts that became brands in their own right, such as The Supremes and The Temptations. Often, well-known personalities become brands: The Beatles, Bruce Springsteen, and politicians Bill and Hillary Clinton are examples. Places have learned to market themselves as brands: Disney World, Colonial Williamsburg, and the Bahamas among them. Increasingly, groups and institutions are learning the value and impact of branding. To compete more effectively, many colleges and universities have invested heavily in updating their brands. Greenpeace, the U.S. Marines, and Republicans are clearly defined brands managed with many of the same formal branding structures as Ivory Soap or *The Simpsons*.

How Brands Should Behave

Here are my expectations. Chances are, they are your expectations, too.

The brand will be honest with me and will not intentionally withhold information.

The brand will provide consistent quality and reliable performance for a reasonable period of time.

If the brand's product or service is unsatisfactory, the brand will do the right thing to correct the problem.

The brand will not harm me. It will not place me or others in danger.

Endnotes

1 Once America's second-largest game and puzzle publisher (Parker Brothers was first), Milton Bradley (Parker Brother) is no longer a stand-alone company. Both are brands owned by the Hasbro empire. Other Hasbro brand assets include: Beyblade, Boggle, Bratz, Candy Land, Clue, Dungeons & Dragons, G.I. Joe, Monopoly, Mousetrap, Mr. Potato Head, Nerf, Pictionary, Play-Doh, Playskool, RISK, Rubik's Cube, Scrabble, Super Soaker, Tinkertoy, Tonka, and Trivial Pursuit.

2 "A Brand New You," by W. Eric Martin, *Psychology Today*, September–October 2003.

3 http://scriptorium.lib.duke.edu/adaccess/rails-history.html

4 http://www.publicpurpose.com/freeway1.htm

5 For a fanciful history of this distant world, watch *The Harvey Girls*, an MGM musical starring Judy Garland. (Look for young Angela Lansbury as a dance hall gal.)

6 Seen annually on *The Macy's Thanksgiving Day Parade,* the site was previously used by Koster & Bial's Music Hall. In 1893, Thomas Edison debuted the Vitascope there, making Koster's (arguably) the first movie theater. Next time you walk by, notice the historical landmark sign.

7 Zions Cooperative Mercantile Institution

8 *The All-Consuming Century: Why Commercialism Won in Modern America* by Gary Cross, p. 31.

9 *Cerealizing America* by Scott Bruce and Bill Crawford, p. 19.

10 *Cerealizing America* by Scott Bruce and Bill Crawford, pp. 78-79.

11 *Cerealizing America* by Scott Bruce and Bill Crawford, p. 99.

12 Geektalk: If the sampling rate is increased, music recorded on the iPod can sound as good as any CD. Increased sampling requires more memory, which means fewer songs per iPod, an unacceptable compromise for many iPod users.

13 http://www.brandchannel.com/features_profile.asp?pr_id=219

14 Along with its sister brand, Silly Putty, Crayola is now owned by Hallmark, a $4 billion company which is also the world's largest producer and distributor of television movies and miniseries.

15 E-mail from Winter, May 16, 2005.

THE MAGIC OF BELIEVING

Susan Fournier, a Harvard Business School professor, described three women with deep relationships to consumer brands, mapped out their lifestyles, and explored their personal "brandscapes." [1]

At the time of Fournier's research, Jean was a fifty-nine-year-old woman who strongly valued family, independence, and hard work. A second-generation Italian American, Jean worked over sixty hours a week in a local blue-collar bar. Jean knew everyone in town and apparently lent a fair number of them money she knew she'd never collect.

Jean took her cooking seriously. Her spaghetti sauce was an extension of herself: "It's like your trademark!" To make that sauce, Jean wholeheartedly relied upon Pastene canned tomatoes (a local Boston brand), Contadina tomato paste, Bertolli olive oil, Progresso breadcrumbs, and her Revereware pans. Jean was convinced that these were the very best products available. How did she know? "You ask me how I know [Pastene] is good tomatoes? I've been making the sauce for forty years and you ask me how I know?" As for the pots, it's the "best I ever had … The sauce doesn't burn in it, or stick to the bottom like it used to do in my old one." Don't bother asking Jean when she last explored alternative products; these products are her life, and she's not changing for anyone. She's the same way about cleaning products: Windex: "No streaks." Bounty: "I buy them by the case." Zest soap: "No tub ring." Spic n' Span: "No residue."

The article went on to describe Vicki. She went through her "Ivory Soap phase" at age fifteen, hoping the combination of Ivory soap, shampoo, and conditioner would send boys her signal of beauty and purity. At the time of the article, Vicki was twenty-three and talked about defining herself by the ways she felt and smelled when using Soft n' Dry ("smells like Vicki"), wearing floral underwear from Victoria's Secret, and washing her hair with floral-scented shampoos. Brands that survived Vicki's elaborate testing acquired an equally elaborate performance mythology. Elevating a mere product to magical status defined the ultimate Vicki. Although she did not consider herself physically beautiful, Vicki used products to express her femininity. Vicki *knew* that others understood the signals that products sent. She explained, "When you are loyal to a brand, you stick by it. Sort of like having a backbone."

I'm Loving It ...

Jean and Vicki were not exceptional. Strong feelings about particular brands and products are extremely common. Strong beliefs about attributes associated with those brands are no less common.

For decades, the cool, calming effects of cigarettes were a stylish addition to a sophisticated person's lifestyle. Ford's Mustang was the ultimate expression of 1967 style. When computers became a part of corporate life, the saying was "nobody ever got fired for buying IBM." Today's parents and children anticipate family vacations to Disney World and cannot imagine a world without Nickelodeon. We love our SUVs and our DVDs. We rely upon Yahoo!, Google, eBay, and Amazon. Life without Starbucks or Levi's is unthinkable. Who among us can get through a year without Ben & Jerry's? No Beatles or Dr. Seuss or Harry Potter? No way! We love our brands for all the practical value, convenience, and pleasure they provide. This passionate connection was the basis of McDonald's 2004–2005 win-back campaign with the simple tagline: "I'm Loving It."

Visit any Ben & Jerry's scoop shop and you'll find yourself in a cartoon world of fun where giant cow spots and bright colors remind you of how whimsical life can be, how you really are a child at heart, and how completely ice cream fits into that experience. Watch daytime television and you'll be reminded that mom can be a family hero when she uses Tide to get stains out of clothes. Want to be a real man? Don't just buy a pickup truck. Buy a Dodge Truck because it's Ram Tough. Dodge's color choices, the style of rough animation, the voice, the music, every creative decision is tested, refined, designed to make real men believe that Ram Tough is more powerful than Viagra. How does Chevy compete? By calling its largest truck an Avalanche.

On the surface, this is all nonsense. Dig deeper and you'll encounter the remarkable power of mythology. When marketers control mythmaking and storytelling, details are left out or modified. Stories are truncated, simplified, told without context, presented as impressions whose cumulative impact really does affect our behavior. We confuse entertainment and marketing so the two become one. Does this craziness work? If it didn't work, why would Procter & Gamble spend over $3 billion a year on advertising? And why would the combination of GM, Ford, DaimlerChrysler, and Toyota (four of the top ten U.S. advertisers) spend $12 billion a year to tell us their stories? Decades of study and analysis allow every corporate penny spent to directly correlate with an anticipated sales yield.

These companies are not advertising in order to provide clear, straightforward information for rational product comparisons. People don't buy on the basis of facts. Instead, people—you and me, not some other people—buy on the basis of our beliefs.

The secret of branding is the manipulation of belief systems. If you understand belief systems and how they work, you will understand what's really at stake when we're branded for life.

Strong Beliefs

Caught in a matrix of values and attitudes, a belief system is a deep-down feeling, a sense of correctness, the result of nature, nurture, observation, upbringing, attraction and repulsion of good and evil, a desire to express individuality, and a need a belong to one or more groups. This is complicated stuff, more so because people don't always behave in a manner consistent with their beliefs. Some beliefs are rational and easily understood; others can be decoded only with therapy; most are somewhere in between.

One fundamental American belief is the individual's right to choose. For decades, this belief has been the basis of the cigarette industry's defensive strategy. The successful strategy is now being used by the food industry to fight off obesity claims. It goes like this: Industry can manufacture and distribute just about anything without concern for public health or liability, but it's up to consumers to decide whether to buy/

> The secret of branding is the manipulation of belief systems. If you understand belief systems and how they work, you will understand what's really at stake when we're branded for life.

use/smoke/eat the products. The right to choose applies to cigarettes, cigars, Big Macs, SUVs lacking automobile safety features, violence in media, and guns. It does not apply to marijuana or other unbranded recreational drugs, nor does it apply to overt sexuality in advertising, curriculum taught to high school students, or to office software used to write documents or prepare spreadsheets. (If at least one of the items in this paragraph made you uncomfortable, your belief in an individual's right to choose is in good operating order.)

What drives beliefs? The quick-and-easy answer is "the best available information." What's "best"? Well, most "credible." Here's a slippery slope. For one neighbor, the answer is conservative talk radio hosts Dr. Laura Schlesinger, Glenn Beck, or Bill O'Reilly. For another, perhaps younger and cynical, the best source is *The Daily Show with Jon Stewart*. Is the BBC World Service more credible than ABC News? Is *Newsweek* more credible than *The New York Times*? Are any of these news sources smarter or more reliable than the guy down the street who reads them all and spews his own opinions? Personally, I trust my wife. She seems pretty smart. For decades, she has shaped many of my political and social beliefs. I think she's done a pretty good job with our kids, too.

Certainly, a well-regarded scientist, an expert in his field who has spent decades studying an issue and researching its implications should be a credible source. Take, for example, Jerry Mahlman, a senior researcher at the National Center for Atmospheric Research, whom *The New York Times* described as a "reluctant activist."[2] Mahlman studies climate, and he says that global warming is a very real and present threat to our existence. He is already seeing a pattern that will destroy the Everglades and may bury the Netherlands; a pattern with dramatic increases in rainfall and in the frequency and intensity of hurricanes; of dangerously hot summers that destroy life and agriculture. Based upon the little I know about global warming, I tend to believe Mr. Mahlman and his fifteen-page resume listing membership in every conceivable meteorological organization, plus dozens upon dozens of published research works.

Unfortunately, I am in the minority. According to *The New York Times* (whose credibility here seems solid), Mahlman has been personally threatened by congressmen and senators who just don't want to hear what he has to say, and by many others who simply refuse to believe what he says. "These people remind me of the folks who kept trying to cast doubt on the science linking cancer to tobacco use," Mahlman said.[3]

Beliefs Are Easily Manipulated

In 1956, the pioneering social psychologist Solomon Asch performed a series of experiments showing cards with lines of various lengths. Working as a group, Asch's confederates were told a claim that lines of different lengths were, in fact, lines of identical lengths. When a naïve newcomer was brought in, the group provided consistently misleading information. Fully 80 percent of newcomers agreed with the group at least once; 33 percent of all tests resulted in a yield to the majority. That is, newcomers did not believe their own eyes; instead, they either conformed with the group or developed an internal conviction that the group was correct.

This phenomenon, and others like it, have repeatedly confirmed the ease with which consistent, credible messages alter reality and vanquish the truth. In another experiment, the subject was shown blue slides, but the group insisted they were green. Here's the intriguing part: subjects reported seeing a red-violet after-image, which is the opposite of green, not blue, an involuntary response manufactured by the brain's visual systems.

Distinguished Professor Dr. Elizabeth Loftus of the University of California at Irvine has written extensively about misinformation, memory, imagination, and the changing of beliefs. In a 2003 article in *Nature Neuroscience*, Loftus described experiments in her laboratory. After visiting Disney parks, subjects were shown advertisements of Bugs Bunny at Disneyland. "When these subjects were … asked to report precisely what they remembered about their encounter with Bugs Bunny, 62 percent remembered shaking his hand and 46 percent remembered hugging him. A few remembered touching his ears or his tail. One person remembered he was holding a carrot." Why is this interesting? Because Bugs Bunny is a Warner Bros. character who did not appear at the Disney theme park. The entire notion was placed in the subjects' minds by a fake advertisement.[4]

To change a belief, facts are not required. Instead, the power of suggestion through vivid imagery, bold statements, and subtle insinuation can be remarkably effective. These bits of trickery have been instrumental for political consultants, who secretly disparage an opponent's reputation. One recent example, cited by the Annenberg Public Policy Center's FactCheck. org: "A group funded by the biggest Republican campaign donor in Texas began running an attack ad Aug. 5 in which former Swift Boat veterans claim Kerry lied to get one of his two decorations for bravery and two of his three Purple Hearts. But the veterans who accuse Kerry are contradicted by Kerry's former crewmen, and by Navy records." The group was called

"Swift Boat Veterans for Truth." Of course, the strategy is not new. A half-century earlier, in 1950, Senator Joe McCarthy grabbed headlines with his undocumented claims that 205 State Department employees were Communists. By 1953, McCarthy's relentless paranoia resulted in more than half of Americans approving of his campaign.

To what extent are our beliefs affected by these manipulations? For a cinematic answer, rent *Wag the Dog*, a film in which a Hollywood producer stages a war. The next time you spend more money to visit Disney World than it would cost for twice as many days in Europe, stop to consider why. The next time you whip out a credit card to pay for something you really can't afford, think about why you behave that way. The next time you vote for a politician based upon his image, not his voting record or his funding sources, consider why you are being allowed to vote at all.

To put this another way (borrowing a clever phrase from a fashionably radical book titled *You Are Being Lied To*): "Reality is a shared hallucination."

Plump Women

In 1878, Thomas Duncan wrote a book called *How to Be Plump*. At the time, plump was desirable. "Plumpness was widely regarded by health experts and by connoisseurs of female aesthetics alike as a sign of good health. Rather than churning out starvation diets, health experts and faddists wrote books ... which recommended eating starchy foods, fats, and sweets in order to achieve ... 'florid plumpness.'" In those days, the female icon was Lillian Russell, who weighed more than two hundred pounds. The media promoted a curvy figure as a picture of health. Corsets made women even curvier, especially in the bosom.

By the 1920s, women wanted to weigh about half as much as Russell. Now, the books were about losing weight. Movies and magazines promoted the flapper: there were pictures of thin women everywhere. Helen's Diet Reducer promised women they would "Gargle Your Fat Away." The 1930s were famous for fad diets. In the 1950s, pictures of Marilyn Monroe (a size fourteen) brought back curves, confounding women who wanted to look like Marilyn but also dieted. Since the 1950s, thin has been in. Branded diets (and diet products)—which prey on hopes and beliefs—are part of contemporary culture. Among the dozens of brand names associated with dieting and weight loss: Weight Watchers, Jenny Craig, Dr. Phil, *Dr. Sears' Zone Diet, Fit for Life, Fit or Fat*, Hamptons, Atkins, Zantrex-3, and

The South Beach Diet. Without much trouble, you could probably add a dozen more.

With so many products available to assist in weight loss, why are more Americans fatter than ever before? And are we any more certain today about healthy eating than they were in 1878 when plump was preferred? Before you dismiss the question as ridiculous, consider why you are so certain of the answer.

Changing a Belief, Creating a Product

For centuries, chefs used butter and lard to cook and to bake. Animal fats were widely available, tasted good, and didn't cost much. With some new-fangled ideas about marketing, the candle, soap, and lard maker Procter & Gamble set out to change all of that. P&G's goal: Replace animal fats with a new product that could be sold as a national brand: Crisco.

Instead of simply advertising the product in the popular women's magazines of the day, Procter & Gamble hired a pioneering behavioral psychologist and assembled the industry's first comprehensive market research plan. Remember, this was 1912. This kind of marketplace assault was a radically new idea.

Crisco was first introduced to chefs in charge of fashionable hotel dining rooms (at the time, among the most popular and classiest restaurants). Then, armed with the chefs' credible endorsements, the launch team systemically attacked the market. They staged in-store demonstrations and gave out free samples of delicious fried foods made with Crisco. They offered special promotional deals to retailers. They presented hired home economists to conduct free Crisco cooking classes. They published Crisco recipe books. There were door-to-door salespeople, streetcar ads, outdoor posters, handbills, calendar books (one Crisco recipe for each day of the year), and, eventually, radio commercials. Since Crisco contained no animal products, it was ideal for kosher homes (which cannot cook or serve dairy and meat products together), so Crisco published a Yiddish cookbook.

In 2002, Procter & Gamble sold its Crisco brand (along with the Jif peanut butter brand) to J.M. Smucker for about $350 million.[5]

Vegetable oils and shortenings now dominate the market, helped by our belief that vegetable oils are, generally, healthier than animal fats. While this may be true when considered out of context, our total per capita fat consumption has nearly doubled since the 1950s and probably quadrupled since the introduction of widely available vegetable shortening earlier in the last century. When Crisco was introduced, the average person was probably taking in about twenty pounds of added fats per year; now, we eat nearly eighty pounds.

Connecting Brands with Beliefs

In 1994, forty-five-year-old George Foreman knocked out twenty-six-year old Michael Moorer, regaining the title of World Heavyweight Champion. After the match, Foreman received more than two hundred endorsement offers and accepted a few of them (Meineke, for example). Meanwhile, the appliance maker Salton, a company in the midst of a slump, was showing trade show visitors an inexpensive indoor grill from Asia, but it wasn't getting much traction. Promoters connected Foreman and Salton in exchange for 15 percent of the action (Salton got 40 percent and Foreman got 45 percent). Then they got to work. Foreman worked the retailers at a 1995 housewares trade show, and Salton sold 200,000 grills. More important, people started coming up to Foreman in airports and bookstores to tell him how much they loved his grill. Cable TV network QVC came in and sold 1.5 million more. By 2004, Salton was a $1 billion company. Bob Garfield, a columnist for the trade magazine *Advertising Age*, told *Fortune* magazine, "There's no explaining it, except that he was a highly charged personality, very likeable, who was selling a good and inexpensive product."

Maybe there is a way to explain it. Foreman caused consumers to *believe* in his grill. Maybe there's more happening here than simple salesmanship or celebrity product endorsement. Once again, Foreman taught people to believe in him. And then he made another comeback with what turned out to be the right product at the right moment. The fact that the product was actually named for him, and on the top lid actually signed by him, satisfied even the most skeptical of nonbelievers.

In May 2005, the American Cancer Society released a report confirming that celebrity encouragement for mammograms and other tests made viewers more likely to schedule those tests for themselves. When we see famous people on television, we are more likely to pay attention, and we are more likely to believe a product's claims. This is true when Robert DeNiro appears in signed print ads with a caption that reads, "My life. My card." Annie Liebowitz's downtown/backstage photography made me believe that if I was an authentic New Yorker, I ought to carry an American Express card.

Brands and Vices

It's one thing to buy into George Foreman's touch of the blarney and pay a hundred dollars for his Knockout Grill. How about Hugh Hefner's blarney, which allowed pornography to be sold on every newsstand in the United States?

As a society, we are not necessarily in favor of pornography or gambling or violence as entertainment. With the addition of a credible brand, our belief system evaporates.

Adult Entertainment

There were men's magazines before Hugh Hefner started *Playboy*, but they weren't mainstream publications. Hefner learned from the best—*Esquire* and the *New Yorker*—and put together a magazine that was young, sophisticated, erudite, and, of course, published centerfold pictures of pretty young women without their clothes on. Many centerfolds contained the suggestion that there was a man around somewhere: a pipe, a necktie. "Hef" (his own personal brand name) developed an elaborate mythology to define *Playboy*, and eventually adopted the Playboy lifestyle as his own. By 1960, Hefner opened The Playboy Mansion in Chicago, debuted the Playboy Jazz Festival (at the time, the ultimate in cool), and the first of thirty-six Playboy Club nightclubs. Playboy's little rabbit logo tied it all together. In 2003, Hefner told *Fortune* magazine, "The notion of using a rabbit in a tuxedo seemed frisky, fun, sexy, and sophisticated."

Look through a stack of old *Playboy* magazines and you'll find a surprising number of Fortune 500 advertisers. That's part of the reason why *Playboy* is a $325 million company.

Where is the line we call "community standards"? It can be hard to find, in part because it moves around a lot, and in part because the ends of the line are held by large corporations.

A few days after Janet Jackson's breast debuted on the network's Super Bowl broadcast, CBS featured a nearly naked young teenaged boy smeared with horse manure, who later suffered for at least a minute as he hung himself, dangling with eyes bulging, gasping for breath. Not a word was written about this episode of the popular CBS series *Without a Trace*. No fines were levied by the Federal Communications Commission. No sponsors pulled their advertisements in outrage.

With the help of advertisements appearing regularly on Viacom's Comedy Central and Comcast's E!, *Girls Gone Wild* products (mostly girls exposing their breasts, etc.), and a record deal with Bertelsmann's JIVE Records, the company has "not only sold millions of units, but has become a bona fide pop culture phenomenon."[6] Apparently, plans for a restaurant chain have been under discussion for some time. Why the popularity? As a company spokesman points out, "It's horny, not porny."

Certainly, the inspiration comes from Hooters, which operates or franchises 375 restaurants, many located in family-friendly locations near major shopping centers. Hooters co-sponsors a National Golf Association tour. The company recently launched an airline. More than fifteen thousand women work at Hooters; those who serve the public are dressed like cheerleaders. From the company Web site: Hooters is "delightfully tacky, yet unrefined." It's the all-American concoction: burgers, partially exposed female breasts, and short shorts. You can dine at Hooters in forty-six states and fourteen countries, including Singapore and Croatia.

As a society, we have determined that *Playboy*, *Girls Gone Wild*, and Hooters are legitimate forms of entertainment. They come professionally packaged as brands, so they are welcome members of our communities.

> As a society, we have determined that Playboy, Girls Gone Wild, and Hooters are legitimate forms of entertainment. They come professionally packaged as brands, so they are welcome members of our communities.

Violence

In television newsrooms and in many newspaper offices, "If it bleeds, it leads" is the conventional wisdom in selecting lead stories. Just before I wrote this paragraph, I checked the lead stories on fifty U.S. newspapers (you can, too: www.newseum.com). I found politics and business to be more common topics for newspaper lead stories. Still, stories about killing, killers, and other forms of violence ranked third.

On the same May 17, 2005, afternoon, a check of television newscasts yielded different results. Of ten ABC, CBS, and NBC affiliates in the nation's largest markets, eight led with stories about murder, child molestation, fire, explosion, or shooting.

The top ten films for the weekend of May 13–15, 2005, included seven films rated R for "strong violence" or "horror violence" or "intense action violence." Week to week, violence keeps the movie companies in the black, but long-term, only two of the top twenty-five all-time worldwide box office champs were R-rated: *The Matrix Reloaded* and *The Passion of the Christ*.

The top ten video games for the first quarter of 2005 included four violent games, including *Grand Theft Auto: San Andreas* and *Mercenaries*.

Whether packaged in an 11 p.m. newscast, a video game or a motion picture, it's clear that violence is a popular form of entertainment. What does this say about our beliefs? It's not a complicated answer. We enjoy watching people in jeopardy, and we enjoy watching destruction. We strongly believe in the forces of good and evil. We finance media brands that provide violent entertainment in several ways: We buy movie tickets, we buy DVDs, and we invest in shares of stock in the corporations that own these violent brands.

Gambling

Next on the list of branded vices is greed, or, in more contemporary terms, gambling. In comparison with gambling, pornography is small change. Every day, slot machines take in an average of $1 billion, but the "hold" from these machines is so enormous that they net more than McDonald's, Wendy's, Burger King, and Starbucks combined. Slot machines—which now account for 70 percent of gambling revenues in the United States—grossed (after payouts) more than $30 billion in 2003. That's three times the total U.S. box office sales for all motion picture films, or three times the size of the adult entertainment industry. Next year, one in five adults will play a slot machine in one of the thirty states where they are now legally available (in the late 1980s, slots were legal in just two states).[7]

For many years, Las Vegas hotels relied upon brand-name entertainers to draw a crowd. They experimented with food, amusement rides, even a full-scale circus above the casino. And then they found their fortunes in slot machines. When gambling discovered branding, gambling became a great business.

"Honey, you were so close!"—those are the words slot machine designers love to hear. Machines are designed to produce many near misses, explained Anthony Baerlocher, chief game designer for industry leader International Game Technology (IGT). Baerlocher explained, "You want to give the newbie lots of positive reinforcement—to keep 'em playing." IGT invests more than $120 million each year so that more than eight hundred designers, graphic artists, script writers, and video engineers can find ways to surround the unromantic computer chips with a colorful matrix of sounds, chrome, garishly painted glass, and video effects. Among the most popular games: "cherry dribblers," which provide the smallest encouragement but still result in players dropping quarter after quarter into these rigged machines.

How to get the newbies' attention? There's a *South Park* game, as well as games based upon *Star Wars*, *Austin Powers*, Drew Carey, *The Price is Right*, Elvis Presley, *Wheel of Fortune*, *I Dream of Jeannie*, *The Munsters*, even Tabasco sauce ("Hot! Hot! Hot!"). WMS Gaming, a top competitor whose history goes back to pinball games, sells slots based upon *Hollywood Squares*, *Men in Black*, *Supermarket Sweep*, *Password*, Pac-Man, and Monopoly. Bally's product line includes products associated with *Saturday Night Live* (Wayne's World, Church Lady), *Playboy*, Rocky & Bullwinkle, and Popeye the Sailor Man.

All of this is comfort food for aging baby boomers and their aged parents. *The New York Times* article "The Tug of the Newfangled Slot Machines" called the casinos "day care for the elderly," a safe environment where, according to Baerlocher, "There are cameras and security guards everywhere. You can go to one place and shop and eat and be in a crowd even if you don't know anybody." Critics call slots an entertainment experience designed to get money from those who can least afford it.

Branded gambling has become an essential source of revenue for many state governments. For Biloxi, Mississippi, one of the most important economic fixes after Hurricane Katrina was the redeployment of the gambling casinos so essential to the local economy. For many state governments unencumbered by possible long-term consequences, slot machines are an easy answer to budget problems. In Pennsylvania, the popular state lottery is positioned with the tagline, "Benefits Older Pennsylvanians." In fact, 34.5 cents out of every dollar spent on lottery tickets goes to benefit programs, subsidizing mass transit, low-cost prescription drug programs, community centers and various agencies—all related to the aged. In the 2003–2004 lottery year, over $800 million was received by these programs. The lottery is seen daily on TV; most people, including children, can sing the jingle.

Pennsylvania's opportunities are modest in comparison with California, a state poised to overtake Nevada as the nation's gambling capital. In 2004, California's tribal casinos generated $5 billion. Around 2010, when the next wave of California's casinos are completed, they will generate $400 billion, including $100 billion for the state government, and gambling will be California's single largest source of revenue. For the "casino tribes," the cash provides opportunity. "We're at the point where we need to take care of our diversified economy," David Quintana, an advisor to the Viejas tribe, told the *Los Angeles Times* in the article "California on Path to Become Nation's Gambling Captial." This economy includes hotels, restaurants, banks, and other investments—and influence. Since 1980, casino tribes have spent about $175 million on California elections—no other special interest group comes close. The article also quoted former Republican assemblyman Bruce Thompson: "You won't find any legislator who will go up against the Indians. That's how powerful they are."[8]

No Matter What Happens, Children Will Be Protected

It would be comforting to believe that children are protected from all of this commercial intent, but we all know that they're not. In today's culture, children see much of what adults see, from scantily clad models on billboards to nasty music videos.

Although child psychologists don't believe children comprehend persuasive intent until age eight or so, children as young as three (some say two) recognize and ask for specific brands. There is a profound ethical issue here, one that we choose to ignore because our children so enjoy Disney, Nickelodeon, Sesame Street, LEGO, *Star Wars*, Super Mario, Blue's Clues, Barney & Friends, and other brands whose merchandise stocks toy store shelves. Still, these media brands, along with up to twenty thousand commercials per year, affect their beliefs. The stakes are high: preschool children represent roughly $15 billion in spending power per year, and that's just a small portion of the $100 billion that U.S. children and teens spend annually on sweets, foods, drinks, games, clothes, and other products (not including their substantial alcohol and tobacco purchases).

For years, my son slept on Thomas the Tank Engine bed sheets. It made him happy to play with a collection of toys similar to the trains he saw on TV. He entertained us by showing us that he knew their names: Percy, the little green engine; James, who wasn't quite so large as Gordon; the twin coaches Annie and Clarabel; and Henry, who felt bad because he needed special coal to run. Like many parents, we bought our son Thomas the Tank Engine videotapes, books, toys, and the occasional T-shirt or beach towel. Certainly, there's nothing inherently wrong with Thomas and his pals. Our son enjoyed learning about the relationships in the microworld run by Sir Topham Hat, and developed a love of trains. Still, there was something vaguely discomforting about it all.

Children believe what they are told to believe. Based upon our behavior as responsible parents, children learn to become active consumers, to respond to television entertainment by purchasing as many products as possible.

Public Relations

To a great extent, all of us are told what to believe. This is the basis of America's advertising business—and perhaps more to the point, the founding principle of public relations.

The advertising business is sixty times the size of the public relations business. Advertising gets the respect, the big money, a weekly column in *The New York Times*, and two well-known industry trade magazines (*ADWEEK* and *Advertising Age*). Most large public relations firms are owned by even larger advertising agencies. Most people seem to understand the work of advertising agencies, but the work of public relations agencies is less obvious.

About 200,000 people work in public relations.[9] Their job is to place stories in the media that will not be perceived as advertising. Day to day, public relations professionals create news by turning commercial messages into messages that make the job of journalists easier. The result: the marketer's story is written and published by a credible third party. The hand of the PR firm or the client company is unseen. Over time, the published material becomes truth. As the story is rerun or quoted by other media sources, the cumulative impact serves to build and sustain brands over months, years, and decades. Done properly, public relations can be far more powerful than advertising, doubly so because these intentionally insidious activities are rarely perceived as marketing. Instead, when Butterball offers a Thanksgiving turkey hotline, news coverage on hundreds of radio and television stations present the campaign as a kind of public service, and not as a marketing scheme by ConAgra to sell more poultry.

This evening (May 18, 2005), *ABC World News Tonight* devoted one story to a new medical product (unnamed, but still a remarkable coup for the public relations firm that pitched the story about its client's product), and another to the superiority of special effects in a new *Star Wars* movie (a big win for Lucasfilm and 20th Century FOX). Both stories were produced by ABC News, working closely with public relations professionals who were neither mentioned nor identified in the stories.

Advertising encourages us to become familiar with products and to buy them, but public relations preys on our belief system: (a) if ABC News is reporting about a medical breakthrough, it must be important; and (b) the special effects in the new *Star Wars* movie make it a film worth seeing.

As marketing strategists Al Ries and Laura Ries point out, advertising is overt, often witty and clever in its call for attention, but public relations is serious business. Advertising often features the incredible. Public relations is all about credibility.

Front Groups

To promote corporate or political concerns, an industry or group of industries night form an organization to pose as an independent voice. These "front groups" are exceedingly difficult to research because they do not typically disclose their purpose, their funding sources (often, large corporations), or their political connections (many are closely aligned with lobby groups and think tanks). In order to affect public policy, shape public opinion, and assist in legislative lobbying, most large public relations firms operate significant offices in Washington, D.C. Often, front groups are organized, managed, or otherwise guided by these well connected public relations professionals.

According to Mike Casey, vice president of public affairs for the Environmental Working Group (www.ewg.org), "People have a pervasive sense that influence peddlers run Washington, D.C. The dirty little secret is that they're right. It's a three-dimensional chess game. Lobbyists spend all day pushing, pressuring, and persuading legislators. Meanwhile, the front groups work in the court of public opinion. They are the propaganda machine that backs up the lobbyists."

Speaking to me about the American Council on Science and Health, Casey explains: "ACSH is essentially a public relations firm disguised as a science organization." In the past, ACSH has published lists of its funders, but no longer does so. According to ACSH spokesman and Associate Director Jeff Steir, "We did that a number of years ago, but the activists took the list out of context and used it against us." When I promised a fair shake in this book, he repeatedly evaded the question and ultimately refused to answer. When asked for any names of corporate funders, Steir would not name names.[10] Why should we care? ACSH's Web site explains why: "ACSH representatives appear regularly on television and radio, in public debates and in other forums. In addition, ACSH hosts media seminars and press conferences on a variety of public health issues. ACSH also provides an in-house internship program for students in health science fields and participates in legislative and regulatory hearings." On the organization's Web site, ACSH Executive Director Elizabeth Whelan explains: "The important thing, though, is not the source of your funding but the accuracy of the points you make, and ACSH's scientific advisors and use of peer review keep us honest."

I specifically asked both Casey and Steir whether their organizations were front groups. Each explained why they were not front groups.

Says Casey: "No, we are not a front group. The people who give us money do not stand to make money if we succeed: people who drink tap water contaminated by farm field runoff and pesticides, for example. That's not true for the front groups. Their funders have a direct financial interest."

Says Steir: "Companies and trade associations recognize the need that ACSH fills. They don't tell us what to say or how to say it; that's why we have scientists. The media relies on us for a balanced scientific view, but they certainly know that we have a perspective on these issues. We go where the science takes us, but often the science lines up with the view of industry."

Often, front groups operate under misleading names. Still, not every organization with a misleading name is a front group with an obscure or misleading purpose.

For example, the Center for Consumer Freedom has a misleading name, but their purpose is stated on their Web site: "... a nonprofit coalition of restaurants, food companies, and consumers working together to promote personal responsibility and protect consumer choices." They go on to say, "The growing cabal of 'food cops,' health care enforcers, militant activists, meddling bureaucrats, and violent radicals who think they know 'what's best for you' are pushing against our basic freedoms. We're here to push back." This is to the point, and not misleading. Whether you agree with their purpose or not, they are being direct and speaking their beliefs in the hope that others will follow.

Front groups play a significant role in the manipulation of media, enabling corporations and industries to affect public opinion in ways that are not entirely upfront or ethical. Many of our beliefs have probably been shaped by these groups.

Manipulated Research

Nearly one-third of university faculty members accept industry funding for their research. Once again, this creates an arm's length relationship rarely seen by the public, allowing university faculty to speak on behalf of a corporations or industry group's agenda. Findings are often reported by the media, typically without much further investigation, and also supplied to lawmakers. Corporations love it because university research costs far less than research done by company employees or expensive private contractors. Professors love the interesting work, the prestige, the occasional consulting contract. Graduate students win because they have something from industry to fill out a resume. The public, however, remains in the dark.

Manipulated Media

With a lot of hours and pages to fill, reporters have limited time and resources to dig, so they go to news sources most likely to provide a viable story. Most often, these sources are tied into public relations agencies, front groups, government spokespeople, or company spokespeople.

Reporters are fed relevant information, then turn it around quickly without undue reflection or research. Some newspapers dig deeper, but who has time to read such long stories? Most people prefer to read *USA Today's* condensation or to catch a few minutes on the TV news unless it's a major story, such as a disaster or celebrity trial.

The objective: keep the public confused, so that belief systems can be manipulated for financial gain. If, after watching or reading a news report, you think, "I don't know what to believe anymore," somebody in public relations has done their job.

Endnotes

1   "Consumers and Their Brands: Developing Relationship Theory in Consumer Research," by Susan Fournier, *Journal of Consumer Research*, March 1998.

2   "Listening to the Climate Models and Trying to Wake Up the World," *The New York Times*, December 16, 2003.

3   From Dr. Mahlman, via e-mail to me on June 15, 2005: "Good luck on your important writing on what people do when they compromise search for truth and hide instead behind unexamined personal belief systems … Admittedly, it is almost always easier to adopt an unexamined belief system than it is to dig to the bottom of things to build firm foundations of understanding."

4   For many more articles describing similar phenomena with regard to family relationships, eyewitness testimony, and implications for marketers and consumers, visit Professor Loftus's Web site: http://www.seweb.uci.edu/faculty/loftus/

5   Based upon data published in J.M. Smucker's 2002 and 2003 annual reports, the acquisition of Jif and Crisco cost approximately $781 million. The peanut butter category provided 26 percent of Smucker's sales for 2003, and the Crisco brand 22

percent, hence the estimated split in favor of Jif.

6   http://www.brandchannel.com/features_profile.asp?pr_id=178

7   Much of the information in this section comes from: "The Tug of the Newfangled Slot Machines," *The New York Times Magazine*, May 9, 2004.

8   "California on Path to Become Nation's Gambling Capital," *Los Angeles Times*, August 25, 2004.

9   *Global Spin: The Corporate Assault on Environmentalism* by Sharon Beder, p. 107.

10   To see a list of funders, researched by a watchdog group, visit: http://www.prwatch. org/improp/acsh.html. This list includes the American Meat Institute, agricultural giant Archer Daniels Midland, Ashland Oil, lumber company Boise Cascade, Dow Corning, DuPont, Exxon, the Monsanto Fund, and many more.

MEDIA, THE EDUCATOR

From jet engines to power generation, financial services to plastics, and medical imaging to news and information ..."[1] General Electric is the fifth-largest company on the Fortune 500. With annual revenues of over $150 billion, GE owns or operates three of the eight broadcast television networks in the U.S. (NBC, Telemundo, PAX), and either owns, co-owns, or operates eight major cable networks (A&E, Bravo, CNBC, History Channel, MSNBC, SCI FI, USA Network, Shop NBC).[2]

With over $40 billion in annual revenues, Time Warner, owner of CNN and *Time* magazine, is number thirty-two on the Fortune 500 list. Time Warner controls one broadcast network (The WB), seven cable networks (CNN, TBS, TNT, TCM, Cartoon Network, HBO, Cinemax), and several of the nation's most popular magazines (Time, Sports Illustrated, many more).

Not far behind, in slot fifty-four, is Disney, which operates ABC and ESPN with nearly $31 billion in annual revenues.

Viacom, owner of CBS and the world's largest children's television network, Nickelodeon, is number sixty-nine with about $27 billion in revenues.

News Corp., owner of the FOX network and FOX News, as well as newspapers throughout the world, occupies slot ninety-eight with nearly $21 billion.

Every one of these companies is larger than Halliburton (101), 3M (105), McDonald's (116), and United States Steel (149).

In fact, every major broadcast network is owned by a Fortune 100 company. These large companies also own seventeen of the twenty largest cable networks (Discovery and TLC are partly owned by Liberty Media (254).[3]

How do these media companies earn money? First and foremost, Viacom sells advertising on CBS, Nickelodeon, MTV, VH1, and other Viacom television networks; on outdoor media (buses, mall signage, billboards, street furniture, sports stadiums, college campuses); and on 180-plus radio stations. In 2004, Viacom earned 60 percent of its revenues from advertising. For many media companies, advertising is the single largest source of revenue. These dollars are spent by advertisers, for the most part, to embed ideas about brands in the minds of consumers.

Who buys the advertising? For the most part, the answer is Fortune 500 companies. Fortune 100 companies own our media and make money by selling advertising time and space to (mostly) Fortune 500 companies. Every year, General Motors pays Viacom several hundred million dollars. Pfizer pays Disney over $100 million a year. Advertising revenues keep the networks alive; without them, there would be no *Desperate Housewives, Pimp My Ride,* or *Fairly Odd Parents.*

Certainly, business relationships between these large companies affect more than the buying and selling of billions of dollars in advertising media. Often, entertainment, news, and sports content are customized to suit the specific requirements of specific clients.

Media companies carefully manage their relationships with the federal government as well. Changes in FCC policy have allowed Viacom, for example, to own five of the largest radio stations in every one of America's largest metropolitan areas (sometimes more than five). Multibillion dollar corporations understand their priorities.

Media Is Not "On Our Side"

From time to time, a local television station will harass a local contractor to fix the roof of a local church or stop polluting a public park. Often, these activities are presented as a branded news segment such as, "News 9 On Your Side." In fact, media outlets are rarely on the side of the viewer. Even a station with the best of intentions is beholden to the advertisers that provide its revenues, the corporation that owns the station, and other corporations that are considered friendly or useful. Certainly, the station cannot upset the federal government, whose friendly treatment has allowed media companies to prosper, or the state or local governments that regularly provide access for important stories, or municipal workers or labor unions. On the list of priorities, the viewer isn't high on the list—except as a portion of a rating point that can be sold, in bulk, to an advertiser.

Do we honestly expect objective news reports from a television news reporter earning $100,000–500,000 per year, working for a boss perhaps earning twice that amount, whose budgets are wholly provided by advertising revenues?

Free Media

In Britain, during a House of Lords argument about appropriate funding for the new television medium, the BBC's legendary leader John Reith compared the idea of broadcasting funded by commercials to the bubonic plague.

Since its inception, Britain's BBC has been funded by an annual tax on every radio and television receiver in the United Kingdom. (In 2004, every British citizen paid two hundred dollars per color TV set.) The per-set tax system allowed the BBC tremendous resources, but it also kept for-profit broadcasters off the British airwaves.[4]

In the United States, early radio was a lot like the early Internet. Hobbyists and budding entrepreneurs were fascinated with a technology that was previously available mostly for government use. In just a few years, commercial radio equipment makers GE, Westinghouse, and AT&T already developed radio stations and network connections between the stations. One of the first networks was NBC, which was, from the start, supported by commercial advertising. Americans thought they got a better deal than the British: their radio programs were "free."

Today, the price of that freedom is exposure to nearly 100 commercials every day, or over 30,000 commercials, year in and year out.[5] (Given the choice, would you prefer to watch 35,000 commercials or pay a few hundred dollars per year to avoid them entirely?)[6]

Americans love a bargain. In exchange for that bargain, we have made it possible for marketing and media juggernauts to grow and to dominate our culture.

Large corporations now control our stories. They define our heroes. They publish our textbooks. They provide our news. They set the topics for national debate. They provide role models and cultural cues that show us how to live our lives.

Selling Ourselves Out

Did you ever wonder why magazines that you buy on the newsstand for $4.99 per issue cost just one dollar per issue when you subscribe?[7] That's an

80 percent discount! With hundreds of pages printed in full color, plus the cost of the staff needed to put the magazine together, how could a publisher possibly afford to sell a full-color magazine with hundreds of printed pages filled with dozens of written and edited stories for just a buck?

Most American magazines cannot support themselves on payments from readers—it's nearly impossible to find enough readers willing to pay enough money to support the combined writing, editorial, design, marketing, printing, and distribution budgets. Instead, advertisers fund magazines by buying readers in lots of a thousand (CPM refers to Cost Per Thousand readers).

In the May 30, 2005, issue of *Newsweek*, the publisher's efforts were funded by Canon, Apple, Philips, Morgan Stanley, Microsoft, Toyota, ExxonMobil, Nabisco/KF Holdings/Kraft/Altria (owner of Philip Morris), Van Kampen Investments, Discovery Channel, T-Mobile, Chase, HP, Colonial Williamsburg, Tempur-Pedic, RBS, Toshiba, Blackberry/Research in Motion, Quaker/Pepsico, LG, Xerox, Siemens, GlaxoSmithKline, GM, US Smokeless Tobacco Co., MSNBC, SONY, Unilever, A&E, and United. With this impressive list of advertisers, one cannot help but wonder how a news magazine can be entirely objective.

Long-time *Ms.* magazine publisher Gloria Steinem explained, "historically, P&G would pull its ads from any *Ms.* issue that contained material about 'gun control, abortion, the occult, cults, or the disparagement of religion'."[8]

Here's another example of a sellout: When cable television was still a new idea, local politicians bought into the promises of entrepreneurs and sold exclusive service rights to wire and provide cable television service to their communities. (Often, local politicians were bought by the cable companies so that these deals could be made.) Promises of new schools, libraries, parks, and local television channels were rarely fulfilled; the cable companies pleaded poverty and kept their valuable franchises. Eventually, about half of these were sold to either Time Warner or to Comcast. Every month, these two companies collect more than forty dollars per month from tens of millions of cable households. Total amount collected: $1.5 billion every month.

Our legislators have given our valuable over-the-air rights to large corporations at no charge. (That's right: ABC, FOX, and the others get to use the public airwaves without paying a penny for the privilege.)

In the 1970s, no corporation was allowed to operate television stations that reached more than 18 percent of the country's television households. Today, each corporation is allowed to operate television stations that serve 39 percent of the United States, including one large and one small station in each city, and up to three stations in larger cities. Assisted by endless spin, industry lobbying has succeeded, and the limit will probably be raised to 50 percent within the next decade or so. The Heritage Foundation explained, "The ability to own multiple media outlets can provide substantial benefits to consumers …" then points out that NBC can compete more effectively with FOX or CNN through corporate synergies."[9] When the spin is unspun, there is no apparent benefit to consumers, but the benefit to corporations is clear.

Not that it matters: NBC does not *own* the two hundred-plus affiliates in its network, but NBC *controls* every affiliated station's most-viewed hours in the morning, afternoon, early evening, prime time, and late night on all of those stations.

Storytelling and Imagination

This afternoon, my college-aged son was reading Jack Kerouac's rite of passage novel, *On the Road*. I considered showing him a photograph of Kerouac, then decided against it. Better for him to read, to develop his own mental picture of the Sal Paradise character than to see the real author.

For the millions of children—and adults—who adored the Harry Potter books, I'm almost sorry that any movie was made. What fun to create your own visual images of Harry and Hogwort's, Dumbledore and Quidditch.

Media provide more and more of the information that was once provided by the reader or listener's imagination. Early radio provided sound, but listeners imagined pictures. Black-and-white TV provided a limited visual view, but we added the colors. When we gain more "free" information about the story, we sacrifice an opportunity for more than passive enjoyment and involvement. Of course, it's tough to sell action figures if everyone's got their own ideas about how a character looks.

Media's Hold on Our Time and Attention

Storytelling is powerful, and in the deepest sense, magical. Skillful storytellers burrow deep into our minds, hearts, and souls. More than we know, we're affected by characters, storylines, context, authority, myths and legends (ancient and modern), storytellers, and messages.

Of the twenty-four hours available each day, adults spend a third of that time sleeping (the national average is 8.5 hours). Total waking hours: 15.5.

We spend 2.6 of them watching TV, and another hour browsing the Web, reading e-mails, browsing magazines, listening to the radio, and catching the occasional billboard, sign, or poster. It would be fair to say that we spend nearly four hours each day—one in four of our waking hours, every day of our lives—in the midst of programs, stories, advertisements, and marketing messages whose content is dominated by Fortune 500 companies.

Our best storytellers are employed by corporations. They are paid to be concerned about shareholder value, not the public good.

Joe Camel didn't become well known by six-year-olds because he was cute. He became well known because the nation's largest billboard companies plastered his enormous puss on billboards in places where children were likely to see him.

Children don't pass a McDonald's and decide they're hungry for a Happy Meal. McDonald's commercials bribe children to take their parents to the restaurants with the promise of a toy (often promoting a new kids' movie).

Lucky Charms teaches children the morning cereal habit by combining fantasy (a leprechaun and a rainbow) with a "magically delicious" cereal that contains colorful marshmallow candy. Through the magic of storytelling, commercials teach, "It's okay to have candy for breakfast."

On A&E's *Biography*, even the most complicated lives are reduced to an hour-long magazine-style documentary. On the Scripps networks (Food Network, HGTV, etc.) and on the Discovery networks (Discovery, TLC, etc.), people who do the hard work are cheerful and get along (or are charmingly disagreeable); results are always handsome and stories always resolve with clear endings. Homes are remade in an hour; gargantuan machine shop projects are planned, built, tested, and launched without serious mishap. We watch these tidy stories because they are nicely packaged and entertaining. We try our best to filter their odd sense of reality, propriety, and proportion. When we watch these stories for a quarter of our waking lives, their skewed reality inevitably affects our perceptions and real-life expectations.

> Our best storytellers are employed by corporations. They are paid to be concerned about shareholder value, not the public good.

For many of us, a nuanced understanding of the American legal system runs as deep as all that we've learned from *CSI, NYPD Blue, Law & Order*, and 11 p.m. newscasts. We know what the bad guys look like, how they behave, and the neighborhoods where criminals lurk because we've watched stories about prostitution, drug wars, gangs, random shootings, and arsonists. Our attention is diverted from other crimes or investigations whose stories are complicated, insignificant, or politically sensitive. A good shooting always aces a tangled matrix of corporate or government misbehavior or an exploration of sometimes-contradictory ethical or social concerns. Night after night, week after week, in Philadelphia and in Buffalo, there are stories of bad black men and their out-of-control gunplay; in Los Angeles and Dallas–Fort Worth, there are stories of bad Latino men and their out-of-control gunplay. We know the bad guys. We know who they are, how they think, and why they ought to be punished.

Stories leave a deep and long-lasting impression, a cumulative impression that operates at a conscious and subconscious level. (This is why advertisers buy flights of many commercials over weeks or months—to lay in lots of impressions.) Effects manifest themselves over time. Gradually, moment by moment and year by year, acceptable levels of sexuality, violence, frank adult storylines, graphic images, shorthand messages, and simple-minded stories become the norm. In time, storytelling changes the way we think about our lives. Kalle Lasn wrote, "We become blunted by all of the hype, jolts, shock, information overload, we never even notice the supermodel, even if she is scantily clad."

It's rare that a story is as simple as one person shooting another. There are always reasons why: reasons the shooter had the gun in the first place, reasons why the shooter became a shooter, why he or she selected a particular target or no particular target at all. Television has no time for context; in order to keep the viewer's attention—our attention—it must keep moving to the next shooter, the next fire, the next human tragedy.

Commercials: Our Most Vivid Fantasies

To produce an hour-long drama, broadcast networks spend about two million dollars per forty-minute episode (the other twenty minutes contain commercials and promos). On average, every minute of prime-time drama costs about $50,000, so every thirty seconds of original prime-time drama costs about $25,000.

The cost of producing a television commercial that will appear in or near that prime-time episode is rarely less than $250,000—ten times the cost of comparable time in the program itself. In addition, every time that commercial plays in prime time, the advertiser invests an additional

$200,000—or more[10]. The total expense for a prime time network campaign is rarely less than $5 million.

There are no guarantees that the commercial's flight will produce sales, but you can bet that sponsor and the agency do everything in their power to get a return on the investment. The process begins with precise market analysis; measurement of the product's strengths and weaknesses among target consumers; statistical evaluations of every word and image in every message; multiple creative concepts with client meetings, revisions, storyboards, more testing; production of the commercial; the best available creative talent; revisions requiring re-shooting and editing; testing the commercial in local markets before going national; point-of-sale research to measure campaign effectiveness in key markets; public relations and/or promotions to support the expensive campaign, to cause you to take action.

Remember: This is done for *every* commercial shown on the major networks, and for just about every commercial seen on cable networks. Imagine the money spent on staff to do this work, the jobs and reputations at risk, the sheer magnitude of these efforts. Failure is not an option. Whether it's Garnier shampoo or Gatorade, *you must buy.*

At $255 billion, advertising represents 2.5 percent of our gross domestic product. It's one of the larger sectors in our economy.

Guiding Light and *As the World Turns* are two of the longest-running broadcast properties in the history of the world. *Guiding Light* debuted on radio in 1937 and debuted on television in 1952. *As the World Turns*, which started in 1956, is TV's second-longest running soap opera. Both of these popular series are produced by Procter & Gamble Productions, part of the $52 billion company that owns Tide, Bounty, Tampax, Ivory Soap, Head & Shoulders, Pringles, Folgers, Charmin, and Pampers. Whether it's toilet paper or dandruff shampoo or a replacement for cloth diapers, each of these lifestyle products was invented or concocted with a change in lifestyle in mind. And what better forum for lifestyle changes than soap operas depicting elaborate fantasies that include instructions and cues about how best to lives our lives. With P&G, the relationship between product, program, storyline, and consumer is intimate.

What If People Stop Watching Commercials?

As the next wave of digital technology sweeps the nation, advertisers are concerned about TiVo and other digital video recorders (DVRs), which allow easy jumps over commercials. The solution? Weave advertising messages into the storyline, but don't tell viewers they're watching paid advertisements.

A *Wall Street Journal* article described soap opera storylines that incorporated a new Wal-Mart perfume called Enchantment, Butterball turkeys, Kleenex tissues, Florida orange juice, Kellogg's Frosted Flakes, and GM's OnStar. Here's how *The Young & The Restless* scripted OnStar's product placement:

Phyllis: Are we just going to wait for the snow to melt?

Jack: Gee, it's a tempting idea. But maybe we better get out of here.

Phyllis: What are you going to do? Dig us out?

Jack: No, I've got OnStar. ... I push that button right there and they come right away.

Phyllis: Wait a second. If these OnStar guys are as efficient as you say, maybe we should just wait to push the button. (THEY KISS.)

Nielsen estimates that television advertisers paid $300 million for product placements in the 2004 season, a number likely to exceed $1 billion within a few years. Coca-Cola, for example, paid an estimated $20 million to be a part of *American Idol's* third season; producer Mark Burnett, who receives a portion of those revenues, explained his rule of thumb: "make it obvious enough that the public doesn't think you're trying to slide it by them." His ask for the 2004–2005 season of *The Apprentice*: $25 million.

The watchdog group Commercial Alert hates the idea: "If advertisers get their way, TV characters will be Pringles potato chips," and suggests pop-up warnings every time a paid placement appears. Paid product placements have been common in motion pictures for more than a decade. One public relations executive called the Tom Hanks film *Cast Away* "a FedEx movie" because the movie could not end until a package was successfully delivered (in other words, the movie's storyline was far more powerful than the product placement or appearance of the logo). The character's only friend, Wilson, was a branded volleyball (in fact, you can buy the Cast Away AVP Volleyball at sporting goods stores).

A World-Class Training Program

More than a million people work in the media and marketing industries— one in every one hundred workers. With communications and marketing ranking among the most popular majors on today's college campuses,[11] the power and sophistication of the media and marketing industries is steadily improving.

Today's marketing majors are taught psychology, sociology, market research, statistics, and technology. Graduates from these programs will be better trained than any previous generation in psychology, sociology, market research, statistical analysis, design, writing, and multimedia. Some will pursue an MBA in Marketing as well.

After they graduate, this next generation of brand managers will spend nearly a trillion dollars a year—as much as we spend annually on education—to market brands to the American people. Colleges and universities are preparing a workforce that will be better equipped to tell stories that persuade you (and me) to buy. The addition of technology and large historical databases containing every credit card purchase and other personal information will dramatically enhance the power of this marketing machine.

Today's communications majors are also being prepared in the most frightening way. They are *not* being taught subject matter expertise in economics, political science, medicine, sociology, world history, American and regional history, and critical thinking. Instead, communications majors are taught how to communicate. They learn how to write and speak persuasively, how to design graphics and animations suitable for the commercial marketplace. They are provided with slim training in statistical analysis or economics, so they are poorly equipped to evaluate the statistical manipulations used by news sources to prove their points. They are required to take few, if any, courses in public health or nutrition, criminology, world affairs, or corporate law, so they are ill-equipped to understand the stories they are likely to report, write, or fictionalize. Without the critical thinking that ought to be applied before delivering any message, communications majors will continue to pass along messages from increasingly sophisticated marketers. Ill-equipped for meaningful investigations, and working in an industry where depth is usually discouraged, they will likely gloss over the most important topics, accept what is told to them by those who seem to know, or make fun of the whole thing (the rampant success of *The Simpsons*, *Family Guy*, and *South Park* attests to the financial rewards associated with making fun of social and economic issues; these staffs routine attract graduates from Harvard University and other top schools). Incidentally, there are few business-oriented graduate programs available for communications majors.

We trust these people who tell us stories for a quarter of our waking hours. Wouldn't it be a good idea to train communications majors so that their stories are honest and complete—as well as entertaining?

You Are a Market Segment

29.4 million Americans watched Carrie Underwood win *American Idol*.[12] It was one of the largest television audiences of the 2004–05 season. Men and women of every age and income level watched the show in large numbers.

Most media properties appeal to smaller, targeted audiences. *Ladies' Home Journal*, for example, attracts an almost exclusively female audience, and is strongest among women aged thirty-five to fifty-four. From a business perspective, the entire reason for the existence of *Ladies' Home Journal* is to deliver just over 13.4 million women per month to brand managers who require a medium to tell women of a certain age and income level to buy Garnier Nutrisse, the Chris Madden for Home Collection, Aveeno Clear Complexion Correcting Treatment, a Chrysler Town & Country Minivan, Jell-O, Nexium, and jars of Dole Tropical Fruit.

Women who browse the June 2005 issue of *LHJ* eventually find their way through the branded advertisements to editorial content written for their demographic: a cover story in which "Reba McEntire opens up about being competitive and a clutter bug, and why she's such a happy wife"; a feature called "Scrapbooking with the Stars," this month featuring television's Leeza Gibbons; and "Crazy for Cupcakes," which promises "a delight for kids of all ages."

Ladies' Home Journal is published by Meredith Corporation. According to the company's Web site, "Meredith's consumer database, which contains more than seventy-five million names, is the largest domestic database among media companies and enables magazine and television advertisers to precisely target marketing campaigns."[13] Meredith also owns a dozen television stations and seventeen magazine brands, including *Better Homes and Gardens* and *American Baby*.

Every contemporary media property is designed to deliver a specific target audience. ESPN was put together to provide advertisers with daily access to the difficult-to-reach male eighteen-to-thirty-four demographic (and, to a lesser extent, other market segments). Nickelodeon took off when it replaced educational programs with Looney Tunes cartoons, dressed itself in a brand defined by orange and green slime, and made it clear to advertisers that they could now reach kids all day long.

For an advertiser, the question is not whether to advertise on *Ellen* or *Meet the Press*, but precisely who the target customer is likely to be, and how best to reach that customer. If your job is buying media space or time for Old Navy and you want to reach young moms with a particular product line ("Sun-sational Styles for the Whole Family," for example), then *Ellen* is one way to reach those target customers.

For advertising agencies, creative teams that devise advertising and media buying plans, America is a collection of market segments.

PRIZM Classifications

PRIZM is one of several database services sold to the marketing industry by Claritas.[14] Generally, these services are based upon a detailed analysis of data from the U.S. Census and from local governments, consumer marketing databases, and postal delivery information. By zeroing in on Zip Codes and adding lifestyle attributes, PRIZM adds sophistication to market segmentation. PRIZM generalizes (or, stereotypes) attitudes, behaviors, and beliefs common within those Zip Codes.

According to PRIZM, "You Are Where You Live."

The largest PRIZM classification, representing 3 percent of the United States, is called *Kids and Cul-de-sacs.* This group is comprised of upscale suburban families, often living in single-family homes (median household income: $80,000). Most are college graduates working in white-collar professional jobs. Technologically savvy, these people overindex (are higher than the national average) on computer purchases, Web, e-mail and IM use, and cell phone use. In the driveways, you'll find Japanese minivans and SUVs, and in the brushed aluminum fridge you'll find imported beers. When the kids are young, these upscale families visit theme parks. As with all segments, you'll find this group scattered throughout the country, but there are significant clusters in eastern Virginia and eastern Michigan, northern Colorado, much of Arizona, and throughout the Greater Seattle area. People in these Zip Codes tend to vote conservative Republican.

Shotguns and Pickups are rural blue-collar families living in central Maine, the Appalachian region of the Virginias and the Carolinas, southern Michigan, and the area around the shared borders of Illinois, Kentucky, and Indiana. They represent 2 percent of U.S. households, and their median income is $47,000. Households are predominantly white. High school educated, they overindex on chewing tobacco, tractor pulls, freshwater fishing, hunting, veteran's clubs, Spam, grits, Diet-Rite, Cap'n Crunch, soap operas, supermarket tabloids, and pickup trucks. They, too, tend to vote conservative Republican.

Which PRIZM classifications are most promising for *Branded for Life*? If I was writing a marketing plan for Emmis Books, I would encourage the publisher to concentrate on:

Kids and Cul-de-sacs (described above).

Money & Brains: Sophisticated urban fringe couples who buy espresso makers with their American Express cards and contribute to public broadcasting. They tend to live around Chicago, New York City, Los Angeles, and San Francisco (1.1 percent).

Young Digerati: Liberal Democrats who support gay rights, hold passports, watch foreign films, and go to the theater. They live in the San Francisco Bay area and in and around the Boston-Washington, D.C., corridor (1.0 percent).

New Empty Nests: College graduates, white-collar professionals who live in the upscale suburban fringe, vote without party affiliation, and live in central and southern New England, the Philadelphia area, or the Pacific Northwest (1.8 percent).

Bohemian Mix: Liberal Democrats who live in city apartments in multi-cultural neighborhoods, rent foreign videos, travel to Europe, and drive interesting cars. They're in cities and towns all over the United States (1.7 percent).

Other promising classifications for *Branded for Life* sales include *Urban Elders, Movers & Shakers, Gray Power, Young Influentials, Suburban Sprawl, Blue Chip Blues, Brite Lights Li'l City, Upward Bound, City Startups, New Beginnings, Urban Achievers,* and more.

Probably less promising are *American Classics, White Picket Fences, Sunset City Blues, Winners' Circle, Golden Ponds, Crossroads Villagers, Park Bench Seniors,* and *Mayberry-ville.*

Marketers also use this information to decline services or information. After analyzing PRIZM data, a bank may decide against opening a branch in a poorer neighborhood in favor of one that may be a better marketing fit, encouraging a marginal neighborhood's downward spiral. In the name of good marketing practices, real estate brokers can exacerbate an already challenging urban development problem. Politicians, whose careers rely upon making the right marketing decisions, may favor more promising precincts. For so many Americans (about one in five who live in unfavorable Zip Codes), the best thing they can do is leave town—and become a part of a different target audience.

Viacom's Four-Billion-Dollar Strategy

Viacom is one of the smartest companies in the media industry (so smart that it will become two successful companies in 2006).

In 1971, the FCC required CBS to spin off its syndication division. Viacom was formed to distribute reruns of *The Andy Griffith Show, The Dick Van Dyke Show, The Beverly Hillbillies, Green Acres,* and other former hits to local television stations and to broadcasters outside the United States.

In 1999, Viacom acquired CBS. By that time, Viacom had also acquired Blockbuster Video, Paramount, Simon & Schuster, and a few promising cable networks from a financially overcommitted Warner Communications in 1986. MTV and Nickelodeon were among them.

Today, Viacom's cable networks offer advertisers a perfect system to reach every demographic age group.

The youngest children are served by Nick Jr. This branded program block (9 a.m.–2 p.m. on Nickelodeon) gets children age two to five into the system. The programs are presented without commercials, but the sale of Nick Jr. toys and other products to preschoolers (*Blue's Clues* merchandise, for example) more than makes up the difference.

Nickelodeon serves advertisers by delivering children age two to eleven in very large numbers. Available in over 300 million households, Nickelodeon reaches more children than any medium in the history of the world. Annual revenues exceed $1 billion. Most of that money comes from advertising to children.

The most widely distributed television signal in the world is MTV, with 380 million subscribers worldwide. MTV delivers the twelve-to-thirty-four age demographic. Annual revenues exceed $1 billion.

To reach men ages twenty-five to thirty-four, Viacom offers Comedy Central. Comedy Central viewers overindex on visiting theme parks; prefer to see movies during opening weekend; buy more sports drinks than the general population; shop at Express; and own an electronic organizer.

If an advertiser needs to buy men ages twenty-five to fifty-four, the solution is Spike TV (now the eleventh-largest U.S. cable network, repositioned from the eighteen-to-thirty-four demographic because Viacom offered too many options to reach younger male viewers).

For men and women ages eighteen to forty-nine, advertisers buy VH1.

If you're over fifty, Viacom is selling you as part of the CBS audience.

To reach black Americans ages eighteen to thirty-four via television, Viacom offers BET. This group dramatically overindexes on purchases of basketball shoes (more than five times the average American!), and also tends to buy feature-rich cell phones.[15]

By design, *every* cable network delivers a specific demographic to advertisers. Each network reinforces a specific, self-perpetuating world-view that includes behavioral and lifestyle recommendations and presents advertised products that encourage each viewer to become part of the story. Are you curious which cable networks target your life and your wallet? Visit http://www.onetvworld.org/ and then click on the CAB Research tab for the current year's downloadable facts regarding each cable network.

Media: It's All About the Brand

Media properties are groomed as brands. They have logos. Like Charmin bath tissue,[16] media properties possess brand attributes, credibility, target customers, and unified visual identities. Most consumers can easily envision the logos associated with *eBay*, *TV Guide*, *The Price is Right*, CNN, and Nine Inch Nails. Every city now has its equivalent of NBC4 or CBS2, the result of national network branding campaigns that decimated the identities of long-time local broadcasters.

Television has become a tangle of brands: branded networks (MTV) and spin-off networks (MTV2), programs (*The Daily Show*), personalities (Oprah), and characters (Homer Simpson). NBC owns *The Today Show* and *The Tonight Show*, but Johnny Carson and Jay Leno have become household names by hosting the latter program.

All major studio films are sold to the audiences on the basis of familiar brand names: actors, directors, or familiar franchises. This week's top films include a *Star Wars* movie, a remake of *House of Wax*, and a picture based on the popular book, *Hitchhiker's Guide to the Galaxy*. The number-two film, *Monster-in-Law,* is not based upon a brand, but it succeeds because two reliable brand names are the headliners: Jane Fonda and Jennifer Lopez. *The Interpreter* was a safe bet because it starred Sean Penn and Nicole Kidman.

Movie actors are infrequently a public problem for the corporations that hire them; they're paid enough money so that they generally behave in the best interest of the brand. Besides, the relationship between actor and corporation lasts only as long as the movie is being promoted.

None of this is new. In the 1930s and 1940s, movie studios controlled and managed the brands of their stars. Today, stars do it themselves. By carefully managing her career, from life as a Fly Girl on *In Living Color* to her jump to movies and her star turn in the *Selena* biopic, to a debut album that went multiplatinum, Jennifer Lopez has become a true star. J.Lo is a top entertainment industry brand.

Among writers and directors, Alfred Hitchcock was a powerful brand name ("a Hitchcock film"). Martin Scorsese, Stephen Spielberg, and M. Night Shyamalan are among the few contemporary directors whose names above the title sell tickets. When Shyamalan was asked why his films were so successful (they've grossed $730 million to date),[17] he answered, "Because they are me." He went on: "Bob Dylan is one of the greatest songwriters of all time because he's him ... the greater the athlete, the more specific they can be to themselves."

When an audience sees Shyamalan's name, they know what to expect.[18] "That's the downside of being a brand: that you have to be the brand. You're stuck with being the brand all the time. You don't get to grow, you don't get to change. They pay you obscene amounts of money to be in your brand and they don't want to pay you when you're not."

When does a musician or author become a brand? At the point where the creator's name is the primary reason why people buy. When people bought "the new Beatles' album," the Beatles became a brand. Nowadays, readers pick up the new John Grisham or Janet Evanovich book, regardless of its title. Since most of you have never heard of me, you probably bought on the basis of this book's subject matter or cover art.

For author David Sedaris—whose schtick is "the charming surrogate loser who turns the tables on his oppressors with caustic and sometimes brutal wit"—brand identity conflicts with his present-day reality. Fans (called "Sedaristas") may not care, but Sedaris has earned enough money for apartments in Paris, New York City, and London, plus a house in Normandy. He regularly sells out symphony halls at $25,000 per appearance. Sedaristas buy into the brand and the storytelling, which is far more fun than the successful author's real estate holdings.[19]

Musicians who are media properties sell more records. B.B. King gets it: he's got a restaurant and club named for him in four cities (so far). Many rappers understand that their corner of the industry demands little delineation between musician and celebrity; they are the musicians who evolved at the end of the previous century, during the great branded age. Russell Simmons's unified approach to music, brands, media, and fashion is hip-hop's ultimate expression of branded sophistication. Bruce Springsteen's persona or brand seems to be a perfect match between the artist and his music. U2 is a strong brand, defined by Bono's combination of musicianship and activism. In fact, U2 was brand enough to cause Apple to produce a U2-branded iPod (all-black with a distinctive red wheel).

How the Rules Changed

When NBC and CBS made their move from radio to television,[20] their new prime-time schedules provided a new home for many of radio's most popular stars and for lesser lights better suited to television, Lucille Ball and Milton Berle among them. Television also provided work for movie stars whose best roles were behind them. One was Ronald Reagan, who hosted the popular dramatic anthology series, *General Electric Theater.* In his eight years as host, Reagan "claimed to have visited GE's 135 research and manufacturing facilities, and met some 250,000 individuals."[21] On Reagan's lecture tours for the company, the actor often spoke about GE causes including deregulation, lower corporate taxes, attacking Communism, labor unions, and social welfare. On one 1957 spot, Reagan told viewers, "When you live better electrically ... you lead a richer, fuller, more satisfying life. And it's something all of us in this modern age can have."[22]

In 1967, the Justice Department turned down ITT's attempt to buy ABC because the deal "could compromise ABC's news coverage of political events in countries where ITT has interests."[23]

In 1986, the federal government approved the sale of NBC to General Electric. It was the first time a television network had been sold in thirty-five years.[24] Also in 1986, the FCC quietly relaxed some laws so that a mother corporation was not responsible for behavior as a good citizen, a requirement that only the corporation's broadcast unit would need to fulfill. At the time, General Electric was one of the major producers of nuclear weapons and energy systems, a top defense contractor, and on the list of the world's top polluters. These issues became nonissues with the relaxation of the good citizen rules. In the early 1980s, then-President Reagan approved tax cuts resulting in a windfall for companies in GE's position. GE's tax burden was adjusted from $330 million per year to negative $90 billion, a tax windfall that helped GE to acquire new assets, including NBC.

Knowing all of this, it's difficult not to interpret GE's recent tag lines, "We bring good things to life" and "Imagination at Work" with a sense of irony.

The Public Trust

There's an old tradition in broadcasting. When the government grants a local broadcast license for a television or a radio station, the licensee gets access to the airwaves at no charge, but agrees to serve the public good. The public trusts the licensee with its valuable broadcast channel, and the broadcaster serves the public.

As a result of other changes made during the Reagan administration, this notion of the public trust is no longer central to broadcasting. We no longer require broadcasters to serve their local communities in a direct and meaningful way.

Clear Channel Communications operates approximately 1,200 radio stations in 300 U.S. markets, reaching more than 100 million listeners every week across fifty states. Every day, Clear Channel reaches more than half of the eighteen-to-forty-nine-year-old population of the United States.

Clear Channel's sheer size and reach has been cause for concern. Visit the corporate information section of Clear Channel's Web site, and you'll immediately encounter a page called "Know the Facts."[25] Here, Clear Channel addresses some of the many accusations made against the company. One is related to a well-publicized incident in which Dixie Chicks records were pulled from some Clear Channel stations after the group criticized President Bush; another discusses a list of songs that were not to be played after the September 11 attacks, which included John Lennon's "Imagine"; yet another describes pressure allegedly applied to artists reluctant to perform in Clear Channel's entertainment venues (concert halls, etc.); and more. There are also links to letters that Clear Channel sent to *Rolling Stone* magazine and to *Forbes* magazine offering corrections to stories that appeared in those publications; unfortunately, the magazines' original stories are not included in those links, so the stories are told only from Clear Channel's perspective.

In January 2002, a freight train derailed near Minot, North Dakota, a city large enough to support four network TV affiliates and a PBS station. The resulting cloud of hydrous ammonia was becoming dangerous, so police called local radio stations, six of them owned by Clear Channel. By the next day, one man was dead, three hundred people were hospitalized, and many were partially blinded by the ammonia. Pets and livestock died. The news story, published with facts that Clear Channel denies, explained that the Clear Channel stations were unmanned. From *Forbes*: "... there was no one available to get the word out. Clear Channel was filling airtime with on-air personalities who were anchoring from thousands of miles away." From Clear Channel: "This is a false statement—the truth is that our stations were manned and the failures here rested with the local authorities, who failed to properly install FCC-mandated Emergency Alert System equipment. This equipment automatically breaks into radio broadcasts. Other public service organizations, including the National

Weather Service, have had no trouble interrupting our Minot stations' broadcasts."[26]

Forbes, and others, may have gotten the facts of the story wrong, but the question of whether the equipment was or was not working is not the significant issue. Instead, the issue comes back to that old idea of broadcasting as a public trust. On behalf of the people of Minot, the FCC granted Clear Channel not one but six radio licenses. With those licenses, the people of Minot should have demanded that Clear Channel, or any radio operator, actively and aggressively use licensed radio stations to protect the safety of their community. Certainly, when there's no emergency, the radio station can be used for entertainment and for information, and the owner can make money selling commercial time. It's unclear whether Clear Channel did anything wrong, but it's apparent that Clear Channel did not take the high road and establish a policy to improve the situation.

What we need is a system that encourages a corporation to do the right thing. This $9 billion company (239 on the Fortune 500) should have checked every emergency system related to every one of its 1,200 radio stations and assured the public that *it was* doing everything it could to prevent a future failure. The problem is, by doing the right thing, Clear Channel might risk some admission of guilt, and perhaps open itself to liability. Instead, Clear Channel acted appropriately, in accordance with the rules and the law, and did what the system demands: It sent a letter with carefully worded statements to *Forbes* and posted the letter on its Web site for the public to see. All of this is wrong-headed and shows just how far off course we have allowed our media to stray. The sad story provides yet another example of the disconnection between the corporations who own and control our brands (in this case, media brands) and their customers (in this case, the local audience that was so poorly served).

Motivation

Like people, corporations behave in predictable ways related to self-interest. If the activity is likely to be profitable, then the corporation will devote the necessary resources. If the activity is likely to be troublesome, then the corporation will steer clear of potential problems.

The marketplace provides little motivation for companies to tell the truth, the whole truth, and nothing but the truth. In the recent case of Merck's problems with Vioxx research—the company was apparently aware of research that connected the arthritis drug to heart attacks—the marketplace rewards pharmaceutical companies whose products sell well, not companies who are cautious or especially communicative about side effects. Maybe there's a public outcry, extensive media coverage about the bad behavior, perhaps a government investigation. In case after case, little change occurs. Corporations are still rewarded for the same fundamental behavior, so they are motivated to act in the same way.

Concerned about excessive violence on the eleven o'clock news? Put together a boycott of every local and national sponsor of that newscast and the station will find other advertisers. The system is not set up to provide for change.

Should there be a law? In fact, there are laws protecting personal privacy; public property; against obscenity, violent acts, libel, and slander; restrictions on the sale of tobacco, alcohol, and firearms; laws against the exploitation of children; and some antitrust activity to limit the most unacceptable mergers (for example, a merger of NBC, CBS, and ABC probably wouldn't be allowed).

Should there be a law that assures the people of Minot that their radio operators will provide truthful, timely, aggressive, and comprehensive local news coverage twenty-four/seven? Or a law that demands NBC put its best investigative journalists on stories related to its present owner, GE? Would radio listeners benefit from a law requiring Clear Channel radio stations to program at least 50 percent of their music from artists who never appear in Clear Channel venues? How about 30 percent or 10 percent? Or does it make more sense for these issues to be worked out in the marketplace?

What is the role of the media? What is the role of the government? Does the corporation have any responsibility besides following the existing laws and providing value for its shareholders? What's your role (or mine) in all of this? If these difficult questions are hurting your head as they are mine, let's move on and return to these issues later in the book.

Public Schizophrenia

National Public Radio member stations understand that their success is built largely upon the franchises whose names and brand identities are well known: Garrison Keillor's *A Prairie Home Companion*, *This American Life*, *Car Talk*, *All Things Considered*, and *Fresh Air with Terry Gross*. PBS member stations are defined by the popularity of *Antiques Roadshow*, *Masterpiece Theater*, *Mystery*, *Frontline*, and *NOVA*—several of these series are more than thirty years old. In order to increase young viewer involvement with *Sesame Street*, *Arthur*, *Barney*, *Clifford the Big Red Dog*, and *Mister Rogers' Neighborhood*, PBS branded its children's programming block as a subnetwork called PBS Kids, which has its own logo and playful identity. Characters appearing on PBS Kids programs are often licensed to manufacturers of bed sheets, children's clothing, books, and other products, all of which are enabled through the powerful branding that television exposure provides. In spite of painful criticism from many of its own member stations, PBS has also announced plans for Sprout, a new commercially supported cable television network in association with Comcast, Sesame Workshop, and H!t Entertainment.

> By the time they finish high school, children have spent twice as many hours in front of the TV as in the classroom: about fifteen thousand in class versus about thirty thousand watching TV.

The preschool series *Teletubbies* was first funded by McDonald's, then by Burger King. Are these the best possible choices for a preschool series? From the corporate marketer's perspective, the answer is a clear yes: it makes sense for these companies to show their logos to very young children. For parents and for PBS programmers, it's a dilemma, but money for programs must come from somewhere, and neither viewers nor government nor purchasers of Elmo's World™ Fun Sounds Video Camera™ pony up enough cash to produce quality children's programming.

Children and Television

On the one hand, PBS provides enriching, culturally uplifting television programs. *Sesame Street*, for example, really does prepare young children to read and to deal with their world. For many parents, *Sesame Street* provides another essential service: it's an effective baby sitter. As children grow, they watch a lot of television. In fact, children spend more time watching TV than any other activity except sleep. By the time they finish high school, children have spent twice as many hours in front of the TV as in the classroom: about fifteen thousand in class versus about thirty thousand watching TV.

In the United States, the average young child watches about four hours of TV each day. These hours of viewing include tens of thousand of commercials often for high-fat, high-sugar, high-salt snack foods. A child who watches sports coverage also watches countless alcohol advertisements.

A child watching TV is a child who is sitting still—only sleep burns fewer calories. Children who are out playing are also less likely to consume unhealthful foods and beverages because they're actively engaged, not passively sitting and staring at a screen. According to Dr. William H. Dietz of the Centers for Disease Control, "TV reduction appears to be the most effective measure in reducing weight gain."

Watching television is a mentally passive activity. When TV is watched in excess, it deprives children of hours that could be spent fostering creativity, self-reliance, learning, and social interaction. Studies have shown that children who watch TV for ten hours or more each week have lower reading scores and perform less well academically than comparable youngsters who spend less time. In one study involving 2,500 children, the more TV watched by toddlers ages one to three, the greater the risk of attention problems at age seven.

For each hour watched per day, a young child's risk of developing attention deficit hyperactivity increased by nearly 10 percent. These children exhibited difficulty in concentrating and organizing and engage in impulsive behavior. Studies of brain functions show evidence of direct harm to brains of young children who watch two hours or more per day. These children exhibited increased aggressiveness, lower tolerance levels, and decreased attention spans. "The two-minute mind easily becomes impatient with any material requiring depth of processing."

"Many parents of children diagnosed with (Attention Deficit Disorders) found the difficulty markedly improved after they took away viewing privileges."[27]

Other issues related to excessive television viewing include poor sleep quality and a greater likelihood of picking up smoking. A 2002 study of children aged ten-plus who watched TV five or more hours per day were six (!) times as likely to start smoking as those who watched two hours per day.[28]

Some advice from the TV Turnoff Network and the American Academy of Pediatrics: (1) Allow your children to select up to two hours of programming to view per day. Stick to the limit. Watch at least some of that programming with your child. Talk about the programs with your child. (2) Don't use television as a reward, a punishment, or as a babysitter. (3) Don't allow your child to just "watch TV." Encourage your child to "watch a TV show" and to turn the set off when the show is over.

Still feeling that this is all no big deal, that there's no reason for concern about children and television viewing? Let's shift the focus away from the programs themselves and into the spectacular business that has grown around merchandise related to children's television.

Nickelodeon, once a free come-on to convince parents to subscribe to cable, is the world's largest television service. Nickelodeon has earned more than $4 billion by selling manufacturers the right to make clothing, toys, foods, and other products based upon its programs. According to the company Web site,[29] "Nickelodeon Consumer Products (is) the world's largest TV-based licensing business and its sixth largest entertainment licensing business. Additionally, Enterprises operates the country's most widely read kids magazine (*Nickelodeon Magazine*); the leading touring live theater business for kids (currently offering *Dora the Explorer* and *Blue's Clues Live*; and the number-one kid-based and parent-based sites on the Internet (Nick.com and Nickjr.com)."

In their prime, *Rugrats* and *Blue's Clues* generated $1 billion in licensing revenues. *SpongeBob SquarePants* has been worth more. Decorating your child's room? Just feed the brand monster. The show becomes a commercial for the merchandise, and the merchandise encourages the child to watch the show. And you pay a buck or so every month to Nickelodeon to bring the show into your home. It's a good deal; your child's happy, you're happy. Nickelodeon is ecstatic. What's more, advertisers pay a premium because *SpongeBob SquarePants* is one of television's most popular shows.

The Printed Truth

Each year, *US News and World Report* publishes guides to the nation's top colleges and universities. "Dig into the data, read the numbers, then use that as a launching point to learn about the nature of the school, the personality," Executive Editor Brian Kelly told viewers of MSNBC. "We say this is a great starting point, but we don't pretend it's anything more than that."

In fact, a positive review in a *US News* annual college guide tremendously enhances the brand value of each top-ranked institution; the result is often seen in an increase in the quantity and quality of student applications. At the same time, *US News*, Peterson's, and other college guides have helped to reduce college choice to easily defined criteria, or in marketing language, easy-to-understand brand attributes. While a numerical rating may be misleading or misrepresentative, parents and incoming students believe the numbers.

What Media Should Be Required to Do

Some of these ideas originated in James Fallows' book, *Breaking the News: How the Media Undermine American Democracy*. I have expanded on some of them.

First and foremost, the media should be straightforward and truthful. Every media message should include information about the company behind it. When I see a baseball player with a mouthful of Skoal smokeless chewing tobacco on TV, it should be easy for me to find out whether he is being paid to drool on national television, and I should know that Skoal is a $1 billion brand owned by the US Smokeless Tobacco Corp. I should also know that the company has entered into an agreement with forty-five state governments that severely restrict the promotion of its brands, particularly in venues where children may be exposed to it.

In fact, every program ought to disclose the corporate interests associated with its broadcast or cablecast. These disclosures should detail network ownership, sponsor ownership, and current business dealings that may, by any reasonable measure, affect program content.

Second, every program should clearly signal the nature of its content. This should be done on the air, before the program begins, and periodically through the body of the program. The message should be clear and direct. For example: "This program contains partial nudity. Its story involves adult situations, such as adultery, offensive language, severe mental anguish, and a scene involving a loaded gun. It is not recommended for children." This information should be included in consumer advertising and in program listings (if not in newspapers and *TV Guide*, then certainly on the Web, where more space is available).

Third, news and information sources should accept their job as America's primary educators and should be held to a higher standard. As viewers, we should demand *perspective*. Why did the story happen in the first place? What is being done to change the situation? Are there contrary opinions? How can I help? We should also demand follow-up, so that stories are not presented in a vacuum, without context. Stories become frozen in time, images that collectively create an impression, a deep impression, that may or may not be true. How important is the event? Does it fit into a consistent pattern? Journalists should explain how stories are connected so that we all understand, more deeply, what is really happening.

Fallows explains that journalists are encouraged to look for the next big story, the next scandal, and along the way they don't attend to "the daily chore of telling us what is important and why."[30] Fallows believes this to be the journalist's real job.

As Fallows points out, life is not a random sequence of car crashes and street shootings. Most stories are told with almost total disregard for history. What were the root causes of the problem? Is this a new issue, or one that's been around for decades? Is this story related to other stories? Storylines branded as complicated never see the light of day.

When Americans watch the outside world on TV, they tend to develop one of these two perspectives about other countries: "That country is so messed up, we shouldn't waste time thinking about them." Or, "That country is so messed up, they threaten our own security or moral sensibility, so we should invade, withdraw, or forget about them."

Fourth, we need more programming that tells us about the large companies that dominate our economy. We should demand far more than news of daily stock fluctuations and CEO changes. Corporations are made of people, not money, and their stories are often interesting. Telling the Enron story in a motion picture with characters based upon Jeffrey Skilling and Kenneth Lay might do more to help people understand corporate greed than any series of stories in *The New York Times*. In truth, I wouldn't mind watching a motion picture about life at Procter & Gamble or Wal-Mart or J.P. Morgan Chase. What's life like in the development labs at Pfizer or Intel? Why can't we all attend a board meeting at Dow Chemical or Tyson Foods? Michael Moore and several other filmmakers have attempted to gain access, often with angry results. Is *The Apprentice* as close as we'll ever get to the ivory tower?

Ted Turner's Perspective

After two decades of attempting to compete with the big media companies Ted Turner sold out to Time Warner. In *Washington Monthly* magazine (July 2004), Turner offered some interesting perspectives on the media business. Some excerpts from his thoughts on big media:

"Without proper rules, healthy capitalist markets turn into sluggish oligopolies, and that is what is happening in the media business today. Large corporations are more profit-focused and risk-averse."

Managers in large media companies must focus on short-term earnings, a type of management that is a polar opposite from the independent owner who must run companies for long-term growth and stability. Independent companies that succeed do so first by selling product to the larger companies, and then selling their companies to the same buyers.

"When you lose small business, you lose big ideas … They know they can't compete by imitating the big guys—they have to innovate so they're less obsessed with earnings than they are with ideas. They are quicker to seize on new technologies and new product ideas. They steal market share from bigger companies, spurring them to adopt new approaches. This process promotes competition, which leads to higher product and service quality, more jobs, and greater wealth. It's called capitalism."

Endnotes

1   From GE web site: http://www.ge.com/en/company/

2   NBC Universal Television owns and operates the NBC Television network and the Spanish-language Telemundo network and controls the marketing for the PAX network. NBC Universal Cable operates and wholly or jointly owns Bravo, CNBC, MSNBC, SCI FI, Shop NBC, and USA, and is a significant investor in A&E, The History Channel, plus a variety of international networks and smaller domestic cable networks.

3   Also in the top twenty, C-SPAN is a nonprofit company.

4   Until 1955, the BBC was Britain's only national radio or television broadcaster. Deregulation in the 1980s opened the door to additional advertiser-supported radio and television services and to commercially supported cable and satellite networks.

5   *Television Week*, May 16, 2005, and U.S. Bureau of Labor Statistics Time Use Survey 2003.

6   In a 2004 survey, CBS asked participants whether they would prefer to buy a pay-per-view program for one dollar without commercials or for fifty cents with commercials. Results were an even split.

7   Example: *Fast Company* magazine sells for $4.99 on the newsstands, but it's available from www.amazon.com for one dollar per issue in a twelve-issue subscription.

8   *Soap Opera: The Inside Story of Procter & Gamble* by Alecia Swasy, p. 198.

9   "The Myth of Media Concentration: Why The FCC's Media Ownership Rules Are Unnecessary" can be read in its entirety at http://www.heritage.org/Research/InternetandTechnology/wm284.cfm

10 Generally, the range is about $150,000 to over $500,000, depending upon the popularity of the program and the "heat" surrounding its upcoming season.

11 According to *The Princeton Review*, Business Administration & Management is the number-one major, and Communications is number eight. For the complete list, see http://www.princetonreview.com/college/research/articles/majors/popular.asp

12 *Idol* is a branded franchise that's a hit in dozens of countries. According to British producer Fremantle Media (part of Bertelsmann), *Australian Idol* was Australia's number-one entertainment show in 2004; *Singapore Idol* was also that country's top

entertainment show in the same year; *Canadian Idol* was Canada's highest-rated locally produced entertainment show ever.

13   http://www.meredith.com/default.sph/pr_user.class?FNC=ViewRelease__ Aextemplate_html___944

14   To learn your own classification, enter your Zip Code: http://www.clusterbigip1. claritas.com/MyBestSegments/Default.jsp?ID=20

15   2005 Cable Advertising Bureau (CAB) Profile, BET.

16   Or, as everybody except P&G calls it, "toilet paper."

17   http://www.the-numbers.com/people/directors/MNSHY.html

18   "The One and Only M. Night Shyamalan," *Philadelphia Inquirer*, January 24, 2004.

19   "Turning Sour Grapes into a Silk Purse," *The New York Times*, June 6, 2004.

20   When NBC was required to sell one of its radio networks in 1943, ABC was born. Another small network, DuMont, started in the 1950s and failed; later, some DuMont stations (then property of Metromedia) provided a foundation for the FOX network.

21   http://www.museum.tv/archives/etv/G/htmlG/generalelect/generalelect.htm

22   http://www.museum.tv/archives/etv/G/htmlG/generalelect/generalelect.htm

23   *Global Spin: The Corporate Assault on Environmentalism* by Sharon Beder, p. p. 200-220.

24   ABC was sold to Leonard Goldenson and United Paramount Theaters in 1951. Generally, television network ownership was perceived as rock-solid fixed. Most people believed the networks would never be sold. (Most people were wrong, as NBC, CBS, and ABC were sold in rapid succession.)

25   http://www.clearchannel.com/Corporate/corporate_ktf.aspx

26   As quoted in the Clear Channel letter to *Forbes*.

27   "TV's Toll on Young Bodies and Minds," by Jane Brody, *The New York Times*, August 3, 2004.

28   "TV's Toll on Young Bodies and Minds," by Jane Brody, *The New York Times*, August 3, 2004.

29   http://www.nick.com/all_nick/everything_nick/press_dunn.jhtml

30   *Breaking the News: How the Media Undermine American Democracy* by James Fallows, p. 134.

GOVERNMENT, THE PROTECTOR

At first, a chapter about government may seem out of place in a book about branding. In fact, there are several ways in which the government is intimately involved in the branding industry: as a regulator, as a promoter, and as a brand manager with its own portfolio of brands to be managed.

Like most national governments, the U.S. government is often faced with two conflicting goals.

On the one hand, the government's most important role is to protect its citizens against clear and present danger, and to take necessary measures to prevent danger from occurring in the future. Many of our laws and much of our annual budget is spent on these concerns.

On the other hand, the government's role is to stimulate the national economy and to encourage trade with other nations.

Often, these goals are in opposition.

When Agriculture Secretary (and USDA chief) Michael Johanns says, in the midst of a mad cow scare, "I enjoyed beef this noon for lunch ... It is the safest beef in the world," is he (a) promoting the beef industry or (b) addressing public health concerns?

Throughout the Federal government, there are overlaps, conflicts, loopholes, and opportunities for lobbyists and smart lawyers to affect outcomes. The same is true of most state and city governments. In our country, there are close personal connections between lawmakers, lobbyists, corporate executives, and leaders of trade associations. This the real world where it's not unusual to find one or several wealthy real estate developers raising money for a local political candidate and calling several influential corporate buddies for cash, contacts, and a few phone calls to the right people. These are not the exceptions: this is the way the system works.

Often, when a politician completes a term, a job as a lobbyist is often an option. From the lobby group or corporate employer's perspective, who better to influence other politicos than a man or woman who served beside them? During the past three decades, one in eight former U.S. senators and congressmen became lobbyists. These lobbyists work hard to affect government policy: they regularly meet with people who write our laws, but they are paid, directly or indirectly, by the corporations that own our most popular brands.

A (Candid) Refresher Course in Government

In general, the executive branch is the one with massive, concentrated power in cabinet departments larger than most large corporations, well-known department leaders who get press coverage, and the freedom to act on behalf of the current president's political agenda.

As a rule, commissions and agencies created and managed by the legislative branch are smaller, with less funding and narrower definitions of required services. Often, their leaders are appointed by the Executive Branch, and then (most often) rubber-stamped by Congress (with occasional, well-publicized disagreements).

The judicial branch is more than the Supreme Court. It also includes the district and circuit courts that make decisions affecting both the rights of consumers and the activities of companies.

Cabinet-Level Departments

Most of the fifteen cabinet-level departments are concerned with what we buy, eat, learn, and believe. Several are concerned with the promotion of American business, and, remarkably, with the regulation of those same businesses.

The Department of Energy's $23 billion budget promotes energy use and protects the nation's energy resources. It's responsible for the activities of some of the nation's most profitable brands, including Exxon, Mobil, Shell, and other fuel companies.

The Department of Commerce, with its $5 billion annual budget and its forty thousand workers, is about the size of Nordstrom's. Its goal is clear, and not at all dubious: business promotion. The patent and trademark office is part of the Department of Commerce, which suggests that patents and trademarks are, mostly, rights associated with commercial entities, not individuals.

The Department of Education was created in 1980 from several other federal agencies. Its objective: "To ensure equal access to education and to promote educational excellence throughout the nation." Along the way, the Department of Education establishes and enforces certain guidelines that permit education on a massive scale. Although Education is relatively small in terms of employees at 4,800 (half the number employed by book and classroom magazine publisher Scholastic, Inc.), its $54 billion budget is massive (most of it pays federal aid to education).

When farming was America's largest industry, Abraham Lincoln established the Department of Agriculture (USDA). The agency calls itself "America's largest company" (critics call it "the plantation," saluting its outmoded ways). The USDA is concerned with economic well being of farmers and ranchers, and, often, this concern lapses into nutrition studies. The USDA also controls farm subsidies and pays out $7.3 billion per year for corn and other feed grains; $1.6 billion for soybeans (often used for feed); $1.5 billion for wheat; a remarkable $1.5 billion for tobacco; and less than a billion for dairy, for rice, and for peanuts. Despite the nutritional recommendations of its own food pyramid, the USDA does not subsidize fruit or vegetable production to any great extent.[1] The USDA's annual budget is nearly $90 billion, about four times the budget of Microsoft. About two million people work for the USDA, more than the total number of U.S. employees working for McDonald's, Burger King, Wendy's, and just about every other fast-food restaurant combined.

Housing and Urban Development, or HUD, is about two-thirds the size of Education. It's an agency that helps with housing and community building for disadvantaged populations (poor, HIV/AIDS, and the elderly among them).

The Department of Labor and the Department of Veteran's Affairs are also concerned, mainly, with individual rights.

The Department of Transportation ensures the safety and viability of our nation's transportation system. The DoT serves both the individual citizen (cars, buses, bikes, accessibility, commuters) and businesses (freight, trucking, rail). It's responsible for the activities of top brands, including Ford, General Motors, Amtrak, American Airlines, and more.

The Department of the Interior's principal role is to protect the environment, but often, environment is a political issue, as corporate interests are often jealous of the economic potential in our land. Interior's range is massive: the department manages 20 percent of U.S. land.

Despite the confusing similarity in names, the Department of Justice is not related to the judicial branch of government. The DOJ is home to the attorney general and the FBI (among other agencies), all of which report to the president. They are part of the executive branch, and their primary concerns are investigation and

No one government body is as deeply involved in the world of branded products as the FDA.

enforcement. The other departments in the executive branch departments are less directly involved with consumers, corporations and branding issues: State, Treasury, Homeland Security, and Defense.

Most of the work done in relation to brands falls under the Department of Health and Human Services, which now oversees the government's health-related activities, notably the National Institutes of Health, The Centers for Disease Control and Prevention (CDC), Medicare/Medicaid, and more. HHS is one of the federal governments largest departments, but the numbers may be misleading. The department's annual budget is $540 billion, but $440 billion belongs to Medicare. About ten thousand people work for the FDA, whose annual budget is $1.7 billion; in comparison with the corporate world, the FDA employs slightly more people than Scholastic or about half as many employees as Mattel Toys.

Food and Drug Administration (FDA)

The FDA was the first government agency or administration formed specifically to protect the average citizen. This model was later used to start the Consumer Protect Safety Commission, the Environmental Protection Agency, and other federal agencies.

No one government body is as deeply involved in the world of branded products as the FDA. Until 1998, the FDA was part of the USDA.

The FDA deals with food safety, nutrition, drug evaluation, drug research, medical devices, safety of the blood supply, vaccines, veterinary medicine, tobacco, and more. In all, the FDA is responsible for $1 trillion in goods each year and keeps tabs on nearly 100,000 businesses. Remarkably, this is accomplished on a budget that works out to four dollars per taxpayer per year, a budget that's a tenth the size of NASA's, and $\frac{1}{250}$ the size of the Defense Department. In other words, we spent 250 times more money to stay safe than to stay healthy.

Throughout its century-long history, the FDA has been limited in its ability to protect the nation's citizens due to inadequate regulation, insufficient staff and resources, an ever-expanding workload, and political pressure from competing government organizations, corporations, and consumers.

The FDA's process frequently involves thousands of pages of data, which may or may not include significant clues to safety, side effects, or other issues. Science and judgment must be considered as gray areas emerge, and uncertainty exists.

From the perspective of pharmaceutical and food industries, the FDA is slow, bureaucratic, and frequently ineffective. From the citizen's perspective, the FDA can be aggravating in its procedures; some of these procedures keep necessary medicines off the market for long periods. Still, citizens hold the FDA to a very high standard: Its job is to protect us.

Regulation is a political process, subject to the whim of every presidential administration. Each administration controls budgets for enforcement, and so sets the FDA's priorities. (Take away the budget for investigator's cars, for example, and the whole process slows down. The Reagan administration did just that.)

Dr. John Nestor, cardiologist with a specialty in pediatric disorders, joined the FDA in 1961. He was one of the people who stopped the Richardson-Merrell's misbehavior in the well-publicized "thalidomide baby" case. His statements ring true today: "You've got to make a choice as to whether you're going to operate under the business and commercial ethic and make a profit for shareholders, or whether you're going to operate under a scientific ethic and make decisions in favor of the patient. You can't be on both sides."

Which brands are regulated by the FDA? In general, the FDA monitors everything we eat and drink, plus pharmaceuticals and cosmetics. An ongoing debate has limited the FDA's involvement in tobacco regulation. Still, the FDA is the single federal agency with the greatest responsibility for products sold as consumer brands.

Centers for Disease Control and Prevention (CDC)

The CDC is also challenged by political forces, and by the tendency of media to make a big story out of a small one. One recent example is mad cow disease, which got a lot of press. ("Mad cow" is a pretty darned good brand name, one that looks terrific in print and conjures images of deranged bovines with mouths foaming and diseases racking their thick bodies just before we eat them as hamburger.) Many other food-related issues are far

more dangerous, but few possess mad cow's impressive brand imagery. ⟵
Each year more people die from issues related to deli meats than the total
number who have died from mad cow or SARS or any number of headline-
grabbing diseases. Political pressure and media coverage divert attention
and sometimes affect priorties.

Internal Revenue Service (IRS)

The IRS may not be a brand we love, but it's certainly a brand that has us
brainwashed. Think about this: we pay a quarter of everything we earn
to an organization that doesn't make much of an effort to tell us how the
money will be used.

Federal income tax was a *temporary* measure during the Civil War.
Around World War I, it became permanent, mostly as a means to tax rich
people. About sixty years ago, the government's policies changed and every
citizen became a taxpayer. America is now 230 years old: for nearly three-
fourths of that time, death was inevitable, but taxes were not.

The IRS is the size of a good-sized bank (Wachovia, for example). With
a $10 billion annual budget, the IRS employs about eighty thousand people
full-time, plus more than ten thousand part-timers. Each year, the IRS
collects about $2 trillion,[2] half of it from individuals, plus about $650 billion
more from employment taxes. Corporations contribute a measly $200 billion.
The rest comes from estate and gift taxes (on individuals) and excise taxes.

Turns out corporations pay far less Federal tax on their income than we
pay on ours—with many more opportunities for deductions. Around WWI,
corporations paid about 50 percent of their revenues in Federal taxes; now
they pay between 5 and 10 percent.

As an individual, your income is taxed from the "top line"—the total
amount of money you take in. As a corporation, taxes are based upon a
bottom line, the total amount of money that the corporation still has on
hand *after* it has paid its other bills. And if a corporation disputes the IRS's
estimate of taxes due, the corporation can and often does negotiate a lower
rate. Individuals rarely negotiate tax payments.

Where does the money go? The answer[3] is convoluted because the Office
of Management and Budget's income categories don't match up with the
IRS, and because there are sources of federal income other than the IRS.
That said, in a typical year, the federal government is working with over
$2 trillion. The biggest bite, about $500 billion, goes to Social Security. If
there's no war, national defense takes about $400 billion, "income security"[4]

takes about $325 billion, and Medicare needs another $240 billion. By now, nearly three-fourths of the money is spent. We use about $300 billion to pay off the interest on loans, and another $260 billion to keep people healthy. Those are the big numbers. Everything else—international affairs, science, energy, natural resources, environment, agriculture, housing, transportation, community and regional development, education, veterans, justice—is funded by what's left. When there's a war, we overspend the budget, usually by borrowing tens of billions of dollars, and more.

When you and I pay our taxes, we blindly provide about twenty cents on every dollar of tax paid for national defense and about twelve cents on Medicare. If you earn fifty thousand dollars and pay fifteen thousand dollars in taxes, you are, in fact, paying three thousand dollars per year for national defense.

Just as we are learning to demand full disclosure from food manufacturers and other corporate marketers, we should demand similar disclosures—in simple language—from our government offices.

Legislative and Judicial Branches

Most of us can name at least a handful of senators and members of congress. Does the legislative branch begin and end with these two bodies? Where does the FCC or the FTC or the SEC fit into the picture? In fact, the legislative branch includes the Senate, the House of Representatives, the Library of Congress, the Government Accountability Office, and The Government Printing Office. The agencies and commissions, including the FCC, the FTC, the SEC, and hundreds more, operate independently and report to Congress.

It's interesting to contemplate why the FCC reports to Congress while the FDA reports to the president. Maybe there ought to be a single federal body to which all monitoring agencies and commissions report? And perhaps another body to which all business promotion agencies and commissions report? If monitoring requires wisdom and judgment, should these activities be situated within the judicial branch?

Federal Communications Commission (FCC)

The FCC oversees the activities of broadcasters and the corporations that own them. It's also concerned with the telephone and telecommunications industries. The FCC is directly responsible for the rules and monitoring of many familiar brands, including ABC, CBS, NBC, FOX, Verizon, Comcast,

Cingular, Clear Channel, Viacom, and more. Many of the activities licensed or regulated by the FCC rely upon brand marketing or consumer subscriptions for their revenue streams. These activities include both the operation of television and radio stations and networks, and the programming and advertising that plays on these stations and networks.

The FCC establishes its own agenda. Often, the results are profound.

In 1981, President Reagan selected conservative activist Mark Fowler to chair the FCC. "He rejected a fifty-year-old principle that broadcasters had a duty to serve the public as well as advertisers because the airwaves were public property. By 1983, Fowler had abandoned public policy that radio and TV stations provided public service, and news programming, and [that they] limit advertising. He also eased the number of TV stations a company could purchase. In the name of free markets, Fowler casually ended the traditional connection that the mass media offer more than commercial entertainment and avoid monopoly control. He insisted that broadcasters should be treated as businesspeople, and not be expected to be trustees of culture."[5]

As with other government organizations, the FCC has a split role. One example: cell phones. The FCC approves every new phone model sold to U.S. consumers. Unfortunately, cell phones are too new to truly assess potential brain damage or other ill effects due to close and extended proximity with radio waves. Rather than insisting upon extensive research, the FCC has gone along with other countries, setting reasonable standards based upon currently available information. By setting higher standards, the FCC might place the United States at a strategic disadvantage, but higher standards might, in the long run, prove to be a far healthier choice. The research is not definitive, so the FCC has taken the side of progress.

There is, however, another aspect of cell phone use where the FCC could set more stringent guidelines. While any reasonable person understands that a driver traveling sixty miles per hour with one hand on a cell phone is a dangerous driver, the FCC has not established any rules regarding the design of hands-free cell phones. These rules have been left for the states to decide; the result has been inconsistent legislation and enforcement.

The FCC also monitors the behavior of broadcasters. Sometimes, the FCC fines broadcasters for inappropriate language or for other violations of good behavior or technical standards. Monitoring is inconsistent and often responsive to public outcry.

The FCC has just two thousand people working at what amounts to a small government commission; large cable networks employ more people.

The FCC works with a budget (a Congressional appropriation) of under $300 million, very small by government standards. Therefore, the FCC's capacity to protect and monitor activities of those under its control is limited. A greater number of employees might make the life of broadcasters more complicated, but a larger staff might also allow for more effective monitoring of the many thousands of hours of programming shown to American viewers each week.

Federal Trade Commission (FTC)

With about one thousand employees, the FTC is also small, about the size of videogame maker Activision. There is a severe limit to the amount of work that one thousand people can do, how many cases they can investigate and prosecute. Brands under FTC scrutiny include all foods, pharmaceuticals, and cosmetics—but only with regard to the claims made on their labels and in their advertising. In general, the FTC focuses on truthful claims and fair competition. It is also concerned with any business engaged in consumer finance, including credit card companies. In the commission's own words: "The FTC is the only federal agency with jurisdiction to enhance consumer welfare and protect competition in broad sectors of the economy. It enforces the laws that prohibit business practices that are anticompetitive, deceptive, or unfair to consumers, and seeks to do so without impeding legitimate business activity. The FTC also promotes informed consumer choice and public understanding of the competitive process ..."[6]

The FTC works at a high level, generally preventing competition through unfair practices. The commission is now paying particular attention to global trade laws. On the consumer level, the FTC focuses on false or misleading advertising. The FTC is also involved in Do Not Call lists, prevention of deceptive or abusive lending practices, curbing e-mail spam, preventing identity theft, consumer privacy, and other issues related to the fair practice of commerce and the protection of individual rights.

> With about one thousand employees, the Federal Trade Commission is small, about the size of the videogame maker Activision. There is a severe limit to the amount of work that one thousand people can do, how many cases they can investigate and prosecute.

Just how important are these issues? For the answer, compare the relative sizes of the Department of Commerce, with its forty thousand employees, to the FTC, with just one thousand. Why do we require an FTC that's a separate organization from the Department of Commerce? Why not a single government agency responsible for American business?

The answer comes down to a kind of branding. We become so accustomed to these government agency brands that these types of questions seem almost blasphemous. Like their commercial counterparts, they are built on a solid foundation of beliefs. Solid citizens should routinely question their government and challenge assumptions. Strong branding discourages these questions: The IRS and the FTC are what they are, and the idea of developing a better way to govern seems almost unfathomable.

Securities and Exchange Commission (SEC)

Although most people's eyes glaze over when the SEC is even mentioned, it's one of the brands in the government portfolio that consumers really ought to know more about. This obstinately protective organization was founded during the heart of the Depression (and several years after the 1929 stock market crash). The SEC now employs about 3,100 people.

In short, the SEC protects your investments. U.S. laws and rules that govern the securities industry in the United States derive from a simple and straightforward concept: All investors, whether large institutions or private individuals, should have access to certain basic facts about an investment prior to investing. To achieve this, the SEC requires public companies to disclose meaningful financial and other information to the public, which provides a common pool of knowledge for all investors to use to judge whether a company's securities are a good investment. Only through the steady flow of timely, comprehensive, and accurate information can people make sound investment decisions.

Unlike bank savings, investments in securities can lose principal. Stocks and other securities should be considered high-risk investments, a fact that is often understated in the consumer marketing of securities through brokerage firms and similar companies.

The SEC also oversees other key participants in the securities industry, including stock exchanges, broker-dealers, investment advisors, mutual funds, and public utility holding companies.

Intellectual Property

There are three types of intellectual property protection: copyright, trademark, and patent.

Copyright

During your lunch hours, you sit at your desk and write the great American novel. When it's published, your employer claims to own the copyright. Since the novel was written on company equipment, using company facilities, while you were an employee, your employer is making a reasonable claim. Work done as an employee does not belong to the individual. It belongs to the company. (You could argue that you were not, technically, operating as an employee because you wrote only during lunch, but you'd probably lose the dispute.)

When the laws regarding copyrights, trademarks, and patents were devised, the business world was a very different place. Creative work was done by individuals. These protective laws were written to encourage creative people to keep on creating. In time, corporations began to exploit the value of these copyrights and trademarks, and eventually, to own them. The rules slowly changed to favor the corporate owner. Today, the majority of valuable media copyrights and trademarks are owned or controlled by large media corporations.

Copyrights are granted to protect the unauthorized duplication or distribution of a creative work, such as Khaled Hosseini's novel *The Kite Runner*; or the picture of a tree, a house, and the sun that your kindergartener drew yesterday (which was, from the first crayon stroke, protected by copyright law). Artists, writers, and producers create and develop copyrights, and, in some cases, media properties that become well-known brands. As a rule, these creators rely upon large media companies to transform their creations into successful money-making products, and ultimately, into brands.

Once a corporation owns the rights to intellectual property, its law department is charged with protecting those rights and making certain that usage fees are collected. Corporations and their trade associations regularly prosecute individual violators. As a result, the Girl Scouts must pay royalties on the songs they sing around the campfire. When you download a song from the Internet, you must pay a copyright fee, and if you don't, you may be arrested.

Trademark

A trademark holder has the right to words, names, symbols, sounds, or colors that distinguish goods and services from those manufactured or sold by others and to indicate the source of the goods. Trademarks, unlike patents, can be renewed forever as long as they are being used in commerce.

Once a trademark is granted by the U.S. Patent and Trademark Office, that trademark is unavailable to others within the product or service category.

For example, consider the trademarks related to the word "domino," a word of French origin, probably related to the Latin *benedicamus Domino,* or "let us bless the Lord." It's also a long hooded cloak worn with a half-mask as a masquerade costume,[7] and a two-thousand-year-old game played with black tiles and white dots.

So, who owns the trademark on the word "Domino"? The answer is not one or two companies, but several hundred. Each owns the use of Domino within a particular and very specific use (in one Domino Pizza filing: "retail pizza store services specializing in pizza for consumption off the premises"), and/or in association with other words in a phrase ("Domino's Pizza Nobody Delivers Better"). Domino Sugar's trademarks are also specific, as are the many other companies for whom Domino is part or all of the trademarked brand name.

So, what happens on the Web, where www.domino.com would help to reach potential customers? That URL belongs to a company that builds Web sites (and was probably smart enough to grab the URL before the pizza or sugar companies caught on). Today, Web URLs are a prominent aspect of branding, so you must visit www.dominosugar.com for sugar cubes,[8] and www.dominos.com for pizza.

Trademarks are not limited to brand names. After Owens-Corning licensed the Pink Panther, it invested millions of dollars to promote color of product and demonstrated that residential customers associated pink insulation with Owens-Corning. After court appeals, Owens-Corning registered the color pink as a trademark. "What Can Brown Do For You?" has been the UPS tagline—and, sure enough, UPS has trademarked[9] the color brown for use on its trucks and also for its uniforms. UPS competitor DHL is now advertising: "Yellow. It's the new brown."

Patent

Accoding to U.S. law, a patent holder has the right to "to exclude others from making, using, offering for sale, or selling the invention throughout the United States or importing the invention into the United States."

Should all types of products be patented? When the modern pharmaceutical industry was young, there was a lot of debate about whether pharmaceuticals should be patented, whether they should become the basis for corporate assets, or available to any company with the means to safely manufacture and distribute the medicine. Ultimately, patents became the property of—you guessed it—major pharmaceuticals companies or smaller development firms that sell rights to these companies for marketing and distribution. (In this regard, developing and selling a cure for cancer is similar to making a movie.)

Where should we draw the line? Computer software can be copyrighted, sold under a brand that can be trademarked, with certain unique processes protected by patent. Should we allow human genes to be copyrighted, trademarked, patented? Would the best genes be branded under a trademark: GreatGenes®.[10]

Brands rely upon intellectual property protection assured by the Library of Congress (for copyright) and by the U.S. Patent and Trademark Office. Without this protection, our branded society might cease to exist.

Endnotes

1   "Feds Aren't Subsidizing Recommended Foods," by Libby Quaid, *Associated Press*, August 10, 2005.

2   http://www.census.gov/Press-Release/www/2003/cb03-ff05se.html

3   http://www.whitehouse.gov/omb/budget/fy2003/pdf/bud34.pdf

4   These are employee benefit plans, resulting from ERISA.

5   *The All-Consuming Century: Why Commercialism Won in Modern America* by Gary Cross, p. 203.

6   FTC budgetsummary05.pdf, page 1.

7   This, according to Merriam-Webster, a brand I trust because it employs dozens of editors and experts who study and think about words all day.

8   Domino Sugar is owned by Domino Foods, not by a conglomerate. All they do is process and sell sugar.

9   For a look at the one hundred or so trademarks held by UPS, go to: http://www.ups.com/content/us/en/trademark.html

10 That ® indicates the trademark has been registered and accepted by the US Patent and Trademark Office. An ordinary ™ means the paperwork has been submitted, nothing more.

BRAND U.S.A.

From around 1775 until 1791, the United States of America was launched, marketed, and ultimately sold to diverse groups of settlers in thirteen independent colonies, plus one independent nation (Vermont). The idea of an invented country was new. Many believed it would fall apart.

Our Branded Nation

In order to sell the idea, activists including Benjamin Franklin, John Adams, and Thomas Jefferson realized the need for a clear definition of the new country's unique vision and attributes. In response to that need, Jefferson wrote the defining document, a declaration of independence from the England.

A successful marketing campaign requires a compelling catch phrase, and Jefferson presented two of history's best: "life, liberty, and the pursuit of happiness"[1] and "all men are created equal." Samuel Adams, John Locke, and others had written about these ideas before, but Jefferson's specific word choices brought these ideas to life, and they have endured. As the heart and soul of our belief system, Jefferson's words have provided a foundation for a nation at war, for the Civil Rights movement, and for tailgate parties.

A new name was adopted: "The United States of America," bringing together the idea of union—a union of previously independent colonies—and the concept of a sovereign state—in which a local authority exercises governing power over a limited sphere. The words were carefully selected by Franklin, Adams, and Jefferson and approved by the Continental Congress on September 9, 1776, replacing The United Colonies of America as the country's name. Soon after, the Latin phrase, E Pluribus Unum ("from many, one") became the nation's motto.

God and Destiny

The newly branded nation was unique in another respect: It was diverse. Settlers from England, Scotland, France, Germany, Sweden, the Netherlands, and other countries held their own religious beliefs. The idea of a national church (similar to the Church of England) was not viable in the colonies, or in the new nation. Still, God was a powerful force in the lives of the colonists. Quoting scripture was a common practice, often in defense of one's position on the slavery question, for example. Bolstered by Divine Providence (roughly: "by God's will"), laws were legitimatized and obeyed.

Evangelical Christianity has always been an attribute of the American brand. When revivalist religion blended with zeal for settling the frontier all the way to the Pacific Ocean, the thoughtful, reverential ideal of Divine Providence was magnified into a bigger idea: the frontiersman's cry of "Manifest Destiny."

With this new slogan defining their belief in a large future, the wilderness would belong to new Americans: European settlers. The American Indians were not part of the plan. American Indians would be removed and, ultimately, killed. Africans and Caribbeans were not part of the plan. They would be put to work as slaves. Slaves worked as household servants, as plantation help, and as laborers. One proud accomplishment built largely by slaves: the U.S. Capitol building.[2] Asians were not part of the plan. They would be put to work building railroads. As it was conceived, the brand called the United States of America was, by and large, for white settlers from England, Germany, the Netherlands, France, and perhaps Scandinavia. A century later, people from Ireland, Italy, and Eastern Europe fought their way into American society, but it would be two centuries after the brand was concocted before large numbers of African-Americans, Asians, and Latinos could call truly consider this branded nation their own.

In comparison with other Western nations, the history of the United States is limited, about four hundred years by the most generous count. The Anasazi people lived in the southwestern desert a thousand years ago, but we've largely decided to tell our history without including too much of the pre-1800s story of the American Indians. Lacking a rich and long history, we built our own story and developed an unusually vivacious form of patriotic attachment to our invented country. American icons abound: the Statue of Liberty, the White House, the Capitol and its dome, the Lincoln Memorial, the Washington Monument, the U.S. Flag, the Presidential Seal, the Bald Eagle, Betsy Ross (who may or may not have sewn our first flag), Uncle Sam, and the Liberty Bell (which had nothing to do with the Declaration of Independence, despite its physical proximity to Philadelphia's Independence Hall). What other country has sculpted giant heads of four favorite leaders into the side of a mountain? And what other country so enraged its natives with this sculpture that they felt compelled to build their own monument—the largest in the world at over 560 feet? (The sixty-foot busts on Mount Rushmore: George Washington, Abraham Lincoln, Theodore Roosevelt, and Thomas Jefferson. The 563-foot sculpture still in progress: Crazy Horse.)

Brand U.S.A.

We have been especially industrious, with more patent applications and Nobel Prizes than the entire European Union. Our per-capita rate for new companies is greater than almost any other Western country; at some time in our lives, one in twelve Americans starts a company. Many of us came from immigrant roots and improvised in order to earn a living, so for many years, "American ingenuity" was a defining national trait.

We remain a nation guided by religious belief and Divine Providence. During the Eisenhower era, "Congress opened a prayer room in the Capitol, made 'In God We Trust' the official motto, and added 'under God' to the Pledge of Allegiance."[3] Despite debate, every public school student says those words— "one nation under God"—every morning before classes begin. Every piece of U.S. paper money and every U.S. coin contains the words, "In God We Trust."

We are patriotic. We love our flag, and we use it in so many ways— including as a bikini. Search the Web and you will find numerous U.S.A. swimsuits, plus the occasional British, Australian, or Canadian two-piece. The selection of patriotic bikinis based upon flags of other nations is quite limited.

We are very protective of our children, but the United States has the highest rate of teen pregnancy in the Western industrialized world.[4] We are among the top spenders on K–12 education, but we rank low on international test results. We spend more money than any other country on education,[5] but we are among the top two among nations whose students "find school boring"[6] (Ireland is first), and we rank below sixty-seven other countries in adult literacy (Mongolia's literacy rate is 99 percent, as is Uzbekistan and

Tajikistan; ours is 97 percent, about equal with Cuba and Argentina). Only four in ten Americans have a college degree.[7]

The millions of Americans who own homes and pay mortgages are the cornerstones of the U.S. financial system. They provide work for builders, electricians, plumbers, landscape workers, and other craftsmen. Despite claims about the importance of the information economy and corporate America, America is largely a nation of blue-collar workers employed by small companies or as independent contractors.[9] For many of our citizens, the nation's health care system fails to provide essential services at reasonable prices.

The CIA Factbook[10] describes current conditions in each of the world's nations. The U.S. economy's "long-term problems include inadequate investment in economic infrastructure, rapidly rising medical and pension costs of an aging population, sizable trade and budget deficits, and stagnation of family income in the lower economic groups."

The perception of the United States as a wealthy nation is generally based in fact, but our wealth is not equally distributed. In the late 1990s, 83 percent of personal wealth in the United States belonged to just 20 percent of Americans. The bottom 60 percent of Americans hold less than 5 percent of the nation's personal wealth. Remarkably, 12 percent of the people living in a country whose brand promises "liberty and justice for all" live in poverty. In the United States, lower wage earners and the unemployed are overwhelmingly black and hispanic. Median income for white households in 1999: $42,504. Median income for hispanic households: $30,735. For black households: $27,910.

> Remarkably, 12 percent of the people living in a country whose brand promises "liberty and justice for all" live in poverty.

From the CIA Factbook, "Since 1975, practically all the gains in household income have gone to the top 20 percent of households."

Our nation is more deeply in debt now than at any other time in its history.

In a 2004 survey about American life conducted by the research firm NOP, the top values attributed to American culture (1999–2004) were wealth and power. These were followed by enjoying life, freedom, and having fun.

The International Perception

"A Chilean woman compares the U.S.A. to a disease that 'doesn't care about your body. It just enters to stay.'"

"... a young English woman says her friends describe the U.S. as 'global earth rapists.'"[11]

The Travel Book: A Journey Through Every Country in the World, produced by Australia's Lonely Planet books, stereotypes the trademarks associated with the U.S.A. as follows: "Burgers, fries, and Budweiser; red, white, and blue T-shirts, sneakers, and jeans; yuppies in SUVs; cowboys in pickups; loud people; gun lovers; dangerous cities."[12]

We are viewed as arrogant. We are considered to be exploitative: We take more than we give. Our companies present and promote products that are not wanted or needed. Our influences are corrupting. We are indifferent to other people's cultures and beliefs. Our heavily promoted commercial and patriotic brands enhance thinking and behavior that clash with local customs or cultural or religious norms. When we visit or live in other countries, many of us make little, if any, attempt to use or understand the local language. We believe other people ought to be more like Americans and lose patience when they behave as natives of their own countries. We are willing to sacrifice almost anything in order to make a profit; our society and country values materialism above all else. For American companies, dollars are more important than people. For American companies, money is more important than humanity.

Still, they buy our products. In Turkey, for example, Coca-Cola became popular because consumers could be certain that the soda was manufactured with clean water. Products from U.S. brands are generally perceived as safe and reliable. Quality materials are used in manufacturing and in packaging. The company behind the product is substantial. Over time, products from the United States and other Western countries often outsell local products. This is due, in part, to perceived product superiority, and in part due to the "elite power and privilege" that people in Zimbabwe, for example, perceived in a 1996 study associated with Western products.[13]

Is the U.S.A. a Violent Brand?

In general, the United States is not perceived as especially violent or hateful. In fact, the United States is a country that caused the death of nearly all of its native people and forced the survivors to live on reservations. We are the only country that has ever dropped a nuclear bomb in battle (and we did it twice).

Admittedly, our role has sometimes been the protector, and sometimes the aggressor. Still, the American story is hardly a peaceful one. We started our country with a war with about twenty thousand associated deaths.[14] In our 230 years of history, we have been at war with Barbary pirates in the early 1800s; the American Indians for much of the nineteenth century; Britain from 1812 until 1814; the Mexicans in Texas in 1835 and 1836; Mexico in the 1830s; and we fought against ourselves and killed a half-million Americans in the Civil War. After a few more decades spent fighting Indians, we were at war again in 1898, this time with Spain; we invaded and subsequently occupied The Philippines, a violent economic occupation that involved the murder of women and children and the inevitable congressional hearings about the atrocities. We helped the British and several other countries subdue the anti-foreign Boxers in China and continued in this century with the First and Second World Wars, which we followed with wars in Korea, Vietnam, the Persian Gulf, and Iraq.

The total body count associated with U.S. wars and similar engagements is difficult to estimate, but it exceeds fifty million people—the largest portion of the dead being American Indians.[15] (This count includes people living in America, but does not include people on foreign soil who were killed in wars involving Americans, such as 100,000[16] people who died in Hiroshima and Nagasaki in 1945.)

Approximately one in eleven American presidents have been murdered in office. There aren't many other jobs with a 9 percent mortality rate. If their potential murderers were competent, one in five American presidents would have been murdered in office.[17] During a slightly longer period (beginning in 1715), Britain has been led by forty-one prime ministers. Only one has been assassinated.[18]

Spreading the Good Word

After the attacks on September 11, executive Charlotte Beers, formerly head of two large advertising agencies, Ogilvy & Mather and JWT, became undersecretary of state for public diplomacy. (How arrogant of the United States to attempt to solve its problems by hiring an advertising executive to produce campaigns instead of dealing directly with the underlying problems of international cooperation and understanding!)

When Beers started the job, she spoke and acted like an advertising executive: "We are going to have to deliver the intangible assets of the United States, things like our belief system and values." She also said, "You'll find that in any great brand, the leveragable asset is the emotional underpinning of the brand—or what people believe, how they think, how they feel when they use it."[19]

Beers produced a fifteen-million-dollar ad campaign showing the successful integration of Muslims into American society. The campaign's commercials were intended to be shown in countries with large Muslim populations. Most of these countries refused to show the commercials. A short time later, Ms. Beers quietly departed.

Beyond Our Borders

The term "Americanization" was first used to describe American ingenuity and mechanical inventions. By the early 1900s, American made telephones, typewriters, cameras, sewing machines, cash registers, elevators, phonographs, toothpaste, and packaged foods. All of these proved popular in Europe. American companies, sometimes working with locally operated subsidiaries, sometimes as partnerships, typically made these products. Ford, GM, Monsanto, DuPont, Kodak, Woolworth's, and Montgomery Ward, along with our advertising agencies, established themselves in Europe.

By 1919, $700 million (U.S.) was invested in Europe. By the 1920s, a quarter-million U.S. tourists, educators, and businessmen visited Europe every year, up from perhaps thirty thousand each year during late 1800s. Our entertainment became their fascination: For more than twenty years, Buffalo Bill's Wild West Shows were popular in Europe.

From the early 1900s until the 1930s, French and German films were considered to be the best in the world. In comparison, the films made in America were generally considered to be lightweight and unimportant. Still, America's output was prodigious. Not long after the film industry began, Germany, England, and France imposed limits, or quotas, on the number of U.S. films that could be shown on their screens. Undeterred, the United States circumvented European rules by producing "Quota Quickies" in Europe to fulfill each country's local requirements. This strategy allowed U.S. films to continue to dominate European screens. By the 1930s, 80 percent of films shown in Britain were American films.

To assure its success, Hollywood studios offered high salaries to Europe's best filmmakers, craftsmen, and performers. Fritz Lang, Alfred Hitchcock, Greta Garbo, and Marlene Dietrich were among hundreds of Europeans who left their countries and moved to Hollywood. Those who were not impressed by American dollars were forced to leave because of the Nazi and Fascist onslaught. In need of work, they, too, ended up in Hollywood. By the end of the WWII, the European film industry was decimated and Hollywood films reigned supreme. By then, Kodak made 75 percent of the world's film and American companies owned three out of every four motion picture theaters[21] in France. We won the war. Now, we had to win hearts and minds, too.

After WWII, we fought a boastful Cold War against our archenemies, the Russians. Their superb ballet companies, symphony orchestras, and circuses traveled throughout Western Europe. In 1957, Russia launched Laika, a dog, into space and welcomed him home, alive. Meanwhile, two of three squirrel monkeys gave their lives so the United States could get its space program started.

The U.S. State Department responded with a bigger and better strategy. "During the late 1950s and 1960s, they flooded Europe with concerts from orchestras from Boston, New York, and Cleveland, and by soloists like Isaac Stern, Rudolph Serkin, and Marian Anderson. The government also offered examples of American dance from the New York City Ballet; plays by Eugene O'Neill, Thornton Wilder, and Tennessee Williams; art exhibitions, photographic collections like Edward Steichen's *The Family of Man* and performances of Broadway musicals including *My Fair Lady*."[22] We wanted to demonstrate to the Russians, to Europe, to the world, that our culture was better than their culture.

> To assure its success, Hollywood studios offered high salaries to Europe's best filmmakers, craftsmen, and performers.

In the midst of this dubious battle was a radio program known as Willis Conover's *Music U.S.A.* It was the most popular program on our propaganda-laden international radio service, the Voice of America. Most of the VOA's thirty-plus million listeners were in Eastern Europe and the Soviet Union. Conover played rock 'n' roll and jazz. He reached the younger generation, and he did so regularly, in their homes. The communist leadership had no idea how powerful American rock 'n' roll and jazz could be. While the State Department was showing off Broadway's best, rock n' roll taught Eastern European and Russian teenagers about freedom.

The State Department is still producing jazz performances. In December 2004, Colin Powell introduced Ravi Coltrane, Earl Klugh, and Al Jarreau in New Delhi. The production was produced for television by Viacom's BET and MTV-India.

And We Won't Go Away!

Americans stay home. Most of us never leave our country, not once in our lives.

Fully 80 percent of Americans do not own a passport. Of those who do own a passport, seven out of eight visitors travel only to large Canadian cities, Mexican resorts or border towns, and nearby Caribbean islands.

Do the math: only 2.2 percent of Americans travel much beyond the nation's borders, and almost 98 percent of us do not travel internationally at all.

For those who do travel, most tourists visit the U.K., France, Germany, and Italy. A far smaller number of U.S. travelers ever go anywhere else.

The United States ranks third among tourism destinations; more people visit Europe and northeastern Asia than visit the United States.

Still, the marketing-savvy United States earns more money from travel dollars than any country in the world: more than $100 billion per year. Fewer people visit the United States than Europe or Asia, but Americans know how to get the most money out of every foreign visitor.

Endnotes

1   Jefferson borrowed and updated the phrase from Locke's "life, liberty and property." By property, Locke apparently intended "the natural rights of man." True to his enlightened age and his confidence in the new American citizens, Jefferson expanded Locke's original idea and allowed Americans to define the new term "happiness" in their own way. —Locke source, *National Review*, January 26, 2004.

2   "Faith of Our Fathers," by Jay Tolson, *U.S. News & World Report*, June 28, 2004.

3   In 2004, the Minnesota legislature passed a resolution honoring the slaves who built the U.S. Capitol. One excerpt: "WHEREAS, public records attest to the fact that African American slave labor was used in the construction of the United States Capitol …" To read the entire resolution, visit: http://www.spokesman-recorder.com/News/Article/Article.asp?NewsID=39647&sID=16

4 According to an AP story from June 1, 2005, "… local farmers rented out their slaves for an average of fifty-five dollars a year to help build the Capitol, the White House, the Treasury Department, and the streets laid out by city planner Pierre L'Enfant. Slaves also were involved in the expansion of the Capitol in the late 1850s."

5 "Faith of Our Fathers," by Jay Tolson, *US News & World Report*, June 28, 2004.

6 http://www.teenpregnancy.org/resources/data/genlfact.asp

7 Based on education as percentage of GDP, per Web site: http://www.nationmaster.com/graph-T/edu_tot_exp_as_of_gdp

8 http://www.nationmaster.com/graph-T/edu_stu_att_fin_sch_bor

9 *The Real State of the Union: From the Best Minds in America, Bold Solutions to the Problems Politicians Dare Not Face*, Ted Halstead, editor, p. 7+.

10 *The Real State of the Union: From the Best Minds in America, Bold Solutions to the Problems Politicians Dare Not Face*, Ted Halstead, editor, p. 27.

11 http://www.cia.gov/cia/publications/factbook/

12 Both quotes from *Business Week*, "Building Brand America," December 10, 2001.

13 Lonely Planet's editors describe their own country: "Bronzed Aussies; dangerous creatures; endless beaches; friendly locals; Outback pubs; sizzling barbecues; Aussie Rules football."

14 "Effects of Brand Local and Nonlocal Origin on Consumer Attitudes in Developing Countries," by Rajeev Batra, Venkatram Ramaswamy, Jan-Benedict Steenkamp, S. Ramachander, *Journal of Consumer Psychology*, Vol. 9, Issue 2, p. 83.

15 The number of deaths includes both battle and nonbattle deaths due to disease and other factors.

16 Without counting the Indians, the total is about three million people. The sources for the Indian casualties include: http://hnn.us/articles/7302.html and http://users.erols.com/mwhite28/warstat0.htm#America

17 http://www.atomicarchive.com/Docs/MED/med_chp10.shtml

18 Lincoln, Garfield, McKinley, and Kennedy were murdered; Jackson, Truman, Ford, and Reagan survived attempted murders.

18 From http://www.spartacus.schoolnet.co.uk/PRperceval.htm: 19 "Spencer Perceval was shot when entering the lobby of the House of Commons by John Bellingham, a failed businessman from Liverpool. Bellingham, who blamed Perceval for his financial difficulties, was later hanged for his crime."

19 More from http://www.absoluteastronomy.com/encyclopedia/l/li/list_of_assassinated_people.htm: Assassination has been more popular in France, with two presidents and two kings killed in office since 1589. Egypt has killed four prime ministers; Afghanistan has killed about three top leaders (depending upon how they're counted); and Iran

has killed about as many; Japan is near the top of the list with five prime ministers killed in its modern era; three Mexican presidents died from assassins.

20 "Building Brand America," *Business Week*, December 1, 2001.

21 *Not Like Us: How Europeans Loved, Hated and Transformed American Culture Since World War II* by Richard Pells, p. 12.

22 *Not Like Us: How Europeans Loved, Hated and Transformed American Culture Since World War II* by Richard Pells, pp. 85+,

BRANDS, INCORPORATED

With few exceptions, the purpose of every public and private corporation is:
(1) to manage the company's assets, and (2) to increase the company's value.

Just about any other activity is a distraction.

It's Always About the Money

A company's assets are, simply, all of the stuff that the company owns or
controls. In the consumer goods and media industries, a company's brands
are often its most valuable assets. For example, Disney's brands are worth
nearly $30 billion, or more than two-thirds of the corporation's total value.
These brands include Mickey Mouse, Donald Duck, Bambi, Disneyland,
Disney World, *The Lion King*, ESPN, ESPN Zone, ABC, ABC News, *20/20*,
and Disney Cruise Lines. In addition, Disney controls *Desperate Housewives*,
Monday Night Football, *America's Funniest Home Videos* ... the list goes on.

As a company increases in value, the value of each share of its stock often
increases as well. Shareholder value is managed with a stunning managerial
focus on "the numbers"—key metrics that guide every corporation. These
key metrics often include the number of customers acquired and retained,
each customer's spending, and more. Individual employees and departments
who achieve their quarterly and annual goals are rewarded with raises,
promotions, and, often, career success. Every well-managed corporation is
run by the numbers.

Inconveniences

Many corporations are large, often high-profile employers, and in order to
attract their facilities, state and local governments regularly compete with
tax incentives and other perks.

Many corporations view legal entanglements as an unavoidable aspect of doing business. Often, lawsuits are seen as business risks, not showstoppers.

Like taxes and legal hassles, social issues are often considered to be something of a distraction. Like a lawsuit, a social issue captures management's attention only when it threatens to slow down or stop business, or if some valuable aspect of the corporation's image may be compromised or damaged.[1]

In many corporations, senior executives may adopt a charity or cause. Often, this is instigated by a personal situation, but it sometimes expands to a kind of corporate sponsorship. Even if you're not a fan of McDonald's hamburgers or their corporate mascot, it's difficult not to acknowledge the Ronald McDonald House program's comfort to families with seriously ill children. Could America's second-largest private employer (438,000 employees in 2004) do much more with its annual profits of over $2 billion per year? Probably. Should every corporation be *required* to provide some significant social service as part of their participation in our economy? (Yes.)

Carnegie and Rockefeller have contributed mightily to the public good. From 1881 until 1917, Carnegie and his company built more than 2,500 public libraries. Wouldn't it be lovely if every Wal-Mart town were provided with a brand-new public library and funds to keep it alive for a century or so? My faith in Verizon (Fortune #14), would improve if the company wired and provided telecommunications services to every public school at no charge. Do less advertising, do more good, and I'll happily give you more of my money.

How Corporations Took Over Our World

The modern corporation is not an American invention. Like so many of our ideas, we imported this one from England. The story begins in medieval times, when the earliest corporate bodies were trade guilds, towns, and universities. Since these institutions were intended to last longer than any individual citizen, they were treated differently than citizens.

In Florence, in the 1100s, a new format evolved, the *compagnie* (translation: "breaking bread together"). Individuals shared liability for the group's enterprise (this required a superior level of trust, because the penalty for bankruptcy was imprisonment and worse). For financing, Florence eventually developed *banchi*, or banks, which loaned money to these enterprises. The Medici operated one of these banks; they "provided much of the capital for the Renaissance."[2]

Eventually, companies were financed through the sale of shares of stock. "In the sixteenth and seventeenth centuries, European monarchs created chartered companies to pursue their dreams of international expansion. One of these, the East India Company, wound up ruling India with a private army of 260,000 native troops (twice the size of the British Army)."[3] The East India Co. was in business for 274 years, until 1874.

By the early 1700s, the market for shares of corporations included options and other mechanisms we associate with modern trading. Then as now, corporations could be mani-pulated to excite foolish investors, and then as now, inevitable bubble bursts caused enormous problems. (Speculation in The Mississippi Co., which occurred primarily in England and France, nearly sacked the entire French economy.)[4]

> Shortly before his death, President Abraham Lincoln foresaw disaster: "Corporations have been enthroned. ... An era of corruption in high places will follow. ..."

In 1636, Harvard University became America's first chartered corporation. The idea quickly took hold: The new approach encouraged investment and permitted the construction of banks, roads, canals, churches, and towns through loans or debt financing. The world had become too complicated for individuals to do the work alone: To build a new university, a corporate charter provided a better way to get the job done.

Corporations also made the slave trade a viable business. The Royal African Co. was granted a monopoly by the British Parliament to import slaves from Africa in 1672. The company transported an average of five thousand slaves per year. By 1698, the industry was deregulated and shipments increased to more than twenty thousand slaves per year.[5] As a result of successful government collaboration with these new corporations, England led the world's slave trade industry.

In the United States, a *coup d'etat* occurred in the midst of the Civil War, and in the period immediately afterwards, when the nation was in chaos. As we all learned in school, the fundamental battle appeared to be a dispute over slavery. The other battle, easily won, was for corporate control of the U.S. economy.

In the early 1860s, two competing governments required massive amounts of materials, manufacturing, transportation, logistics, and money.

Corporations took advantage of the situation, provided the necessary resources, and along the way, bought legislatures, judges, senators, congresspeople, and probably cabinet members.

Shortly before his death, President Abraham Lincoln foresaw disaster: "Corporations have been enthroned ... An era of corruption in high places will follow, and money power will endeavor to prolong it, reign by working on the prejudices of the people ... until wealth is aggregated in a few hands ... and the republic is destroyed ..."

During this era, the U.S. Supreme Court elevated the corporation beyond the reach of most citizens. Although corporations could not participate in the political process, under-the-table deals with politicians allowed corporations to become monopolies. Corporations were not permitted to buy stock in other corporations, so markets and deals were manipulated out of public view. Meanwhile, the Supreme Court set the stage for modern American business by reinforcing a concept known as "corporate personhood;"[6] an interesting (if difficult to understand) series of Supreme Court cases that eventually granted corporations the same rights as U.S. citizens. In reality, corporations were granted far more power than all but the richest citizens (who controlled the corporations). Corporations possessed vast financial resources, political connections at every level, and large (often mistreated) workforces. In fact, these resources were unavailable to individuals.

The courts consistently favored corporate interests over individual interests. Employment law was based upon voluntary service and personal acceptance of the risks, not upon employer responsibility or provision of safe working conditions. If you got hurt on the job, that was your problem. Railroad and mining companies annexed huge tracts of land at minimal cost, then worked with the U.S. Army to move Indians from the land or kill them.

Railroading America

In fact, it was the railroads that set us on the path we're on today. Railroad magnates invented modern stock markets. Railroads needed organizations that separated management from workers. Railroads demanded flexibility from government officials in order to get the job done. Railroads required investment and beneficial relationships with shareholders. Railroads built the fortunes of business bullies like J.P. Morgan, Cornelius Vanderbilt, Andrew Carnegie, Jay Cooke, and many of the richest men in 1800s America. These people set the standards and the stage for corporate America.

As was common practice during the railroading of America, shares were given to legislators to assure the necessary support. Stock fraud was among the many issues that allowed railroads to pass into the hands of bankers, particularly the House of Morgan (four of the six national railroad systems) and Kuhn, Loeb, and Co. (the other two).

In the 1850s, "Railroad men traveled to Washington and to state capitals armed with money, shares of stock, free railroad passes. Between 1850 and 1857, they got twenty-five million acres of public land, free of charge, and millions of dollars in bonds—loans—from state legislatures."[7]

Like many of these wealthy men, J.P. Morgan started by selling dubious railroad shares, a short step from his other cons. In one deal, he bought five thousand defective rifles from an army arsenal for $3.50 each, and resold them to a general in the field for $22 each. Soldiers who used them shot off their own thumbs. A federal judge upheld the contract.

By 1900, Morgan controlled half of the rail mileage in the United States, some 100,000 miles. "He linked railroads to one another, all of them to banks, banks to insurance companies."[8]

John D. Rockefeller built upon his success as a merchant, bought his first oil refinery in 1862, and in 1870, set up Standard Oil Company of Ohio. He drove competitors out of business through secret discounts with rail carriers, who essentially subsidized his success while driving his competitors out of business with higher prices. Dirty tricks were part of Rockefeller's game: explosions set at competitor's refineries, for example.

Andrew Carnegie, a Wall Street broker selling railroad bonds for large commissions, traveled to London in 1872, saw a Bessemer steel plant, and used the method to build a U.S. steel plant. With a high tariff, Congress kept the competition out. J.P. Morgan bought Carnegie's company to form U.S. Steel (in combination with several other companies). Foreign steel was kept out, and wages were kept low "by working 200,000 men twelve hours a day for wages that barely kept their families alive."[9] As a result of the U.S. Steel deal, Andrew Carnegie became the richest man in the world.

By 1900, large conglomerates, protected by government leaders who were nicely compensated for their protection, controlled the telephone system (American Telephone & Telegraph); farm machinery (International Harvester, which made 85 percent of farm machinery); and every conceivable commodity, from beef to sugar to tobacco.

This system was unfair to consumers and to workers. Companies that held monopolies fixed prices: if you wanted to buy sugar, you had to buy it from a store that bought it from the trust, regardless of the price. If you were a steelworker, you had to work for the steel trust or you would not work at all. In an industry where fair work practices, fair wages, and safety were nonexistent, steel workers risked their lives. Workers who complained were blacklisted, so no one in the industry would hire them.

The late 1800s were filled with strikes, unions, and violent outbursts. By the 1890s, it was clear that the federal government needed to become involved—but on whose side? Beginning with the 1890s Sherman Anti-Trust Act, laws were passed, but every attempt at enforcement was struck down by the Supreme Court. Corporations remained in control.

If corporations were analyzed as individuals might be, many would be considered psychopaths. They can neither recognize nor act upon moral reasons to refrain from hurting others.

By 1919, corporations controlled 80 percent of U.S. employment and most of the country's wealth (gee that happened fast!).

By 1929, only two hundred corporations controlled half of all American industry.

In 1997, fifty-one of the world's largest economies were corporations. The top five hundred corporations controlled 42 percent of the world's wealth.

For more than four hundred years, corporations have been the dominant economic and political force in the world. By their very nature, corporations are impersonal, acting with a fixed gaze on money in a world where individual citizens often operate with other motivations. It is with this single-mindedness that most successful brands are managed.

Corporate Psychopaths

If corporations were analyzed as individuals might be, some would be considered psychopaths: they can neither recognize nor act upon moral reasons to refrain from hurting others.[10]

Robert Hare's PCL-R test evaluates psychopathy by measuring a total of twenty traits. A simplified version, based upon eight traits, can be used to measure what Hare calls an individual "corporate psychopath.[11]" It's instructive to apply this same scale to evaluate overall corporate activities as well, particularly as they apply to brand marketers of, say, Marlboro cigarettes or McDonald's hamburgers or ExxonMobil gasoline.

"Is he glib and super-charming? Does he have a grandiose sense of self-worth? Is he a pathological liar? Is he a con artist or master manipulator? When he harms other people, does he feel a lack of remorse or guilt? Does he have a shallow affect (is he cold and detached even when someone dies, suffers, or falls seriously ill)? Is he callous and lacking in empathy? Does he fail to accept responsibility?"

As Kalle Lasn wrote in *Culture Jam: The Uncooling of America,* "We go to corporations on our knees. Please do the right thing, we plead. Please don't cut down any more ancient forests. Please don't pollute any more lakes (but please don't move your factories and jobs offshore, either). Please don't use pornographic images to sell fashion to my kids. Please don't play governments against each other to get a better deal."

Of course, it would be unfair to label every corporate brand owner as a psychopath. Unfortunately, with the castle walls so very high, it's difficult to see clearly into any large corporation. Home Depot, for example, has fixed up hundreds of troubled schools, not for public relations reasons, but because it's been the right thing to do. Still, it is difficult for the average consumer to understand the real power and motivation of such a large company.

Defining Success: The Growth of the MegaMarket

Home Depot is the thirteenth-largest company in the U.S., larger than Boeing, Time Warner, or Procter & Gamble. With annual revenues of $73 billion, it's about the size of Verizon Communications, and twice the size of its nearest competitor, Lowe's.

One way Home Depot measures success is by evaluating the "average ticket"—the amount of money spent by every customer on every trip to Home Depot's cash register. Currently, the average ticket is $58.25;[12] that's up from $55.11 in the first quarter of 2004, and $51.29 in the first quarter of 2003.

One can't help but wonder whether local hardware stores or lumberyards measures their customers in terms of average ticket, or establish annual goals to increase per-customer take.

Do you prefer a small-town hardware store where everyone knows your name and your business, where just about everything you need for day-to-day projects is available at somewhat higher prices, where friendly service is assured by a long-time member of the community where you live? Or do you prefer a Home Depot not more than a few miles from where you live, where every conceivable product is available, for a fair price, and all systems are standardized by a major world-class corporation? The question is not new.

It's the mid-1800s. With several small, family-owned grocery stores on a two-block-long Main Street, mother did not go shopping in the way we do today. Instead, she sent one of the children to fetch a chunk of cheddar cheese or a pound of sugar. If the product was unacceptable, she sent the child back to the store. The child carried no cash; instead, the grocer kept a running tab, and the bill was paid, in cash, every week or so. There were few, if any, brands; the grocer stocked commodities (milk, cheese, butter, beets), not brand-name products.

By the late 1800s, Main Street started to change. Some local storekeepers affiliated with national chains, whose numbers increased as they opened their own stores. By 1880, there were one hundred A&P grocery stores; by 1950, there were fifteen thousand. As A&P moved into Main Street, so too did its branded merchandise. Procter & Gamble, for example, became a large A&P supplier. A&P also developed its own brands, including Eight O'Clock Coffee, Jane Parker White Bread, and Ann Page salad dressings and ice creams. In the United States, consumer brands and large grocery chains grew up together.

In the 1920s and 1930s, consumers, storekeepers, and local governments grew concerned about the rapid, relentless growth of chain stores and their devastating impact on the local economy. About half the states imposed special taxes to limit the growth of chain stores. The FTC investigated. Not much happened. Americans voted with their wallets and purses in favor of Woolworth's, JC Penney, Sears Roebuck, Rexall drugstores, Winn-Dixie groceries, and more.

After the Depression and WWII, consumers had more money to spend, and the stores became larger. In the 1950s and 1960s, old-style grocery stores (where countermen picked each product off a nearby shelf) gave way to newer supermarkets (where consumers selected their own merchandise).

Founded by two brothers who had grown up in their parents' Rochester, New York, grocery store, Wegman's opened a twenty-thousand-square-foot showplace store in 1930, complete with a three-hundred-seat cafeteria. In 1972, Wegman's opened its first pharmacy. Two years later, it was opening larger supermarkets with a Wegman's-owned Chase-Pitkin home-improvement center next door. In 1992, Wegman's debuted a fresh foods restaurant called Market Café, and now the chain is experimenting with upscale, full-service, high-quality restaurants—as part of a supermarket. For many people who live in Rochester, Wegman's is a one-stop center and a family shopping tradition. In New Jersey, where Wegman's has operated several large upscale markets, the Wegman's experience includes a well-stocked wine and liquor store.

Modern supermarkets stock about forty thousand individual items and typically employ more than a hundred, or several hundred, people. Despite Wal-Mart's $31 billion in annual supermarket sales, regional chains dominate the business.

In most areas, a handful of brand-name supermarket chains compete for local customers. In southern New Hampshire, for example, it's a battle between Hannaford's and Shaw's. Like most local and regional supermarkets, these are owned by much larger companies: Hannaford's is owned by Belgium-based Delhaize Group, a New York Stock Exchange-listed company with over 1,500 stores and over $15 billion in revenues. Shaw's has been in New England since 1860, but today, it's part of Albertson's 2,500 store empire whose annual sales exceed $40 billion.

Supermarkets are only one example of the relentless evolution toward larger retail stores. In the United States, we like our stores large and well stocked, and we don't mind driving to a shopping mall or shopping center, even if the decision contributes to the death of local retail stores. Very few of these large stores fail. We've supported this sort of phenomenon in many retail categories, including hardware, pets, books, toys, clothing, cosmetics, appliances, electronics, records/CDs, musical instruments, furniture, arts and crafts supplies, fabrics, and office supplies. Every one of these categories was once represented by a store on Main Street. Today, every American can name at least two or three national brands that dominate their retail category. (Try it.)

The Scoop on Wal-Mart

Since the late 1950s, Lowell Conrad has owned Conrad's appliance store at 125 Main Street in Geneseo, New York. His store is quiet and old-fashioned; it's the oldest store on Main Street. Every fifteen minutes or so, a customer drops by to buy a part, to check on an order, ask a question, or just to say hello. There's a Wal-Mart up on the main highway that gets most of the area's appliance business, but Conrad isn't concerned. Wal-Mart is only the latest in a series of interlopers. Conrad's began to suffer in the 1960s when a small chain discounter called Big N opened on the highway; it was the first of several discount chains that sold appliances for less than Conrad's could buy them. By the time the local Wal-Mart opened in the 1990s, there was little more that discounters could do to hurt Geneseo's appliance store. Still, Conrads has a strategy: he's fairly certain that people buy just one appliance from Wal-Mart. After they realize that Wal-Mart's support is nonexistent, Conrad usually hears from the unhappy customer, and he sells them their next refrigerator or dishwasher.

For residents of Geneseo and the farm towns around rural Livingston County, whose shopping options are limited, Wal-Mart offers the widest range of merchandise and at least the promise of quality merchandise at the lowest possible prices. The alternative is nearly an hour's drive to the nearest city, Rochester, New York, where they will likely end up at either another Wal-Mart or some branded big-box retailer. So, they might as well shop at the Geneseo Wal-Mart.

Facts about Wal-Mart

With more than $288 billion in sales for 2004 and more than $10 billion in profits Wal-Mart is the world's largest retailer. With more than 1.6 million employees (called "associates"), Wal-Mart is also the world's largest private employer.

The company operates more than three thousand large discount stores in the U.S., and more than one thousand in Mexico, Canada, South America, Asia, and Europe. Every other day, Wal-Mart opens a new store. Every week, Wal-Mart opens a new store in the United States.

Wal-Mart is the largest food retailer in the U.S. It is our second-largest jeweler (after QVC), and our third-largest pharmacy. Wal-Mart is an industry leader in nearly every retail category: if not number one, then usually in the top five.

The average Wal-Mart discount store stocks 80,000 items; the average Wal-Mart Supercenter stocks over 100,000. To stock the shelves, Wal-Mart works with thousands of suppliers. Wal-Mart is a very tough buyer because it demands an extremely high level of performance and extremely low wholesale prices from every vendor.

Wal-Mart's current revenues roughly equal with Belgium's GDP (Belgium is the twenty-eighth largest economy in the world). If the 12-percent growth continues, it will overtake Australia (currently ranked seventeenth) in 2010, and will be on par with the largest economies (Germany, etc.) in the 2020s.

From an investor's perspective, Wal-Mart is a superb performer. The company's earnings have been extraordinarily consistent. The twenty-five-year graph of Wal-Mart revenues resembles a flight of stair steps—evenly paced, every step higher than the one before.

Wal-Mart is the United States' largest corporation, but others come close: notably Exxon Mobil ($213 billion) and General Motors ($196 billion).

Wal-Mart accounts for more than 10 percent of China's U.S. imports. It's probably unwise for a single company to control such a high percentage of trade with the United States' largest creditor. Wal-Mart does not deny that it imports $18 billion in Chinese products, but its Web site quickly changes the subject to discuss Wal-Mart's $150 billion in U.S. product purchases every year.

Wal-Mart is not without its issues—enough issues, in fact, to keep a site called www.walmartwatch.com busy and to require a company-owned site called www.walmartfacts.com to address troublesome issues.

With so many employees, many paid very low wages, Wal-Mart lives in the midst of official denials, employee lawsuits, news stories about illegal immigrants mopping the floors, gender discrimination, allegations of causing low wages at other retailers, workers locked-in overnight, and, perhaps most dismaying, a real and substantial impact on public assistance—because many Wal-Mart employees ("associates") are not paid a living wage or provided with suitable benefits.

Wal-Mart is hushed about the wages it pays, but a 2001 court case[13] revealed that the average hourly pay was under $9 for more than half of Wal-Mart store employees, and under $10 for just under three-quarters of store employees. By comparison, retailers with more than one thousand employees average $14.01 per hour.

According to one University of California at Berkeley study, the state paid an estimated $86 million in public assistance in 2001 because Wal-Mart wages were so low that its employees required $32 million in health-related costs plus $54 million in other assistance. If other large California retailers adopted a similar wage and benefit policy, the cost to California taxpayers would be $410 million per year in public assistance. In a report prepared for former Seattle Congressman John Miller: a typical Wal-Mart store with two hundred employees may cost federal taxpayers $420,750, or $2,103 per Wal-Mart employee. Many such reports are available; Wal-Mart finds a way to discredit every one of them.

Wall Street is encouraging other retailers to study and adopt Wal-Mart's low-wage, low-price approach.

Should you buy from any low-price retailer if you know that they pay their employees and suppliers poorly in order to maintain low prices? Should you buy from a retailer that maintains low prices largely by squeezing their suppliers to a point where they must either change their own business practices or risk losing their largest account? Is this progress? For many of us, the answer is yes.

Keeping Wal-Mart out of Town

An increasing number of communities simply do not want Wal-Mart stores in their area. Wal-Mart usually finds a way to bulldoze its way into the area amidst accusations that the store will destroy local retailers and the special sense of the local community. Despite efforts to support local causes, to employ the elderly, and to be a good neighbor, Wal-Mart is despised. Does Wal-Mart destroy local stores? The answer is unclear because Wal-Mart is not the only force that affects local retail. (It certainly isn't helping.) Worse, however, are the customers who, when offered the choice to shop at a local store or to spend the money at Wal-Mart instead, always seem to do the latter.

Controlling the Variables: The Science of Starbucks

Manage every step of the process. Nothing is left to chance. Nothing is left unanalyzed. Every decision improves efficiency, lowers costs, or improves profitability. Starbucks is a phenomenally sophisticated coffee machine. A friendly neighborhood companion, but a machine just the same.

Founded as a geeky source of fine coffees not available in the United States, Starbucks transformed high-priced, high-potency coffees into an experience incorporating affordable luxury, "an oasis" offering casual social interaction, even a "dose of romance" in the words of long-time Starbucks CEO Howard Schultz. Stores are designed to stimulate all of the senses, to provide the richest possible retail coffee and relaxation experience.

By design, Starbucks has become the U.S. version of the English pub and the French café, an informal neighborhood gathering place. Before Starbucks, our Main Street was sleepy; now, there are people strolling, sitting on benches, chatting day and night. Despite venomous reactions to branded retailers in my hometown, Starbucks has become a welcome member of our community.

The average Starbucks sale is about four dollars, and Starbucks customers return an average of about eighteen times per month; in other words, Starbucks customers are worth, on average, one thousand dollars per year.

Starbucks is not just a brand—it's an importer, manufacturer, retailer, wholesaler, licensor, and direct mail business. So much can go wrong when making high-end coffee. That's why Starbucks buys and roasts the beans, manages every detail of the customer experience, and worries about the shops it has licensed Marriott to operate in airports and Aramark to operate on college campuses.

Customer Relationships

Of course, the reason for the success of Starbucks and Wal-Mart is not just low prices or high-octane coffee. It's the relationship that the customer has built with the retailer (and vice-versa). When my friend Charles slows down in the afternoon, he leaves the office for a tall thin latte at Starbucks. It's a habit.

"Always" is a concept that brand managers like a lot. It's "Always Coca-Cola," and it's "Wal-Mart: Always Low Prices."

In my house, it's *always* for my wife when she watches the ABC affiliate's eleven o'clock newscast, and in her sister's house, it's always for QVC's midnight special sale; neither woman likes to go to sleep without the branded routine. For me, the morning seems strange if I miss my *New York Times*.

When I worked in an office, my assistant always had a candy dish on her desk. People would stop by for a brief, friendly chat and grab a small bit of chocolate. Sincerely, we loved her for being so nice, so friendly, so caring. And she was doing her part in our national campaign for sugar addiction. Last year, Americans ate more than 10 billion Hershey's Kisses.

Make the Emotional Connection

Professor David Loy of Japan's Bunkyo University writes: "A corporation cannot laugh or cry; it cannot enjoy the world or suffer with it. Most of all, a corporation cannot love." [14]

There's a particular shade of turquoise that, when wrapped around a small box, can mean only one thing: a gift from Tiffany & Co. The color makes the heart beat a little faster ...

For a while during the 1990s, when people saw polar bears, they thought, "Coca-Cola." A talkative white duck is associated with AFLAC, and a gecko represented GEICO, both of which were faceless insurance companies before the campaigns. In the 1950s, when NBC wanted to communicate the beauty of its new color programs, designer John J. Graham designed a peacock.

How to encourage adults to make an emotional connection and drink more milk? The California Milk Processor Board answered the question by hiring beloved celebrities and encouraging them to pose with milk moustaches. From Spike Lee to Buffy the Vampire Slayer, everybody seemed to be sporting a white moustache. With so many celebrities promoting milk, the campaign felt like a global cause, not an advertising campaign.

Early on, brand managers learn an important lesson: Don't rely upon practical need to maintain the relationship. Instead, reinforce the emotional connection between brand and customer by using color, typestyle, animal imagery, celebrity endorsement.

Make Sure the Logo Appears Everywhere

Familiarity breeds success. The next time you're out and about, count the number of Coca-Cola logos you see in a single day: I tried this a few times, and typically counted between five and fifteen, day in and day out.

Public relations people are paid to get the product's name mentioned in news stories. Advertising managers and agencies are paid to show the logo and the product in paid advertising spaces on TV, billboards, magazines, and on the radio. Licensing agents are paid to get the logo on clothing and other merchandise. Promotion people are paid to set up relationships with other companies and brands. At the retail store level, detailers and other direct sales people set up store displays and arrange for the best merchandise positions. Together, for the average national brand, there are probably a few dozen people working all day, every day, to do nothing but get that brand in front of your face. They want you to *see that logo*!

Play to Beliefs; Nurture Emotions

Hallmark Cards (and other greeting card companies) is expert in identifying the emotional component of every event and, remarkably, they've convinced thousands, and often millions of people to celebrate every family event, life cycle event, and annual holiday with a piece of printed cardboard. When someone is born, we buy a card. When someone dies, we buy a card. When someone gets a new job or buys a new house, we buy a card. And for at least five holidays every year, we buy a card (Mother's Day, Father's Day, Christmas, Valentine's Day, and for most of us, at least one more). When we buy a card, we are absolved of the responsibility to take the time to think, write, and present our feelings in a direct and personal way. Cards are a quick, convenient shortcut, sold by brands we trust to communicate our deepest feelings.

New Year's Eve is the holiday for champagne; no respectable party would be complete without Moet et Chandon, Mumm, Taittinger or for the upscale, Dom Perignon.

About $13 billion is spent on roses for each Valentine's Day.[15] Certainly, more Godiva chocolate is sold on the days preceding February 14 than any other week of the year. Still, Valentine's Day candy sales are second to Easter, when about $1 billion in candy is sold for the one-day celebration. M&Ms, Jelly Belly jellybeans, and the seasonal marshmallow Peeps are brands that enjoy annual windfalls.

For Oscar Meyer, Hebrew National and many regional hot dog brands, there is no better way to celebrate the signing of the Declaration of Independence. (You understand the connection, right?)

Candy companies get a third jolt in the autumn. Halloween has become a profit festival for Hershey's and M&M/Mars, which dominate Trick-or-Treat bags nationwide. (Halloween is primarily a children's celebration, and children eat less candy than adults, so specialized Halloween candy sales are worth only about 30 percent of Easter candy sales). Still, to offer, say, an apple or some other healthful treat is considered both sacrilegious and a potential terrorist act because some harmful object might be concealed in the fresh fruit (did the chocolate companies spread this rumor to increase their share of the child's plastic pumpkin?)

Butterball owns Thanksgiving. Nearly every news organization provides a report on turkey preparation from Butterball, a public relations coup. Nearly every household cooks a turkey for a holiday that originally had little to do with the birds we call turkeys today (at the time, the word "turkey" referred to any variety of wild fowl).

The annual Christmas shopping orgy is covered later in the book.

Study Consumer Habits

In the popular book, *Why They Buy*, author and retailing expert Paco Underhill explains that the more time each of us spends in a retail store (excluding time wasted standing in line), the greater the likelihood that we will buy. For his company's clients, Underhill regularly adjusts the number of words on signs in stores and the paths that customers are taught to move through stores. He even studies what we do with our hands. If, for example, both of your hands are free, you are more likely to shop for a longer period of time, or to buy more merchandise. By providing customers with a basket, stores increase both the likelihood of a purchase and the size of the purchase. Stores designed for older customers are more brightly lit: a fifty year old requires about 25 percent more light in order to see clearly. For Underhill and his clients, the retail environment is a place to be manipulated to alter behavior. Retailing has become a science.

Hire Celebrities, or Build Your Own

Although celebrities seem to be randomly scattered throughout the brand-scape, they are most often hired for one of two very specific reasons: (1) to encourage first-time buyers to sample the offering, or (2) to encourage current consumers to switch to the client's brand. In the lingo of professional brand managers, celebrities are most useful in encouraging customer acquisition.

Jason Alexander, for example, was hired by KFC to encourage switching to fast-food chicken. Weight Watchers campaigns are always aimed at new customers; Sarah Ferguson is one of a long line of celebrity endorsers.

When a company wants to build a deeper belief system, the chief executive might speak on the company's behalf. Wendy's Dave Thomas set the standard for the "ordinary guy" spokesperson (the way he looked, people believed he was a regular Wendy's customer and dismissed the logic that said he was a multimillionaire selling fast food). Thomas was able to embody the brand, connect with the viewer on an emotional level, and positively affect the belief system that people used to form their opinions about Wendy's.

Whenever Possible, Go for the Children

For many brands, the target audience is children. They are the customers, they buy the products. For other brands, children exert a strong influence over their parents. For many brands, kids are considered "consumers in training." The habits and buying patterns they establish as children and teens will help to shape their lifetime relationship to brands. (This is especially true when marketing alcohol and tobacco to children and teenagers.)

"The mass marketing model is dead. *This* is the future," said James Stengel, P&G's global marketing officer.

"This" is P&G Tremor, a new kind of marketing agency that employs children and teenagers as stealth marketers. Tremor employs over a quarter-million boys and girls, ages thirteen to nineteen years, and promotes the service within its own company and to clients as "The Power of Word of

Mouth." AOL, Coca-Cola, Kraft, and Toyota have been clients.

Tremor seeks out teenagers with unusually large numbers of personal relationships. The organization's questionnaire asks potential Tremor marketers how many friends and family members are communicated with each day, and how many names are on their buddy lists (the average Tremor kid has about 180, about six times as many as the average teen). Tremor's system is selective: only 10 percent of survey respondents are asked to join the sales force. Tremor seeks out teens who will talk up their products to friends.

What do the kids get in return? They receive free samples, coupons, the occasional DVD player, and the thrill of being an insider. True, they are selling out their friends, but this is rarely discussed.

Record companies and movie companies participate in similar shenanigans. For years, they have recruited on-campus shills to hand out free movie passes, T-shirts, and other items designed to encourage brand awareness through the magic of peer contact.[16]

Brands Outside the U.S.A.

Of course, brands are popular throughout the world. In many cases, U.S. travelers recognize their own brands sold in other countries, sometimes with variations on the packaging, presentation, or ingredients.

When traveling, sampling the local brands is often a rewarding adventure. In Japan, Pocari Sweat is a popular soft drink. In Italy, people enjoy the bitter lemon taste of San Pellegrino Limonata. In Mexico, Jarritos is a very popular brand of local soft drinks. These local brands sell beside international brands, including Perrier and Coca-Cola.

Most Western countries actively develop, promote, and market local brands. In England, France, Germany, Italy, Spain, Brazil, Mexico, South Africa, China, Korea, Japan, Greece, Turkey, Russia, the Netherlands, and the Scandinavian countries, local companies work with local advertising agencies and build brands. Often, these companies are international, and the ad agencies are local branches of large agencies headquartered in London or New York City.

Among the United Kingdom's top brands: Andrex Toilet Tissue (U.K. households buy over ten million miles per year; the brand is notable for the Andrex puppy); Boddington's (175 million pints sold throughout the world annually); Hamley's ("The Finest Toyshop in the World"); Macleans (toothpaste); Manchester United (soccer team); Sellotape (Europe's biggest-selling clear cellulose tape; each year, every person in the U.K. buys at least one roll, on average); *The Sun* (tabloid newspaper in a very competitive market); Thomas Cook travel; Virgin; Walker's Chips (potato chips); Wedgwood; and many more.

In each country, a brand's success may be based, in part, upon local preference, and in part upon the clout of the transgressor from abroad. In one study of South African consumers, researchers found that a preference for South African products translated to trust in products well suited to one's own type of hair, trust in the safety of local products, paying less for hair care, and pride in a local company. Preference for foreign products (most often, products from the U.S.) indicated a desire for higher quality, ease of use, and a desire for the long, shiny look of American hair. A skillful marketer with a budget could probably gain considerable market share for the foreign brand, but it would be more difficult for them to transform the more down-market local brand into a major winner: the market almost always pushes upstream.

Going Global, Part I

Corporations have been seriously global for a half-century or longer. Doubt it? Try this global soap opera ...

In 1898, in Germany, Siemens founded Deutsche Grammophon, which continues today as one of the world's top classical record labels. In 1950, the Dutch electronics firm Philips created a record label of the same name, also to record classical music, which was merged with Deutsche Grammophon to form a new joint venture owned by Philips and by Siemens in 1962, then reorganized in 1972 to become PolyGram, which acquired the U.S. jazz label, Verve. As it happens, that was the year that MCA acquired Decca Records, which had bought a controlling interest in the U.S.'s Universal Pictures in 1949. In 1980, PolyGram bought Decca records, and in 1987, the Dutch bought out the Germans, and PolyGram became a part of Philips. In 1989, PolyGram bought Island Records (which was based, partly, in the Caribbean), and a year later bought A&M Records, which was based in LA but made its fortune with owner Herb Alpert's recordings of Mexican-inspired music. A year after that, the Japanese company Matsushita (you known their Panasonic subsidiary) bought MCA, and a year after that, in 1993, PolyGram bought Motown Records, bringing Detroit's legendary catalog under Dutch control. In 1995, the camera swings around to Canada, where Seagram is based; it bought most of MCA from the Japanese. In the same year, PolyGram bought Rodven, the largest independent record label in Latin America. And in 1998, Seagram acquired PolyGram, bringing the entire story under control of a company that was previously known for its beverages.[17] In 2000, the French showed up as shareholders of Générale des Eaux (a utility) and acquired Seagram's interests in Universal. And so, Vivendi Universal was born. By 2001, the new company had sold off Seagram's beverage business to the French company Pernod Ricard, and to the British company Diageo. In 2004, the multinational U.S. company GE entered the picture, merging NBC with Vivendi Universal to create NBC Universal, which GE is likely to own completely in 2006.

Going Global, Part 2

About twenty years ago, an outdoor enthusiast created Teva sandals because flip-flops were flimsy and shoes became too heavy and cumbersome when wet. Teva has long been a company associated with extreme sports. It is committed to the environment and to good corporate deeds. Teva's products are made in China. The company is unapologetic about the decision—Teva provides jobs where they are badly needed, and it costs a lot less to produce shoes overseas. On the surface, the decision seems so modern and so uncomplicated.[18]

In the book *WTO: Whose Trade Organization*, authors Lori Wallach and Patrick Woodall take aim at the World Trade Organization. "Taken as a whole, the WTO and its agreements are a powerful mechanism for locking-in corporate-led globalization." Key themes in WTO agreements encourage and enforce privatization to generate revenues from commodities such as water and power; deregulation, which includes designating environmental and food safety rules as trade barriers to be eliminated; harmonizing local rules so they are consistent with worldwide corporate standards; liberalizing investment and banking policies to allow corporate investment flexibility; foreign ownership; and intellectual property protection so that investors can enjoy trademark, patent, and copyright protection often at a level unavailable to local individuals or companies.

Often, the market gets a lot of help from big corporations and the governments that benefit from their money. Yvonne Smith, communications director of the Port of Long Beach, California, explained to PBS *Frontline* producers, "We export cotton, we bring in clothing. We export hides, we bring in shoes. We export scrap metal, we bring in machinery." Standing amidst acres of shipping containers, Smith explained that the United States had become the source of raw materials for manufacturing in China, that our status was similar to a Third World country, that the situation was growing more extreme every year. Once the goods were manufactured, they were shipped back to the United States, mainly for sale to U.S. consumers who shop at discount stores, including Wal-Mart. "Back in the 1990s, the politicians and multinationals pushed free trade with China ... The picture they painted was of an emerging Chinese market, 1.2 billion consumers eagerly awaiting American-made products." In fact, a small percentage of China's citizens can afford to buy those products. Instead, with the help of China's government, Chinese manufacturers not only undersold American makers, but managed to replace them as low-cost suppliers to the discount stores. As a result, many U.S. factories have gone out of business, and many of the former factory workers are now employed at the discount stores that started the cycle in the first place.

How is this crazy cycle related to brands? When you buy an RCA or Phillips television set from Wal-Mart, you are funding Chinese manufacturing. RCA is now a brand owned by the French, and Phillips has always been a Dutch brand. For years, American TV sets sold in American stores were made in American factories by American workers. Today, only the stores (and many of the raw materials) are American.

Endnotes

1   One notable exception is the responsive and generous support provided to disaster victims associated with the 9/11 attacks, Hurricane Katrina, and so many others.

2   *The Company* by John Micklethwait and Adrian Wooldridge, p. 9.

3   *The Company* by John Micklethwait and Adrian Wooldridge, p. xvi.

4   For more info: http://mshistory.k12.ms.us/features/feature22/law2.html

5   *The Company*, 40–41.

6   This tricky concept is explained, along with early history and specific Supreme Court cases: http://en.wikipedia.org/wiki/Corporate_personhood

7   Howard Zinn, *A People's History of the United States*, 215.

8   Zinn, 250.

9   Zinn, 251.

10 *The Corporation: A Pathological Pursuit of Profit and Power* by Joel Bakan, various pages.

11 *Fast Company*, July 2005, p. 48.

12 According to the company's quarterly results press release for the first quarter of 2005.

13 According to "Hidden Cost of Wal-Mart Jobs: Use of Safety Net Programs," UC

Berkeley Center Briefing Paper Series, by Arindrajit Dube and Ken Jacobs, 2004, this data was provided in testimony by Dr. Richard Drogin.

14 David Loy, *A Buddhist Critique of Transnational Corporations:* http://www.bpf.org/tsangha/loy-corp.html

15 http://www.americanprofile.com/issues/20050206/20050206_4439.asp

16 http://www.cmomagazine.com/read/070105/making_waves.html and "The Hidden (In Plain Sight) Persuaders," by Rob Walker, *The New York Times,* December 5, 2004, and "Kidnapping," *Fortune,* February 2, 2004.

17 Source up to this point: http://new.umusic.com/History.aspx

18 "Teva: Making Tracks," Brandchannel, September 1, 2003: http://www.brandchannel.com/features_profile.asp?pr_id=142

CARS, MONEY, AND BRANDED MEDICAL CARE

As a rule, Americans concentrate their energies on a pleasant home, family, and personal lives. Half of us work outside the home.

We're busy. We never have enough money to do everything we want to do. As a result, we are easily wooed by convenience and by low prices.

When thinking about the future, anything beyond about five years is vague, so we tend to think ahead in terms of years, not decades.

We laugh when Jay Leno goes "Jaywalking" to ask Americans easy questions about history and other topics that they cannot answer. The bit is funny because it rings true: Many of us are pretty much clueless when it comes to major issues. What most of us know about global warming or stem cell research or U.S. relations with Indonesia (the world's largest Islam nation) would not fill an index card. Still, we are clear on our beliefs, and we're stubborn and resistant when anyone tries to change our thinking.

Most of us are aware that our country has some pretty serious problems—always has had serious problems—but the majority of us are too busy and feel as though we are poorly equipped to solve major problems. Instead, we hope someone else will solve them.

While some of us try to make a difference, most of us just follow our daily routines. The rest of us go shopping.

We have enormous respect for leaders and for power. We learn about respect from our parents, our textbooks, our teachers, our co-workers and our bosses. Americans who question power and authority are viewed as unfriendly, or as crybabies whose political party is out of office.

We believe what we are told by the media.

We are predisposed to trusting and buying almost anything with a brand. We buy without considering consequences.

And ... you ain't seen nothin' yet. Let's go for a drive.

Cars and Driving

You sink into the leather seats of your air-conditioned, leather-upholstered Honda Accord EX-V6 and switch on your Sirius satellite radio to laugh at Howard Stern. You're on your way to the interstate. It's a beautiful day for a drive. Here in America, life is sweet.

The $25,000 car is probably one of the most expensive things you own. Add the cost of gas, oil, licenses, maintenance, repairs, and maybe the total cost of ownership adds up to about $45,000 for about five years, maybe $7,500 a year. All things considered, this is a reasonable price for freedom.

In our branded world, we've convinced ourselves that this is the whole story. It isn't.

Car Culture, Brands, and Spin

There's this notion of a "car dealership," or in 1950s/1960s lingo, the "showroom." This clever use of language suggests a distinction between this type of retail establishment and others. In fact, every car dealership is a fancy store that sells cars, usually with a repair shop out back.

Why choose one car brand over another? Logic, price, and recommendations from trusted sources all play a role, but the most significant factor is "the car you see yourself driving." When GM was king, many Americans aspired to a Cadillac, but those who couldn't swing it bought a Buick instead. One step down was the Oldsmobile, then the Pontiac, then the lowly Chevrolet. Nowadays, the choices are simpler: if you can afford the Acura, you buy one. If not, you buy a Honda. And if you cannot afford a Honda, you buy a Saturn or maybe a used car. As the carmakers constantly remind us, you are what you drive.

Some cars are fun. It's fun to spend a sunny afternoon at an antique car show, or to see an Ohio main street filled with nothing but Corvettes in every color. NASCAR, Mustang, Mini Coopers, Hummers, Indy 500, Daytona 500—the car culture has become a defining aspect of American life.

Our exceedingly high level of brand recognition in the automotive sector is impressive as a marketing achievement. By focusing our attention on brands, new models, DVD players, and navigation systems, the car industry cleverly misdirects our attention away from larger issues about cars and driving. This skillful magic allows us to know that Dodge Trucks are Ram Tough, the Chevy cars and trucks represent an American Revolution, and that GM's Saabs provide a State of Independence. We know what Ford's Land Rover looks like, and we can easily recognize a Chevy Corvette or a GM Hummer because of their distinctive features, nameplates, and brand attributes.

You Are a Target

Just by driving onto the Honda lot, you're announcing that you're willing to spend about twenty thousand dollars on a new car (give or take a few thousand dollars), that you can be sold on the basis of quality, that you are steering clear of American brands, and, more than likely, you have owned a Honda before (quite likely, the car you are driving into the lot is a Honda). Within seconds, the well-trained salesperson evaluates you as a target customer. If the car you're driving into the lot is three to five years old, you'll likely buy the new version of the same car. If you're coming in with a spouse and a young child or two, you'll be leaving with a CR-V or an Odyssey. Traveling with a daughter who just graduated from college? The salesperson is already calculating the commission on the Civic. Like Viacom's cable networks, Honda's automobiles align with target customers: there is a car for every age and demographic, but there is a consistency in terms of price, quality, style, and consumer expectation across the entire product line.

As you browse, the salesperson pretends not to watch, but the gaze is predatory. When you are either seated in the new car or studying its price sheet, the moment is right. He wanders over, casually, and offers to answer your questions. In an instant, you are "qualified." If you're in the early stages, he'll hand you a card and ask you to keep in touch. If you've brought the family, he'll press harder because he knows you don't want to drag the kids to even one more dealership. He'll play it friendly, a bit high-handed. He'll draw you out by casually asking about features; this allows him to refine his target in terms of price point and profit potential. Within minutes, he'll suggest that you sit down at a table, just to get some information. He anticipates that you'll begin with a conversation about sticker price or some price you found on a Web site. No problem. In the friendliest possible way, he'll ask about your trade-in. Just as soon as that conversation begins, he has won the game. When we buy a car, we feel the pressure in a game that's tough to beat.

No other type of U.S. retail store engages in price negotiations. A combination of lax government regulation, auto industry unity, and consumer stupidity have allowed this practice to thrive.

When I go into a car dealership, I want to know how much the product costs, and I want to see a list of every available accessory, with its price. I would expect all prices to be openly displayed, clearly stated, and not misleading in any manner. The black magic is in the trade-ins. Dealers work with extensive databases, but these are unavailable to the consumer. As a result, the dealership has an unfair advantage. Why can't I have a look at my own car's wholesale value? This dubious business practice really ought to change, but we're all too lazy, foolish, or complacent to do anything about it. Besides, we're impressed and a bit overwhelmed by the sheer size and power of the dealer's retail establishment; we're a bit too comfortable with the familiarity of the brand. I want the same fair shake for a loan or a lease. No shenanigans. I hate feeling as though I've been a duck in a duck shoot for the past hour or two. Time is a key ingredient in the strategy: If the dealer can get you to stay in the store for more than about a half-hour, there is an extremely high likelihood that you will buy a car on that very day.

We should demand full disclosure, honesty and integrity, and a reasonable return policy for vehicles that do not operate properly. When you buy a product in a store, and you are not satisfied, you can return the product for a refund. Why is this not the case for cars? The generally accepted truth is that the car loses value just as soon as it wheels off the dealer's lot. Whose truth is that? Most likely, it's central to the branded-for-life behavior perpetrated by the car industry. Just as in any other retail industry, a car should be returnable if it does not operate properly and cannot be quickly and easily repaired to operate as new.

There should be no Lemon Law. Faulty cars should be returnable.

Why do the rules favor multibillion-dollar car manufacturers and not the consumers who buy the cars? Look for the answer in the century of government and industry interaction.

The Real Cost of Cars[1]

For every car on the road, we each pay enough money on costs of roads, bridges, tunnels, parking, police protection, and environmental damage to buy a second car. These costs are buried in the hefty taxes we pay on gasoline, or within our property taxes. The larger and heavier the vehicle, the greater the cost.

With the manufacture of a typical compact car, thirty tons of waste are produced, plus enough polluted air to fill a McMansion. Engine blocks are made in a foundry, an old-style, high-pollution factory (typically tucked away in places like Massena, New York, a blue collar town north of the Adirondacks where people are happy to have the work). Making tires is nasty business, too. Every car requires about ten tires. Roughly 25 million new cars purchased in the United States every year—that's 250 million tires a year, or a *billion* tires every four years.

A *billion* tires? Where do they all go when they're worn out? Is Goodyear responsible for their safe and pollution-free disposal? (No.) Engine blocks aren't recyclable. Nor are many car parts.

Twenty million cars are discarded every year. The car manufacturers aren't responsible for cleaning up their mess. That's somebody else's problem. That's not okay. Every kindergarten student knows that.

On the road, over the course of, say, 100,000 miles of useful life, your car spews over 1,300 cubic yards of pollution into the air, plus about fifty pounds of road gunk (bits of worn asphalt, tires, tiny pieces of your brakes).

Mining and refining petroleum is a nasty, messy business. Oil refineries are discretely located away from places where most people live, but BP's new logo, suggesting both a flower and the healthy warmth of the sun, isn't fooling anyone, nor is Shell's environmentally conscious ocean floor imagery. Just about every active American car cranks through about fifty gallons of gas each month, or more than five hundred gallons per year. With one hundred million U.S. cars on the road, that's fifty billion gallons of annual gas consumption by cars alone (trucks add to the figure). Most of it we buy from America's largest and most profitable corporations: Exxon Mobil (Fortune's #2 in revenues and #1 in profits), Chevron/Texaco (3 in revenues, 5 in profits), and ConocoPhillips (7, 5). Apart from Wal-Mart and General Electric, the seven largest corporations in the United States either make and sell cars (GM and Ford) or sell the gas to make them run.

And then there are the highways, the roads, the parking lots, the garages, and the driveways. We've paved enough of America to easily cover Indiana. Americans have more paved roads and highways (four million miles) than any nation on earth.

Americans spend about 20 percent of our income on transportation—one in every five dollars we earn. We've been taught to drive just about everywhere, convinced to live in sprawl, branded and brainwashed by the car culture to support an economy whose largest and most profitable corporations are in the car business. People in other countries, with longer traditions and more common sense, spend less than half as much on transportation (9 percent in Japan, 7 percent in Europe). Even our food travels long distances: in the United States, the typical American meal has traveled over 1,300 miles, mostly via long-haul trucks.

Hijack

Is there a better way? Well, there was a better way, but that was long ago, long before GM and large-scale branded transportation took over our world. From the 1890s until the 1920s, America's *public* transportation system was the envy of the world. Today, Americans who travel to Western Europe or Japan marvel at the network of connected trains and the delights of easy train travel. Two generations ago, it was America's system that thrilled world travelers. There were 250,000 miles of railroad lines—sixteen times as long as the road system. If you wanted to get from place to place in the United States, railroads were your answer. Today, there are just ten thousand miles of railway track—and the road/highway system is four hundred times as long.

How did that happen?

In the era before car (and bus) manufacturers decided to decimate the public rail system, WWI was ending, and Americans moved by rail. Everyday, streetcars located near their homes connected their surroundings, their neighborhoods to a downtown center.

"In 1933, General Motors, the manufacturer of buses and the owner of the largest share of Greyhound, formed a consortium of tire, oil, and highway men to buy and shut down America's streetcar system. ... Attacking the trolley mile by mile, the syndicate of GM, Firestone, Mack Truck, Standard Oil, all allied as National City Lines, cajoled and bought off city officials."[2] Subsequent Congressional hearings proved that there had been a conspiracy to destroy the streetcars and related public transportation, but it was too late. The streetcars were gone. So too were so many local train lines. At the same time, car manufacturers perfected their consumer marketing. They convinced Americans that cars were status items and essential modern conveniences, that cars were part of what made America great. These corporations then manufactured the car culture and taught us to think of it as the American way.

Faced with limited alternatives, a desire to move out of the cities (motivated by new roads, new homes, and new shopping centers), Americans bought more cars than people in any other country. No matter how many roads and bridges were built more cars were bought and driven, which caused more congestion. In *The Power Broker*, Robert Caro wrote about New York City's relentless road builder, Robert Moses: "Watching Moses open the Triboro Bridge to ease congestion on the Queensborough Bridge, open the Bronx-Whitestone Bridge to ease congestion on the Triboro Bridge, and then watching traffic counts on all three beecome as congested as one [bridge] had been before, planners could hardly avoid the conclusion that "traffic generation" was no longer a theory, but a proven fact: the more highways were built to alleviate congestion, the more automobiles could pour into them. ..."

Economist Todd Litman surveyed Americans by providing two choices. One was investment in more road capacity. The other involved lifestyle changes (more uses of walking, bicycling, car pooling and public transportation, plus increased density in urban areas). Most people wanted to build more roads, even though they knew that theirs was the wrong answer.[3]

The Cars We Drive

What do we want? Heavier cars (three thousand pounds in the early 1980s; around four thousand pounds today), with more horsepower (steady rise from about one hundred horsepower to nearly two hundred) and more speed (from zero to sixty miles per hour in fourteen seconds thirty years ago, now ten seconds). Although we complain when gas prices rise, we don't much care about miles per gallon. From time to time, we express concern about safety, but we've bought millions of family vehicles with safety standards associated with trucks.

In Europe and in Japan, a nimble car is considered a safe car. In the United States, a safe car is thought to be a larger car, more of a buffer between the driver and the theoretical brick wall. With a larger car or the higher driver position associated with an SUV or pickup truck, the driver is made to feel like an American king of the road. Unfortunately, SUVs and pickup trucks are more difficult to control than smaller cars and require longer braking distances. Add the aggressive driving that a powerful pickup truck often encourages, or the inattentive driving associated with a soccer mom driving an SUV while cradling a cell phone, and the situation becomes more dangerous. Better to own a nimble midsized car such as a Honda Accord, Toyota Camry, or VW Jetta. These cars are easier to control and maneuver, more responsive to the road, quicker to stop, less likely to roll over in an accident, and yet, they are large enough for a family.[4]

Just as Americans love their cars, so too do they love their credit cards.

Consumer Credit—The Opposite of Savings

In 1974, my father had no credit card. He paid by check or with cash. Then he needed a rental car. Without a credit card, none of the car rental companies would allow him to rent a car. Reluctantly, my father signed up for a Master Charge card.

Earlier this year, we decided that our son, a college freshman, needed a credit card. When I explained how credit cards worked, my son thought I was joking. My side of the conversation went something like this, "Basically, a credit card is a way to borrow money from a bank. It costs about fifty dollars a year to use the card, and then there are penalties if you don't pay them back on time. If you're not careful, you could spend a few hundred bucks a year just for the right to borrow the money." He wondered why he wouldn't just pay cash instead. He also realized that someone could use the card to borrow a lot of money that they could not easily pay back. For the first time in his life, he began to comprehend the concept of personal debt.

For more than five thousand years, individuals have borrowed money. Without Alexander Hamilton's restructuring of the Revolutionary era debt accumulated by the new United States of America, the country would probably have fallen apart. Without mortgages—the largest debts for most Americans—few families would own their own homes, and far fewer people would have been employed to build them. In 1925, three quarters of radios, phonographs, cars, and furniture were purchased "on time," on installment plans. Department stores allowed their best customers to sign for products, often using a metal charga-plate to imprint the form they signed. In recognition of the high cost of airfares, airlines set up an industry-wide credit system whose initials (UATP) are still found on tickets.

The idea of a charge card that could be used by everyone was kicking since the 1920s, but the Depression and World War II delayed progress. In 1949, Diner's Club introduced the first branded credit card to upscale business travelers. A decade later, in 1958, Carte Blanche (previously a Hilton hotels perk) went national, and so did American Express, initially as an extension of its Traveler's Cheques business. The same year, two of the country's largest banks, Chase Manhattan and Bank of America, joined forces to create Bank Americard, the first charge card for the general consumer, Soon after, Bank of America played a key role in creating the Interbank Card Association and its Master Charge cards.

Still, there were two seemingly unsolvable problems: how to get consumers to use the cards and how to get merchants to accept them. Unable to
come up with a better solution, the two associations dumped tens of millions of
cards into the mail in the late 1960s and hoped for the best. By 1970, the
FTC caught up with the banks' irresponsible practice and banned the mail-
ing of unsolicited cards (a ruling
since rescinded), but the deed had
been done. Consumers opened the
envelopes, used the cards, and some
got into trouble with debt. By 1978,
more than fifty million Americans
carried two credit cards in their
wallets, and billings were up to $44
billion for more than eleven thousand
banks in the credit card networks. The
scheme worked![5]

> Credit cards are a brilliant marketing scheme. They make consumers feel powerful: With a credit card, consumers learn they can buy anything they want.

Since that time, names have been changed (Bank Americard became
VISA, suitable for international expansion, and Master Charge became
Master Card to bury the distasteful word "charge."). Department stores
learned to use credit cards to acquire and retain customers ("10 percent off if
you sign up for the card today …"), and the Discover card tweaked the offer
by handing a tiny (about 1 percent) cash reward to loyal customers.

Today, there are 1.25 billion credit cards in use throughout the world,
and in the United States, annual billings are nearly $400 billion. U.S.
household debt is over $8 trillion, and now exceeds our disposable income
(that is, we owe more than we can afford to pay).[6] In the past four years,
more people declared personal bankruptcy than graduated college. With the
help of government regulators, loan rates that were once considered usury
are now commonplace for every credit card.

Credit cards are a brilliant marketing scheme. They make consumers
feel powerful: with a credit card, consumers learn they can buy anything
they want. MasterCard's campaigns have been especially clever: showing
the many things that (borrowed) money can buy, and then intimating that
borrowed money also helps to buy happiness. In fact, the tag line could be
changed to: "Convincing millions of Americans to borrow money from our
company: Priceless."

For lenders (the branded card companies), the key is to encourage
the use of the card for every conceivable purchase—to overcome my son's

instinct to avoid unnecessary charges. MBNA's five thousand-plus client companies offer branded credit cards associated with Hard Rock Café, Elvis Presley, The National Wildlife Federation, Ducks Unlimited, The Humane Society, The Nature Conservancy, L.L. Bean, Star Trek, Major League Baseball, Ty (for Beanie Baby collectors), the Fraternal Order of Police, or any of dozens of universities. A special offer, incentive, or small payment to a nonprofit group encourages program participation. Your credit card can now tell the world whether you prefer to shoot small feathery creatures or save them. Naturally, this data is used to further refine information about you, allowing direct marketers to more successfully build their customer databases and their brands.

The scheme is brilliant because consumers buy without considering the real costs (in this regard, using a credit card taps into the same dumb part of the brain as buying a car). The key to credit card fortunes is the APR (annual percentage rate). This compounding of interest enriches lenders (making the rich richer) and places borrowers even deeper in the hole.

In time, credit card companies will work together with their merchant network to wear my son down. It won't be long before he, too, uses a credit card for every purchase, without thinking about consequences. He'll consider using a debit card instead, but he'll soon fall into line and spend money he doesn't have to buy products he probably doesn't need.

Investing, Saving, and Branding

Most consumer marketing is about short-term consumption and immediate gratification. It is contrary to the interests of corporations—and very much in the interest of consumers—to discuss the long-term value of saving or conserving money as a valuable resource.

"Consumption may help fuel the economy in the short term, but it is savings, not spending, that provides the capital for productive investment and long-term growth."[7]

By allowing everyone to buy whatever we want and pay for it later, credit cards have displaced the idea of saving money. We have been taught to live beyond our means (just as the federal government does). Today, our government and our country is deeper in debt than ever before, and the situation is steadily worsening.

Americans now save at less than half the post-WWII average of 8.5 percent of after-tax income. Many households save nothing at all.

In place of traditional savings, we gamble on larger returns by "investing" (not gambling, but investing) in the stock market. To "manage" our investments, we turn to high-falootin' firms like Merrill Lynch and Morgan Stanley that sell stocks, bonds, and mutual funds, and offer free advice. Shrouded in powerful words and imagery, these retailers are known as "brokerage firms" and their salespeople are called "brokers." Research, though frequently self-serving, is offered as if it was objective. With marginal basis for trust, these firms focus instead upon mystique and imagery. That's why the king of the jungle prowls Wall Street on behalf of Merrill Lynch; and why Price Waterhouse pays Sam Waterston, the trustworthy *Law & Order* assistant district attorney, to encourage people to trust them with their money.

In fact, we do trust these companies, but when we act upon their recommendations, we do not hold them accountable when the market drops and we lose not only our interest but part of our principal as well. Such is the power of our trust and belief in major financial brands.

Branded Medical Care

I don't know about you, but I don't want my medical industry to spend much time, money, or effort on marketing or branding. I want them to concentrate on keeping people healthy, and making people better when they get sick. Everything else is a distraction.

I don't want Pfizer spending money on Viagra commercials, and I don't want to tell my doctor which drug to prescribe to me.

I wince when I hear a radio commercial that ends with the tag line, "The Best Cancer Care. Anywhere." I understand why the Memorial Sloan Kettering Cancer Center advertises—to fill beds and to maintain visibility among donors and civic leaders. Is it necessary for Blue Cross to advertise with a giant right field sign in a major league baseball stadium in order to compete effectively against CIGNA and Aetna? Will they not get the business from my employer if they cease advertising? I don't want to see HMOs advertising. I want them out of the marketing business. Period.

I'm not wild about doctors who pay professional sports teams to treat their players. These services are provided at no charge or at a deeply discounted rate. In return, the medical group or hospital gets the right to bill itself as the team's official hospital, HMO, orthopedic group, whatever. "People believe if a team doctor or official hospital is good enough for their favorite athletes, it must be good enough for them," said Dr. William O. Robinson, president of the American College of Sports Medicine. "But the purchasing power of these groups doesn't necessarily reflect their abilities." Despite concerns among doctors and players' unions, about half the teams in the four major sports are contractually committed. The New York Mets are paid one million dollars per year by New York University Hospital for Joint Diseases, plus the team receives doctor services at no charge. "It's bad for the sport, and it's bad for the community it serves," said Troy Vincent, president of the NFL Players Association.[8]

The Roots of Branded Medicine

In fact, we got off to a very good start. Six thousand years ago, in India, Ayurveda took a holistic approach to healing and personal health. Among its successes: inoculations to prevent smallpox. In China, acupuncture and the fundamentals of Eastern medicine were discovered and developed around two thousand years ago. At about the same time, Hippocrates laid the foundation for modern medical science. Greek (and subsequently, Roman) medicine emphasized hygiene and proper diet. Then, things fell apart, at least in the West, and we have yet to recover. Enter the charlatans ...

Charlatans were traveling performers who performed comedy and pulled teeth for the entertainment of assembled crowds on castle grounds or in market squares. They also sold elixirs (alcohol-based cures) and salves. Always one step ahead of the law and the church, their performances became known as medicine shows.

Medicine shows succeeded because, at the time, there was no better way to get well.

Dr. Benjamin Rush was generally considered the finest physician in the American colonies. He treated infection and other medical problems by the common practice of bleeding his patients. When George Washington visited Rush for a treatment of an infection, Rush bled thirty-two fluid ounces of Washington's blood. The former president died a short time later.

Early medicines were often worse than the diseases they were supposed to cure. Calomel, for example, was a tasteless white powder of mercury chloride that caused heavy saliva flow, bleeding gums, mouth sores, tooth loss, and, according to one source, "unfettered bloody evacuation of bowels." Opium, morphine, and other addictive drugs were widely prescribed and freely available at apothecaries, and often found in family medicine cabinets. Laudanum (alcohol plus opium) was especially popular. By the 1860s, it was clear that these substances were being abused (authors and painters, for example, were using opium and hashish to generate and enhance fantasies).

Through the first half of the 1800s, there were fearsome epidemics of cholera and yellow fever. To combat yellow fever, people fired cannons to scare it away or carried amulets filled with garlic and pieces of tar. Poor sanitation and hopeless hygiene made people sicker. Bathing was considered eccentric. The water supply was impure. In season, fruits were eaten, but vegetables were far less popular. At best, meat was unclean. Salt pork, a popular dish, was made from swine that wandered the streets consuming all manner of trash and sewage. It was decades before the emerging professional medical community was trusted. In the meantime, people did what they had always done: they bought and trusted patent medicines.

Illiterate consumers learned to recognize their favorite patent medicines by the shape of the bottles and the illustrations on the labels (for example, Hercules wrestling a Hydra on the label of Swain's Panacea). Making liberal use of Native American recipes, secret formulas, alcohol, opiates, and other dubious substances, patent medicines were a far better option than going to a doctor.

By the middle of the 1800s, there were more than fifteen thousand patent medicines available in the United States. Among the most popular and most heavily advertised: Lydia Pinkham's Vegetable Compound (forty proof alcohol); Dr. Kilmer's Swamp Root; Bonnore's Electro Magnetic Bathing Fluid; any products from the Kickapoo Indian Medicine Co., which staged very popular medicine shows. In addition to handbills that were so widely distributed and pasted on so many walls and buildings that they caused public debate, advertisements for patent medicines filled between a quarter and half of the ad space in many newspapers and magazines.

By the late 1800s, it was not unusual to find one-fourth of the pages in a newspaper or magazine filled with patent medicine advertisements. There was no stopping the patent medicines—these branded products had won over America. Unregulated brands were filled with alcohol, cocaine, opium, and other feel-good substances, so most Americans were sure this was a far better way to deal with personal health than visiting a doctor.

In 1905 and 1906, Samuel Hopkins Adams wrote a series of muckraking articles that were supposed to take down the patent medicine industry. The articles, which appeared in the popular *Ladies' Home Journal* and *Collier's* magazines, resulted in the formation of what became the FDA. There were all sorts of new regulations about, for example, fair labeling (listing ingredients on the bottle, for example). From 1906 until 1933, the agency's effectiveness was gutted by "ripper amendments added by Republicans intent on making these regulations disappear."[9] What's more, the industry fought back hard. In one case, manufacturers of Lydia Pinkham's sent pink slips to customers saying, "This new bill would make it very hard for you to buy Lydia E. Pinkham's Vegetable Compound or any other medicine which you are now in the habit of using and which you know helps you. We are trying to stop the bill ..." (This tactic is currently used by today's successor to patent medicines, the food supplement business.)

By the early 1930s, patent medicines were a $350 million business, one that would not go away. It wasn't until 1938 that the new Food, Drug and Cosmetic Act finally allowed the FDA to test every drug before it was sold to consumers—with real scientists working in real laboratories doing the testing. In the 1920s, the drug companies employed a few thousand scientists; in the early 1940s, nearly sixty thousand scientists worked in the more modern pharmaceutical industry.

Today's Patent Medicines: You Gotta Believe!

Although the term "patent medicine" is no longer used, plenty of products are left over from the patent medicine era—not drugs, exactly, but branded products that we have come to trust because they make us feel better. These include Bayer aspirin, Ex-Lax and other laxatives, cough drops and cough suppressants, antacids, liniments, vitamins, antiseptics for small wounds, deodorants, toothpastes, and mouthwash. Most have never been tested or approved by the FDA or any other agency. Until the 1970s, Listerine (whose name is derived from germ-killing scientist Joseph Lister, an innovator who had nothing to do with the product) falsely advertised that it killed germs that caused diseases such as colds and viruses (these are caused by viruses, not bacteria, so the claim was simply false).

Vitamins

In the 1800s, scientists suspected the presence of certain nutrients in foods and other substances. In 1912, biochemist Casimir Funk isolated the substances and called them "vital amines."[10] Funk, and others, demonstrated that some diseases were related to deficiencies in these substances. In order to persuade the masses to buy vitamins, Merck, Hoffman-LaRoche, Squibb, and Pfizer formed the National Vitamin Foundation. The purpose of the foundation was to develop a mass market for vitamins. No more "dreary health food stores and corner pharmacies"[11]—there was big money to be made by selling consumers on the vague promise of preventative health.

And so, children and adults were encouraged to take a daily vitamin tablet; in branded form, this established the One-A-Day brand that has been popular for decades (and is now owned by Bayer). Flintstones vitamins were introduced (with some added sugar for improved taste when chewing), and they've remained popular for decades. Both One-A-Day and Flintstones are owned by Bayer, and both brands are now represented by numerous brand extensions including nine different One-A-Day adult multivitamins and six One-A-Day Kids brands. One-A-Day Kids

> Today, there's a new breed of vitamin and supplement company, mostly unregulated ... Just so long as the claim is not a blatant lie, or a promise to cure a specific disease, the manufacturers can say whatever they like.

Complete are the ones with Scooby-Doo on the box; the sugar-free version of One-A-Day Kids Complete has Bugs Bunny on the box, and so on. (Bayer is also home to other not-exactly-a-drug products such as Aleve, Alka-Seltzer, Bayer Aspirin, Campho-Phenique, Midol, Neo-Synephrine, and Phillips [Milk of Magnesia], etc.)

Supplements

Today, there's a new breed of vitamin and supplement company, mostly unregulated. Many are located in Utah, home state to Senator Orrin Hatch, a principal sponsor of DSHEA (Dietary Supplement Health and Education Act of 1994), which deregulated the industry. The DSHEA allows companies to put health remedies on the market with no safety testing or review by FDA. As of 2002, the vitamin and supplement business is worth approximately $30 billion per year, perhaps more (the industry is dominated by private firms that are not required to disclose revenues).

Many of these products are positioned as "natural," so people feel as though they control their own health—not an HMO, a doctor, or a pharmaceutical company. There are no standards to regulate the manufacture of the pills, no scrutiny over safety, no testing. Companies need not prove effectiveness, nor safety. Just so long as the claim is not a blatant lie, or a promise to cure a specific disease, the manufacturers can say whatever they like. For further information, visit the Office of Dietary Supplements Web site at http://ods.od.nih.gov/factsheets/dietarysupplements.asp#h1.

When a supplement law may change, companies encourage public support and their own survival with a "Write to Congress today or kiss your supplements goodbye" campaign that emphasizes personal freedom and individual choice, and recalls tactics employed by patent medicine firms.

"This really is a belief system, almost a religion," said Loren D. Israelsen, member of the Utah Natural Products Alliance and principal architect of the 1994 law. "Americans believe they have the right to address their health problems in the way that seems most useful to them. ... They are willing to believe anything if it brings them a little hope."

According to an investigative report that appeared in *New Yorker* magazine,[12] Zantrex-3 is one of most popular weight loss supplements. The manufacturer's claim: "The most advanced weight control compound available ... period." Favored by many celebrities, a month's supply of Zantex-3 pills costs fifty dollars. Millions of bottles of Zantex-3 have been sold through GNC, Wal-Mart, CVS, and by phone and on the Web. Protected by DSHEA, Zantrex-3 is not subject to the laws that regulate pharmaceutical sales. Daniel Mowrey, who earned his PhD in psychology from Brigham Young University, developed Zantrex-3 by reading a study about the effects of caffeine on sleep-deprived Navy Seals, and by extrapolating ideas from a few other research studies. The product has not been tested in any scientific manner, but it apparently contains a lot of caffeine, some green tea, and three South American herbs: guarana (a stimulant used in popular Brazilian soft drinks), yerba mate (also a stimulant as well as a diuretic, it's a popular tea-like drink in some South American countries, long associated with good health), and damiana (possibly an aphrodisiac, certainly a relaxant). Mowrey says he does most of his research in a cost-effective way: He surfs the Web, relying upon public databases such as the ones offered by the National Institutes of Health.

Zantrex-3 is distributed by Basic Research, in which Mowrey is a partner. Since Basic Research understands the importance of branding, it often sells its products under impressive-sounding company names. One is Klein-Becker USA, whose products include PediaLean (weight control for children), and Mamrälin-AR (prevent breast shrinkage due to weight loss). [It's unclear why there's a Euro-style umlaucht over the letter "a," but it seems authentically Nordic). Apparently, the company names were devised to sound like traditional pharmaceutical companies; neither Klein nor Becker is or was part of the company.

Unlike products sold by pharmaceutical companies, products from Basic

Research come with a money-back guarantee. If the product does not produce the desired results, you get your money back. It's an impressive scheme, but I'd prefer a more reliable test that assures me of these products' effectiveness and safety. (Wouldn't you love to see the traditional pharmaceutical industry institute a money-back guarantee?)

"You cannot determine whether they are safe or effective without doing studies. And with supplements, studies are almost never done."[13]

When JAMA studied more than four hundred children during a four-month period, it found that a placebo worked every bit as well as echinacea. It also found that many of the children who took echinacea developed a rash. Such studies are rare because they are not required by any government agency.

Who to believe? On the one hand, it's good to see natural remedies on the market, but it would be better if they came with reasonable protections. On the other, Merck first heavily advertised and then pulled its very popular Vioxx because the drug increased the risk of heart attack. Critics take aim at the supplement industry and the government's hands-off stance and see, in the words of former FDA commissioner David Kessler, "a colossal failure to protect the public health of this country!" Why? Kessler told the *New Yorker*, "The supplement industry doesn't have to report adverse events, so the FDA doesn't have the data it needs to protect people. You cannot prove something is unsafe if you don't have the data. It's the ultimate Catch-22." [14]

Modern Pharmacy's Marketing Machine

In the 1850s, chemist Edward R. Squibb, who founded the pharmaceutical company that still bears his name, wrote, "I myself do not think anything should be patented by either a physician or a pharmacist; I am sure the patient could not be benefited thereby." At the time, it was considered ethically wrong to withhold medicines in order to profit from human suffering, an action akin to patenting bread and exacting a crippling price for it, ensuring some people would not get any bread at all.

Despite the objections, Squibb's sons built a modern pharmaceutical company. With penicillin, the Squibb company became a major player as the pharmaceutical industry grew from a "handful of chemical companies with no interest in research and no medical staffs to a huge machine that discovered, developed, and marketed drugs of real use in disease."[15] By the 1940s, 58,000 scientists were engaged in drug industry research, compared with a few thousand at the top two hundred drug companies in the 1920s.

By the early 1950s, a stunning 90 percent of prescriptions were for drugs that did not exist in 1938. Life expectancy increased from fifty-plus in the 1920s to seventy-plus in 1960. Thanks to the new drugs, tuberculosis, dysentery, whooping cough, and diphtheria—all major killers—stopped killing people.

Still, there were horror stories, mostly the result of inadequate research. S.E. Massengill (a respected pharmaceutical company) killed more than one hundred children when the chemical equivalent of antifreeze was used to provide a sulfa drug in liquid form. At the time, there were no laws or government agencies to deal with the problem. Ultimately, the company was found guilty of mislabeling and fined about $240 per death.[16]

Despite high regard for the valuable prescription drugs developed and produced by the pharmaceutical industry, questions about business practices remain. In 1960, an investigation led by Senator Estes Kefauver revealed drug industry markups of more than 1,000 percent; prices in the United States 400 percent higher than in other countries; and a four-to-one ratio between revenues spent on advertising (24 percent of budget) versus R&D (6 percent). In more recent times, according to the FDA, only 13 percent of the 569 new drugs approved between 1995 and 2000 offered a significant improvement over already available drugs and therapies.[17]

Pharmaceutical companies spend more on lobbying than any industry except insurance. This $250 million expense is best understood over time—and fortunately for the pharmaceutical industry, media rarely bothers with a news story that involves a period of decades. "In 1981, the drug industry proposed that the FDA allow advertising directly to consumers, arguing that the public should not be denied access to the 'knowledge' that would be provided." In 1985, the industry got its foot in the door (with strict limitations since rescinded). Drugs could be mentioned in advertisements, but any mention of treatment had to include information about side effects. In 1997, another rule change allowed television and radio commercials, but the side effects requirement was lifted, provided that the side effects information was published in magazines.[18]

The Miracle of Claritin

Armed with an advertising budget larger than Coca-Cola's, Claritin made use of the over-the-counter laws and grew sales from $1.4 billion in 1997 to $2.6 billion in 2000.

Schering-Plough's own tests show Claritin to be only 11 percent more effective than doing nothing at all. It's not that the drug is not effective, it's that the drug is not effective in low dosages. Therein lies the problem. Claritin's brand is based upon the idea of an allergy medicine that does not cause drowsiness. With doses of ten milligrams, Claritin doesn't do a whole lot, but the brand can make the nonsedative claim. At forty milligrams, Claritin would be a lot more effective, but it would make you drowsy, and so Claritin would lose its marketing edge. Ultimately, Claritin may be more of a marketing concept than an anti-allergy formula.[19]

What about Clarinex? It was developed just as Claritin was going off-patent (taking with it a $2.7 billion business for Schering-Plough). Clarinex is, basically, Claritin with an additional claim that it could be used to minimize the impact of indoor allergens as well. Based upon the additional claim, the FDA approved Clarinex and Schering-Plough was able to continue to sell its prescription, nondrowsy allergy formula.

Winning the DTC Game

Drugs advertised directly to consumers are the fastest growing medicines, and among the best revenue producers. These drugs provide the annual growth for the industry, both in unit sales and in dollar volume (because they are often higher priced than older drugs).

You've seen the commercials, so you know where the big money has gone: Claritin, Celebrex, Prilosec, Xenical, Zyrtec, Lipitor, Zyban, Flonase, Viagra, Nasonex. The annual advertising budgets for nationally known products like these are usually in the $50 million to $150 million range, but the money is well spent, resulting in sales in the $500 million to $1 billion-plus range. In the marketing trade magazines, it's not unusual to read, for example, "Lipitor sales shot up 56 percent after its maker spent $55 million advertising the drug."

Thanks to effective advertising, Nexium is now known by most consumers as "the little purple pill." According to *Overdosed America* author Dr. John Abramson, Nexium is "chemically almost identical to the acid-blocking drug Prilosec. Both are manufactured by AstraZeneca. In 2001, the patent was about to expire on Prilosec. This basically means that a drug's "recipe" enters the public domain and other companies can manufacture generic equivalents of it that sell for a small percentage of the price of a brand-name drug. (When) AstraZeneca sponsored head-to-head studies between Prilosec and Nexium...the catch (was)...the dose of Nexium in the study was forty milligrams and the Prilosec was only half of that." Nexium's twenty-milligram dose costs about $4.90; Prilosec's twenty milligrams, without a prescription, costs about sixty cents. How to encourage consumers to make the more profitable choice? Color the new pill purple and buy a whole lot of advertising time. Then, let the direct-to-consumer machine work its magic.

The National Institutes of Health has expressed a concern that, over time, the benefits of raising consumer awareness of (mostly new) drugs will cause inappropriate demand. Studies show that doctors overwhelmingly try to satisfy their patients' requests. There is also concern that so much advertising of drugs and pills in general will teach a powerful lesson (one that clearly runs to the benefit of drug makers): that the best way to prevent disease and improve health is to take a pill.

Marcia Angell, PhD, the former editor-in-chief of the *New England Journal of Medicine*, said, "The huge amount of marketing ... raises the question: If prescription drugs are so good, why do they need to be pushed so hard? ... The answer is that truly good drugs don't require much promotion. Cancer doctors treating patients with the kind of leukemia that responds to Gleevec know all about the drug from professional meetings and journals. And they use it. No sales pitch is needed."[20]

Angell's analysis of the pharmaceutical industry's dilemma is also on point: "If I'm a manufacturer and I can change one molecule and get another twenty years of patent rights and convince physicians to prescribe and clients to demand the next form of Prilosec, or weekly instead of daily Prozac, just as my patent expires, then why would I be spending money on less certain endeavors (such as) looking for brand-new drugs?"[21]

For pharmaceutical companies, the pursuit of brand excellence and clever marketing has always been part of the game; nowadays, it seems to be overtaking research and development as these companies' primary contribution to medicine.

Endnotes

1   Much of this information, and much of the inspiration for my further research and calculations, come from *Asphalt Nation: How the Automobile Took Over America and How We Can Take It Back* by Jane Holtz Kay, p. 92.

2   *Asphalt Nation*, pp. 213, 241.

3   *Asphalt Nation*, p. 213.

4   "Big and Bad—How the SUV Ran Over Automotive Safety," *New Yorker*, January 12, 2004.

5   *The Credit Card Industry: A History* by Lewis Mandell (various pages).

6   *The Real State of the Union*, p. 34.

7   *The Real State of the Union: From the Best Minds in America, Bold Solutions to the Problems Politicians Dare Not Address* edited by Ted Halstead, p. 34.

8   "New Sports Trend: The Team Doctors Now Play the Team," *The New York Times*, May 18, 2004.

9   *Protecting America's Health: The FDA, Business, and One Hundred Years of Regulation* by Philip Hilts, p.77.

10 Apparently, Funk got the story only partly correct. Strictly speaking, the substances were not all amines, one reason for the name change from vitamines to vitamins.

11 *Paradox of Plenty* by Harvey Lowenstein, p. 167.

12 Generally, the source for this section is "Miracle in a Bottle" by Michael Specter, *New Yorker*, February 2, 2004.

13 "Miracle in a Bottle," *New Yorker*, February 2, 2004.

14 "Miracle in a Bottle," *New Yorker*, February 2, 2004.

15 *Protecting America's Health: The FDA, Business, and One Hundred Years of Regulation* by Philip Hilts, p. 97.

16 *Protecting America's Health: The FDA, Business, and One Hundred Years of Regulation* by Philip Hilts, p. 89+.

17 *Overdosed America: The Broken Promise of American Medicine* by John Abramson, MD.

18 Source for this section: "DTC Research Brief: Prescription Drugs and Mass Market Advertising," September 2000. A publication of NIHCM Foundation (National Institute for Health Care Management) written by Steven Findly, MPH.

19 The Claritin story can be read, in more detail, in *Overdosed America*.

20 *The Truth About Drug Companies: How They Deceive Us and What We Can Do About It* by Marcia Angell, PhD, p. 133.

21 *The Truth About Drug Companies: How They Deceive Us and What We Can Do About It* by Marcia Angell, PhD, p. xvi.

DRINKING AND SMOKING

Is Coke *the real thing*? (What the heck does that *mean*, anyway?) (Don't worry too much about it. Not much in this chapter makes much logical sense.) Welcome to a chapter about drinking, smoking, and paying dearly for the privileges.

Soft Drinks

Soft drinks are American's single greatest source of refined sugar.[1] On average, a twelve-ounce can of soda contains twelve teaspoons of sugar. On average, each of us consumes the equivalent of a fifty-five-gallon drum of soft drinks every year! At least 75 percent of children enjoy a soft drink every day; among children, soft drink consumption has doubled during the past twenty years.[2]

With an annual marketing budget of $600 million, the soft drink industry gets results. In one much-publicized outrage, Mountain Dew and several other soda brands were licensed for use as baby bottles. In another, less-publicized campaign called "H2NO," Olive Garden servers and managers met their monthly beverage sales goals by steering customers away from water and toward soft drinks.[3]

Regarding the 2005 legislative action that would ban soft drink sales in California, the American Beverage Association, which represents more than 211,000 people who produce U.S. sales of nonalcoholic beverages in excess of $88 billion per year, told *The Christian Science Monitor*,[4] "While well-intentioned, the [passage] is unfortunate." The soda legislation, it says, "is an ineffective means of addressing obesity, a complex problem with many

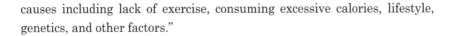

causes including lack of exercise, consuming excessive calories, lifestyle, genetics, and other factors."

History[5]

If you stop to think about it, sugared bubbly water sounds refreshing, but it's hardly the sort of thing that you'd bet on as a century-long worldwide phenomenon—and the basis for more than one of the most popular brands of all time. How did this product, with no nutritional value, become so popular? Why do people drink so much Coca-Cola?

This saga begins in the early 1800s, when the wealthy visited spas for health and recreation. Taking the waters at Saratoga Springs or Ballston Spa was satisfying and popular, so more than one entrepreneur attempted to bottle their water. Bubbly mineral water contains gases that pop (hence the term) the caps off bottles, so spa water was stored and served from pressurized tanks. These tanks were tapped (like kegs of beer) in fancy soda fountains, often with polished marble countertops, mahogany facades, and ornate silver fountain tops. Many of these soda fountains were built into taverns and apothecaries (or, if you prefer, drug stores).

Once people slowly accepted the scary practice of drinking cold water (the sources—icy ponds and rivers—were badly polluted), they convinced themselves that icy soda water promoted health. In the South, where anything cold during the summer was a godsend, fountain owners added fruit flavors (one Alabama fountain advertised rose, lemon, pineapple, strawberry, vanilla, sarsaparilla, sassafras, ginger, almond, peach, and more). By the 1850s, soda fountains were open in just about every American city and town. The flavored syrup industry was booming, but syrups were local specialties, not national brands. Some syrups were, however, promoted as healthful; during this patent medicine era, many made medical claims.

Made from Bordeaux wine infused with cocaine, Vin Mariani was introduced in Europe in the 1860s. Through advertising and celebrity endorsements, Vin Mariani became wildly successful in the United States as well. Founder Angelo Mariani collected hundreds of endorsements from more than seven thousand doctors, plus notable citizens including Thomas Edison, William McKinley, Emile Zola, John Philip Sousa, Frederic-Auguste Bartholdi (Statue of Liberty sculptor), actresses Lillian Russell and Sarah Bernhardt, Buffalo Bill, even Pope Leo XIII.

After the Civil War, Dr. John Smith Pemberton was a respected Atlanta doctor known for his patent medicines. He became interested in the properties of a nut grown in Ghana that supposedly boosted energy and served as an aphrodisiac. Pemberton developed an "invigorator" made from the kola nut, and called it French Wine Cola. Unfortunately, his hopes were dashed by Atlanta's move to prohibition. He reworked the drink, replacing the alcohol with distilled fruit flavors and adjusting the taste with sugar and citric acid.

> By 1925, Cola-Cola was selling six million drinks per day, even more during Prohibition, when sugar and chemicals offered the best available substitute for unavailable alcohol.

Quite likely, he was influenced by Vin Mariani's formula and by its success. Sadly, by that time, Pemberton was a weak, needy man, addicted to morphine. Pemberton took on a new partner, Frank Robinson, who named the drink Coca-Cola and sold it as a treatment for headache and depression. By 1888, Pemberton was dead. By 1891, the company had been sold to Asa Candler, also an Atlanta pharmacist and patent medicine man. Candler understood advertising, marketing, and distribution.

Apparently, at first Coca-Cola contained both cocaine and caffeine (apparently, caffeine increases cocaine's impact). By about 1900, the cocaine was supposedly removed or replaced. Coca-Cola was able to outperform its many competitors and copycats through effective, wide distribution and aggressive advertising. At that time, Coca-Cola was often promoted with pretty girls on its handbills: in fact, some say Coca-Cola was the Viagra of its era, one of several concoctions that supposedly improved sexual power. Also, Coca-Cola's logo was everywhere. The company provided retailers with signs for their stores, provided that the red Coca-Cola circle could appear on the sign as well. For most of the twentieth century, thousands of these signs dotted both the small-town and urban landscapes. By 1925, Coca-Cola was selling six million drinks per day, even more during Prohibition, when sugar and chemicals offered the best available substitute for unavailable alcohol.

Candler's Coca-Cola business was, essentially, the sale of flavored syrup. The finished soda was concocted at the local fountain, where syrup was mixed with cold soda water. Whenever anyone suggested that the product be bottled, Candler shooed the person away. Liquid in bottles was costly to manufacture, too heavy to ship, and far more trouble than filling and transporting tanks of syrup.

Then came the brilliant idea that shifted Coca-Cola from a fountain drink to an international phenomenon: the independent bottling plant. By selling the exclusive rights to bottle Coca-Cola, and then selling its franchisees the syrup, Coca-Cola headquarters avoided the nasty parts of the business, made franchisees fabulously rich, and assured local distribution throughout the United States and, ultimately, the world. By 1940, there were bottlers in forty countries. During World War II, believing that Coca-Cola was good for troop morale (we'll see a similar theme for cigarettes), bottling plants were built behind the front lines in North Africa, then in France, and ultimately in Berlin. By 1954, Germany had ninety-six plants, making it the most important non-U.S. market. When French wineries and beverage makers joined with the Communist Party to force a government ban against Coca-Cola (they claimed potential damage to French agriculture, and enough sugar to rot children's teeth), Coca-Cola pressured the U.S. State Department and kept the French market open. The dark secret in France: People were buying Coca-Cola because they liked to drink Coca-Cola.

Today, more than nine million stores sell Coca-Cola,[6] and the beverage is also sold in vast numbers of stand-alone soda vending machines. As with many American brands, the big push is now overseas. Coca-Cola now makes more money and projects far more growth outside the country than at home. The company is now moving toward total control—its bottling plants are now owned by a second Fortune 500 company, Coca-Cola Enterprises (123 on the Fortune 500)—while strenuously campaigning to place a Coca-Cola within easy reach of every person around the world, at every moment of the day or night. That's why Coca-Cola machines are showing up in schools and other unexpected places. The goal (seriously) is world domination. This, from a food that is a nutritional nightmare.

Coke and Nutrition

Depending upon your daily calorie intake, a twelve-ounce serving of Coca-Cola meets or exceeds the total recommended daily allotment of added sugar. Since this allotment includes the hidden sugars in breads, fruits, milk, and dairy products, a can of Coke will *always* exceed recommended intake.

A twelve-ounce serving of Coca-Cola contains over 160 calories, comparable to a twelve-ounce serving of orange juice or one-percent milk. Soda and orange juice contain about the same amount of sugar: forty grams (one-percent milk contains half as much). The difference is in the other nutrients, which are provided in abundance by both milk and orange juice. Here, Coca-

Cola scores a zero in every category except phosphate. Still, Coca-Cola scores high on refreshment, convenience, and for its many fans, taste.

Coca-Cola's executives are not focused on nutrition. They are paid to sell more Coca-Cola. There are two ways to do this: (1) sell more servings, and (2) increase the size of those servings. That's their focus, all day, every day.

Always. Coca-Cola.

Tea

Although it would be impossible for many of us to get through the day without coffee, tea is the world's most popular beverage—people drink more tea than *all* other beverages (except water) combined. In fact, more than two-thirds of the world's population drinks tea every day. Today, tea is benign. Its history is anything but: Coffee was never the cause of a major war, nor did it cause an entire nation to become addicted to opium.

Two thousand years ago, tea was associated with sacred ceremonies. A thousand years ago, tea became popular in China. An eighth century book, *The Classic of Tea*, instructed tea producers and consumers for a thousand years. Tea became popular in Japan in the 600s, and subsequently developed into a ceremony central to formal Japanese life. Tea was used as a currency along Asia's Silk Road and made its way to Europe in the 1600s with a long list of health claims. Thomas Garway translated these claims from Chinese and listed in his coffee house: "vanquishes heavy dreams; purifies blood; eases brain of damps; purifies defects of bladder, kidney; eases headaches; prevents dropsie; dries moist humors in head; clears sight; cleanses and purifies humors and hot liver; prevents consumption; sharpens and quickens understanding; purges safely the gout; strengthens use of due benevolence; drives away dizziness; makes one 'nimble and valiant;' vanquishes superfluous sleep."[7]

Tea became a popular alternative in London's coffeehouses, but developed a life of its own when Thomas Twining converted Tom's Coffee House into The Golden Lyon, London's first teashop (the Twining tea brand celebrates its three-hundredth anniversary in 2006). With the change in venue came new customers: women. Tea was welcomed in London's pleasure gardens, where it refreshed middle class families—including women and children—amidst groves, arbors, and stylish gazebos. Tea became a family drink, associated with social meetings and friendship. Before long, the average British laborer was spending 10 percent of his income on tea and sugar (tea's effectiveness is enhanced when sugar is added).

As tea became a British necessity in England and throughout the far-flung British Empire, China, the sole source of good English tea, became increasingly difficult to control. When small quantities were required, various commodities were traded for tea: cotton from India and silver from the New World among them. When the American Revolution cut off trade to Mexico, silver's price soared. The solution was opium. In 1758, the British Parliament gave the East India Tea Co. the monopoly for the production of opium in India: a government inducement to a private corporation to assure a steady flow of tea.

In 1776, China imported sixty tons of opium; by 1790, the amount doubled, and by 1830, the British were exporting 1,500 tons. This was enough opium to employ nearly a million workers in Bengal with today's equivalent of several billion dollars in business (the size of the operation would have made the bottom reaches of today's Fortune 500).[8] While the likes of Twining's London tea operation flourished, the Chinese grew increasingly poor and docile due to widespread opium addiction that cut across all classes. For nearly a century, opium consumption in China increased seventy-fold, all to keep England and the British Empire in tea (and to make the East India Co. wealthy). At the same time, the British government grew rich by taxes and tariffs on opium and tea.

Taken without sugar or honey or milk, tea has no calories and far less caffeine than coffee. What's more, researchers have found that tea really does do a body good, as tea has been linked to decreased skin cancer and other cancers, and helps with blood pressure and diabetes. Green tea seems to protect against heart and liver disease. To make the most of these protections, it's best to drink fresh tea, made with recently dried berries or flower petals. Branded, packaged tea sits in warehouses or on store shelves for months. Despite the promise of the comfortable bear in pajamas warming himself by the fireplace on boxes of Celestial Seasonings' Sleepytime tea, and a label that honestly says "100% Natural Herb Tea," it's tough for branded tea to compete in terms of flavor or health value with loosely packaged fresh tea. That's why tea brands expend so much energy on branding and packaging—without the freshness, the next best idea is to sell on brand image.

Coffee

According to the National Coffee Association, half of U.S. adults drink three cups of coffee every day.[9]

According to the National Institutes of Health, coffee (or, more precisely, the caffeine in coffee) is a stimulant and a diuretic. It provides short-term relief from fatigue or drowsiness. If you're a heavy coffee drinker—you drink more than a half-dozen eight-ounce cups per day—and if you suddenly stop your caffeine addiction, you will probably experience headaches, drowsiness, irritability, nausea, or vomiting. Pregnant women and people with heart disease should avoid caffeine entirely.

Supposedly, coffee's story begins with some hyperactive goats. The goats were eating berries, so their keepers gave the berries a try. The extra kick of the caffeine proved useful in prayer, so the goat-herding monks recommended the stuff to their friends. By the mid-1400s, coffee was popular all over the Middle East. By the mid-1600s, coffeehouses were popular in England, and by the mid-1700s, there were more than two thousand coffeehouses in Vienna, Austria. Coffee wasn't always a liquid drink; the beans were also popular.

As a rule, coffee is grown on plantations in tropical climates. Brazil is, by far, the world's largest producer. Colombia is second on the list, with about half as much production, followed by Indonesia, Vietnam, Mexico, Ethiopia, Guatemala, and several other Latin American nations.[10] In half of these countries, coffee production is closely aligned with dubious or dangerous political or economic situations.

Still, when Maxwell House claims it's good to the last drop, and Folger's claims to be the best part of waking up, it's unfair not to think about poorly paid workers cutting beans off trees in extreme heat, often in an abusive work environment. Most of the time, the location of coffee plantations is either ignored or romanticized (as it is in Starbucks stores). When Procter & Gamble heir Jamie Gamble turned eighteen, he learned of human rights abuses in El Salvador, then a large supplier for P&G's Folgers coffee. There were accusations of connections between death squads and coffee growers. Jamie asked P&G to stop buying Salvadoran coffee, but the company's CEO followed the first Bush White House's instructions to continue. By now, Jamie was a member of an activist group that produced a commercial showing a bloody cup of Folger's coffee ("brewing misery and death"). The ad ran on Boston's WHDH, and P&G pulled one million dollars in advertising from the station. "Such economic intimidation comes very close to an effective corporate censorship over content," wrote Massachusetts Senator Ted Kennedy. Mainly due to pressure from its large customers (Pizza Hut, etc.), P&G changed its ways.[11]

Incidentally, a dose of Anacin or Excedrin packs more caffeine than the average cup of coffee. On the plus side, there is some early evidence that coffee and/or caffeine may be helpful in reducing diabetes, the likelihood of developing Parkinson's disease, gallstones, colon cancer, and cirrhosis of the liver. Additional research points to its potential in treating headaches and preventing dental cavities and asthma.

Beer, Wine, and Liquor

Most twenty- and thirty-somethings have been exposed to the cleverly designed Absolut vodka ads (all sorts of objects were arranged to resemble the Absolut bottle). When Absolut's adman, Richard Lewis, resigned, he jokingly told *The New York Times*, "I have the obviously shaped tombstone already ordered for me."

Those who buy vodka would instantly recognize the names of Absolut's competitors, all strong brands: Stolichnaya; Grey Goose; Belvedere; Ketel One; Chopin; Smirnoff.

People who buy Scotch whiskey know Ballantines's and Bell's, Chivas Regal and Cutty Sark, Glenfiddich and J&B. Upscale consumers of single malt scotch know the more commercial brands such as The Macallen, but warm to lesser-known discoveries. Several of today's favorite Scotch whiskey brands are nearly two hundred years old[12], including Laphroaig (1816), and Glenlivet (1824). Many familiar brands are over a century old, such as Glenfiddich (1886).

You know Jack Daniels, if not from the print advertisements, then from their promotional deal with the family-oriented restaurant chain, T.G.I. Fridays, which features Jack Daniels's flavor and imagery in their barbecue sauces.

After-dinner drinks are especially well known, with every brand name recalling a particular flavoring: Bailey's Irish Cream, Harvey's Bristol Cream, Grand Marnier, Kahlua, Amaretto. Close your eyes, and you can probably envision the shape of the bottle and the design of the label. That's branding at its best!

The branding of the brewer or distiller is an old practice that has resulted in some of the world's oldest brand names, and the world's oldest brand preferences among consumers.

From the U.S. Treasury's Alcohol and Tobacco Tax and Trade Bureau (whose role involves the collection of revenues from these substances): "Alcoholic beverages date back to the very early part of man's history. Many archaeologists believe that wines made from grapes have existed for more than ten thousand years and that drinks such as mead and beer have existed for even longer. The Celts, ancient Greeks, Norse, Egyptians, and Babylonians all kept records of production and consumption of alcohol beverages."

During the Middle Ages and the Renaissance, monks made beer and mead in monasteries and sold some to the public. Private brewers and distillers operated local inns, taverns, public houses (pubs), and also distributed alcoholic beverages. In Colonial America, alcohol was extremely popular, even among children. "Alcohol was consumed at every meal, between meals, at polling booths, barn raisings, weddings, funerals ..."[13] On July 4, 1837, novelist Frederick Marryat visited Times Square for the Independence Day celebration, and found it was filed with booths selling porter, ale, cider, mead, brandy, wine, ginger beer, pop, soda water, whiskey, rum, punch, gin slings, cocktails, mint juleps, and other compounds.[14]

Beer

Stella Artois dates back to 1717, or, depending upon how you interpret the story, back to the 1300s. For more than two hundred years, the British have been enjoying Bass ale. The brew's familiar red triangle has been in continuous use since 1876—it was Britain's first trademark. Bass was enjoyed on the Titanic, a tribute to its upscale reputation in 1912. (According to Bass's Web site, five hundred cases remain on the ocean floor.)

In the United States, beer became a workingman's drink, an inexpensive high. Here, it's sold ice cold, so flavor matters less than what food scientists call "mouth feel." Throughout the northern part of the country, every city of any size brewed its local beer, mostly for local laborers: Yuengling in Philadelphia; Iron City in Pittsburgh; Rheingold and Schaeffer in New York; Blatz in Milwaukee; Old Style in Chicago (though it came from Milwaukee); Budweiser in St. Louis; and Genesee in western New York.

On average, every adult in the United States drinks six gallons of Budweiser per year. That would be one-fourth of America's total beer consumption, but the figures are misleading. If you figure that half of U.S. adults drink no beer at all (my estimate), then the average beer drinker is downing nearly fifty gallons of beer a year (not quite the fifty-five-gallon soft drink total, but awfully close).

Beer drinkers are wooed by brand names. Samuel Adams, for example, is a brand that pretends to be associated with the successful colonial brewer.

In fact, the brand dates back to 1984. The real Samuel Adams bankrupt his father's brewery while rabble-rousing on behalf of the American revolutionaries—the Boston Tea Party, for example, was an Adams affair. Better to go with an authentic microbrew that makes great beer but can't afford to advertise. In the Philadelphia area, these include Yards, Flying Fish, Iron Hill, and if you shop in the right stores, Ommegang Belgian-style ales imported all the way from Cooperstown, New York. Or go regional. In Portland, Oregon, many of the coolest restaurants, hotels, and clubs are owned by a megabrewery that's become a local tradition: McMenamin's. In this world, brand loyalty is far less interesting to beer drinkers than trying the next delicious beer, preferably one that's from a far away place and has a ridiculous name.

There's another contingent of brand-aware beer consumers: those who travel the world by sampling beers, ales, and similar drinks from the Czech Republic (Pilsner Urquell), England (Smith's Nut Brown Ale), Belgium (Stella Artois), India (Singha), and more. Having tasted a particular brand becomes a badge of honor, one more label for the collection. Is Pilsner Urquell the best beer brewed in the Czech Republic? For a while, I believed the answer to be yes, and then I realized it was probably the only Czech beer widely distributed in the United States. Now, I wish I had spent more time tasting other Czech brews on my three-day tour of Prague. I was branded.

Wine

Contradictions abound. In the 1990s, the USDA and HHS published Dietary Guidelines for Americans and wrote, "Alcohol in wine, beer, and spirits has no net health benefit" and "has physiologic drug benefits and is harmful when consumed in excess." At about the same time, CBS's *60 Minutes* reported on "the French paradox"—Frenchmen who ate foods with lots of saturated fat and drank a lot of red wine lived very long lives. Wrote Dr. Serge Renaud in the journal *Epidemiology*, "Wine protects not only against heart disease, but against most cancers."[15]

Together, France and Italy account for about one-fourth of the world's annual wine consumption. The French and the Italians drink, per capita, around thirteen gallons of wine per year—half as much wine as we drink beer. In both countries, consumption is dropping as fewer meals are taken at home.

In the United States, our average consumption is less than two gallons per year. Wine was never the U.S. workingman's drink.[16] One reason: The branding of wine hasn't been especially successful (particularly in comparison with beer or coffee or soft drinks).

Some vintners have established trust with consumers, principally through consistent product quality and recognizable labels. One example is Barton and Guestier, whose crested B&G logo is now an asset owned by the global beverage conglomerate Diageo (which also owns Johnny Walker, J&B, Guinness, and lots more). Another French vintner whose label has become well known is Louis Jadot. The vintner's consistent quality has resulted in loyalty among consumers who frequent better wine shops.

Serious wine lovers become very familiar with individual brands, down to the year that each product was made. What's more, they seek out brands ripe for discovery. Their bible: *The Wine Spectator*, a magazine whose own brand name is far better known than most wines described on its pages.

Branded to the Last Drop

Americans may recognize the brand names, but we are conflicted about alcohol.

On the one hand, we're a God-fearing nation, and so there are many places in the country where alcohol is prohibited. One such place is the Tennessee county where Jack Daniels sour mash whiskey is made. In Kentucky, where there are many dry counties, distilleries employ 6,500 people, and bourbon is the state's leading export (more than tobacco). It is illegal to buy bourbon where it is made.

On the other hand, we permit the widespread advertising of alcohol, even in places where children are likely to see logos (sports events, for example). We routinely connect sports with beer. We celebrate major sporting events, and just about every pro football game, with tailgate parties. Budweiser's frogs were fun, but they also resulted in 99 percent brand awareness[17] among junior high and high school students. This was no accident.

The alcohol industry understands the statistics. Undoubtedly, these statistics are used to define marketing strategies and spending. According to *Consuming Kids* author Susan Linn, "Lifetime alcohol abuse and dependence is greatest for those who begin drinking between the ages of eleven and fourteen (or younger) and the alcohol industry depends upon alcoholics for a significant portion of their profits."[18]

She continues, "In combination, adults who drink excessively and underage drinkers account for almost half of the alcohol sales in the United States."

In fact, underage drinkers drink almost one-fifth of the alcohol consumed in the United States and spend about $22 billion of the $116 billion Americans spent in 1999 on beer, wine, and liquor. This should be no surprise in a country where one in four children "live in a household where a parent or other adult is a binge or heavy drinker."[19] Each year, approximately 3.3 million students between the ages of twelve and seventeen start drinking. The statistics will not surprise high school students, but they may surprise parents and other adults: 41 percent of ninth graders currently use alcohol, as do 50 percent of tenth graders, 51 percent of eleventh graders and 62 percent of twelfth graders.

To cope, families are provided with (branded) solutions such as Al-Anon and AA, but these measures are weak in comparison with the billions of dollars spent by alcohol marketers each year.

Where do our lawmakers stand? Typically, they don't stand, they sit with a cool brew or a fancy Scotch in their hands, watching a pro football game from a skybox.

There is one consolation ... at least alcohol's not as bad as tobacco.

Tobacco

Just in case you missed the press release, Altria is the new name of our largest tobacco company, Philip Morris, and one of our largest food companies, Kraft. Before an Altria employee makes a decision, Altria now requires four questions to be answered. They are:

1. Is it legal?
2. Is it consistent with company policy?
3. Is it the right thing to do?
4. How would it look to those outside the enterprise?

For reasons lost on me, the sale of cigarettes remains legal in the United States, so Altria can't be faulted for selling or marketing cigarettes. It's the answers that employees have given to the other three questions that bewilders me. I don't work for Altria, and I'm not a shareholder, but to me, selling billions of cigarettes each year seems like a lousy idea. A company as large and rich as Altria ought to change company policy. By any reasonable measure, selling cigarettes is the wrong thing to do. And while we're talking about change, the altruistic sound of the name Altria sounds so insincere, I'm cutting down on my consumption of Tang, Oreo cookies, Jell-O, Maxwell House coffee, and Kool-Aid. And Velveeta.

Why hasn't the government placed Altria (and the other cigarette makers) on a timeline, requiring the end to cigarette sales in, say, ten years? How powerful is the tobacco lobby? Why are these companies still advertising in the likes of *Newsweek*? And how did we get ourselves into such trouble in the first place? The answer, of course, is successful brand marketing.

History

As a rule, humans don't smoke plants. We do smoke cannabis, and we do smoke opium poppies. However, we have smoked tobacco for at least five thousand years.

Tobacco has been sniffed, chewed, drunk, smeared over bodies, blown into warriors' faces before battle and into women's faces before sex, used in eye drops and enemas. It's been used as a mild analgesic for toothache (leaves packed around tooth). Sha-mans smoked cigars large enough to require support; they either blew smoke on hopeful patients, or simulated their own near-death experiences. The Mayans enjoyed their tobacco with blood; tobacco was popular in self-mutilation rites, probably involving young women Native Americans smoked pipes filled with tobacco to feel at peace, to meditate and feel at one with

> Why hasn't the government placed Altria (and the other cigarette makers) on a timeline, requiring the end to cigarette sales in, say, ten years? How powerful is the tobacco lobby?

the spirit[20]. Columbus received tobacco on the day he arrived; his crew threw the tobacco leaves to the fish because they didn't understand the gift. Gonzalo Fernandez de Oviedo, the military governor of Hispaniola,[21] wrote, "Among other evil practices, the Indians have one that is especially harmful: the ingestion of a certain kind of smoke they call tobacco, in order to produce a state of stupor. Their chiefs employ a tube shaped like a Y, filled with the lighted weed, inserting the forked extremity into their nostrils ... in this way, they imbibe the smoke until they become unconscious and lie sprawling on the ground like men in a drunken slumber."

In Europe, tobacco became popular when Jean Nicot treated a tumor with its leaves. He sent a letter to Catherine de Medici. Soon, her court (and the Pope and various Monks) were promoting tobacco's health benefits. In *Claims in Joyful News of Our Newe Founde Worlde*, Nicolas Monardes promised all sorts of benefits: for those short of the wind; grief of breast; bad breath; any illness of an internal organ; wounds; curing cattle of foot and mouth disease. England's King James I was decidedly anti-tobacco. In 1604, the king wrote *A Counterblaste to Tobacco*: "Smoking is a custom loathsome to the eye, hateful to the nose, dangerous to the lungs, and in the black stinking fume therefore nearest resembling the horrible stygian smoke of the pit that is bottomless." When devil-worshipping savages refused to listen, the king claimed tobacco was addictive, and when that didn't work, he decided to shared in the profits through taxation.

Meanwhile, in the Colonies, tobacco proved a godsend. The Virginia Colony was a bust until Jamestown's John Rolfe successfully grew the first tobacco crop in 1617.[22] With only about one thousand people living in Virginia, the colony shipped twenty thousand pounds of tobacco in 1618. In 1620, Rolfe decided to brand his tobacco. He called the first tobacco brand "Orinoco," and he even had a slogan: "Sweeter than the breath of the fairest maid." By 1622, Virginia's shipments were up to sixty thousand pounds, thanks not so much to the colonists, who were dying, as to the shipments of disposable humans who could work in the heat until exhausted. In 1619, the Dutch brought the first "negars" from Africa to work in the tobacco fields. By 1627, shipments were up to 500,000 pounds, and they were three times that much by 1640, thanks in large part to slave labor. By 1700, shipments were up to 38 million pounds, a major piece of Colonial commerce, our contribution to the growing British Empire.

In France, there were rumors of girls in their underwear making little cigars. (Seriously.) The girls were gypsies, and when the Seville factory got hot, as it did every summer, the gypsy girls stripped down. They also smoked a smaller cigar they called a *papelote*. When French writers visited, they loved the girls, but took the *papelotes* home. By the 1840s, the gypsies' (or, gitanes') small cigars were the rage of Paris. By 1845, the French government was in the tobacco business, encouraging its citizens to buy and smoke cigarettes. Emperor Louis Napoleon III said "I will certainly forbid it at once—as soon as you can name a virtue that brings in as much revenue." The British picked up the habit during the Crimean War.[23]

In the 1870s, the United States was both the largest tobacco producer and the largest tobacco consumer. In 1875, U.S. consumers bought 42 million cigarettes, usually in loosely tied bundles. In 1880, they bought eleven times that number. What happened? Baseball cards! Or, to be more precise, collectible cards in each newly wrapped package of cigarettes that featured baseball players, cyclists, runners, pugilists, and other athletes.

Children encouraged their fathers to buy the packages so they could have the cards inside.[24] Bull Durham cigarettes published cards dad was more likely to keep for himself; pictures of buxom actresses, for example. By 1889, cigarette sales were up over 2 billion, a number that increased to 200 billion by 1920—the direct result of the U.S. War Department's provision of cigarettes to WWI soldiers (in 1918, the War Department bought out all of Bull Durham's output, plus large numbers of cigarettes from Lucky Strike and Camel). That's when the big marketing push really began, as cigarette companies figured out how to reach really large audiences via a new medium: radio. Philip Morris moved from England to the United States and introduced a new brand called Marlboro, for women. Despite the promise that it was "mild as May," it failed, and was later relaunched as a man's product. FDR's administration further promoted relaxation and a feeling of home among WWII soldiers by purchasing billions of cigarettes. Soon after, the bad news about cigarette smoking began to materialize.

Through much of the 1800s, people thought tobacco and nicotine (named to honor Jean Nicot) were healthy products. The first major voice to express a contrary opinion was botanist Luther Burbank (later responsible for the development of the Idaho potato). In 1889, he wrote that tobacco was "nothing more than a slow but sure form of lingering suicide." Further research was scattered, and it wasn't until 1939 when German scientists began to notice parallels between increasing cigarette sales and increasing lung cancer rates. The Nazi government even printed and distributed some anti-smoking materials, but moved on to other concerns. In 1950, the *Journal of the American Medical Association* published an article establishing a statistic linkage between lung cancer and heavy, long-term smoking. Additional studies followed, prompting a secret meeting of the leading cigarette companies in 1953 at New York's Plaza Hotel, the apparent starting point for a half-century effort to mislead the public about the dangers of cigarette smoking.[25] Allegedly, the companies worked together to keep their current customers addicted, and they also worked together to engage new customers, often children as young as fourteen.[26] And they discovered television advertising.

The new medium was perfect for cigarette advertising (*I Love Lucy* was sponsored by Philip Morris, and the characters smoked a good many cigarettes). On TV, Old Gold dancing cigarette packages were popular, along with so many memorable campaigns ("Winston Tastes Good Like a Cigarette Should," "L&M Means Fine Tobacco," "Benson & Hedges: Just a

Silly Millimeter Longer," "Come to Where the Flavor Is. Come to Marlboro Country," and more). Tobacco companies were among television's largest advertisers until 1971, when the practice was banned.

Through the 1960s, as more people smoked cigarettes and more people died of lung cancer, the cigarette makers were bent on developing a more comfortable smoking experience. One such attempt was Kent cigarettes, whose Micronite filter promised a "smoother smoker." Along with the promise came asbestos poisoning, which killed not only the smokers who used the filter but also nearly all of the factory workers who made the Kent cigarettes.

In 1957, the Surgeon General published a report that confirmed, "prolonged cigarette smoking was a causative factor in the etiology of lung cancer." The industry's denial ran in 448 newspapers with a circulation of over 43 million; it explained that there were many possible causes of lung cancer, that there was no proven link between lung cancer and cigarette smoking, that the experiments were inconclusive, and confirmed "We believe the products we make are not injurious to public health." Meanwhile, both cigarette sales and lung cancer rates were increasing in tandem (29,000 deaths in 1956, up from 7,000 in 1940). The 1964 Surgeon General's report was released on a Saturday morning, perhaps in an effort to avoid media attention. In 1965, the Cigarette Labeling and Advertising Act was passed. It required each package of cigarettes to include the not-so-scary warning, "Cigarette smoking may be hazardous to your health." The phrase "Smoking Causes Lung Cancer, Heart Disease, Emphysema, and May Complicate Pregnancy" did not appear until 1984, the result of a 1981 law.

It's an odd marketing problem: 440,000 customers die each year, largely due to the purchase of the marketer's own products. In order to remain financially viable, the marketer must replace the dead people with 440,000 new customers.

The Tobacco Marketer's Dilemma

Given that nearly one in five American deaths are due to cigarette smoking,[27] it seems incredible that cigarettes aren't being phased out, made completely unavailable by, say, 2025. Certainly, the tobacco companies have fought hard, kept their customers addicted, added as many new addicts as possible, and kept everyone confused about the issues. The obfuscation worked: No substantive action was taken until 1998, when the states required tobacco makers to sign a Master Settlement Agreement: Make payments in perpetuity to cover all of each state's medical expenses incurred in treating sick smokers.

Cost to the industry over a twenty-five-year period: $246 billion, an average of about $10 billion per year. To put this figure into context, Philip Morris's U.S. revenues are usually in the tens of billions, so the settlement is meaningful. The hurt will be deeper if the United States wins its racketeering case, essentially doubling the penalties to cigarette makers.

In addition to financial penalties, there are (finally!) limits on targeting underaged smokers (why are these companies allowed to advertise at all?). And there's funding for a foundation to reduce teenage smoking and to investigate diseases.

How will the cigarette companies pay for all of this? By charging more money for cigarettes. And, by focusing on places like China, where one-third of the planet's 1.2 billion smokers live. No matter where you go, boys want to look cool and girls want to look sexy. Already, Philip Morris makes twice as much money outside the United States as it does domestically. They've begun to make their move through a global marketplace where unified regulations are shaky at best.

2004 was the fortieth anniversary of the U.S. Surgeon General's statement that cigarettes cause cancer and other fatal diseases, and that Americans should stop smoking. This year, we celebrated by purchasing 400 billion cigarettes. In a land where one in four people smoke (despite the hubbub, a steady rate since 1990), personal choice trumps public health. Here, personal choice is supported by a $100 billion industry with everything to lose if Americans ever kick the habit. Most Americans equate liberty and pursuit of happiness with personal choice. While we acknowledge that brands manipulate our thinking, we know final decision will be our own.

So why are cigarettes so popular? Short of a hypodermic needle, smoking is the quickest way into the bloodstream."[28] Within a half-hour, nicotine has left the brain for other organs, just about the time that a smoker needs another cigarette; this explains the two-pack-a-day habit: a cigarette for each half-hour that the smoker is awake.

Buying Marijuana from Sears

What about marijuana? One theory: Tobacco companies make so much money with tobacco, there was never any reason to pursue another product line.

From the early 1800s until the 1930s, marijuana was not only legal, but for decades, it was sold as a branded candy bar in the Sears Roebuck catalog (Ganja Wallah Hasheesh).

By the time mainstream (white) Americans discovered marijuana, it was the topic of sensationalist stories in Hearst newspapers and some very strange government maneuvering involving prejudice against Mexicans, who enjoyed smoking marijuana. Beginning in the 1920s, marijuana was popular among jazz musicians, who were mostly black and always viewed skeptically. By 1937, a Congressional panel outlawed marijuana, but the evidence and investigative rigor were weak.

By the late 1960s, the substance was popular among college students, protestors, hippies, professors, and suburbanites. People became familiar with brands of rolling papers: most likely, you would recognize the logos associated with Bambú, Zig Zag, and Job rolling papers.

By 1978, marijuana was decriminalized in eleven states. When Reagan conservatives reinstituted Nixon's war on drugs and Clinton took his own surprisingly conservative stance, it was clear that marijuana would not soon become a commercial product. In 1997, the World Health Organization reported marijuana was less harmful than tobacco or alcohol. But it's been branded a "gateway drug," so it's now introduced to junior high school students in association with harder drugs.

Marijuana is caught in a very peculiar drug war that allows politicians to blame drug abuses for many of America's social problems. Economist Milton Friedman wrote, "Had drugs been decriminalized, crack would never have been invented and there would today be fewer addicts. ... The ghettos would not be drug-infested no-man's-lands. ... Colombia, Bolivia, and Peru would not be suffering from narco-terror because of [it]."[29]

Once the tobacco companies find themselves locked out of cigarette sales in an increasing number of countries, one cannot help but wonder whether we'll be seeing Super Bowl commercials for Marlboro Marijuana or *Newsweek* advertisements for Camel Cannabis. Would you be surprised to find out that lobbyists are laying the groundwork? (Neither would I.)

Endnotes

1   Report from Center for Science in the Public Interest: "Liquid Candy: How Soft Drinks Are Harming America's Health."

2   *Food Fight: The Inside Story of the Food Industry, America's Food Crisis, and What We Can Do About It* by Kelly D. Brownell, PhD, p.77 and *Journal of American Dietetic Association*, 2000; 100:43-51, Guthrie, Morton.

3 "When You're Here, You're Thirsty," *Harper's*, October 2, 2002, p. 14, as quoted in *Food Fight* by Kelly D. Brownell, p. 25.

4 "California says 'no' to junk-food sales in schools," by Daniel B. Wood, *Christian Science Monitor*, September 6, 2005.

5 In general, the sources for this section were: *Sundae Best: A History of Soda Fountains* by Anne Cooper Funderburg and *The Real Thing: Truth and Power at the Coca-Cola Company* by Constance L. Hayes.

6 "Coke's Sinful World," *Forbes*, December 22, 2003.

7 *The Empire of Tea: The Remarkable History of the Plant That Took Over the World* by Alan and Iris MacFarlane, p. 65.

8 Here's how it worked: The East India Co. sold opium to British merchants in India, who sold it to China in exchange for silver coins. The coins were sent to England, then back to China to buy tea. The circuitous route allowed for deniability.

9 http://www.coffeeresearch.org/market/usa.htm (Note that this three per day is based only upon coffee drinkers.)

10 http://www.allaboutcoffee.org/id26.htm

11 *Soap Opera: The Inside Story of Procter & Gamble* by Alecia Swasy, p. 193.

12 http://www.scotchwhisky.net/history.php

13 *Snake Oil, Hustlers and Hambones* by Ann Anderson.

14 *Drink: A Social History of America* by Andrew Barr, p. 45.

15 http://www.askmen.com/sports/health/14_mens_health.html

16 http://www.winespectator.com/Wine/Daily/News/0,1145,2052,00.html

17 http://www.mediafamily.org/press/20010419-2.shtml

18 *Consuming Kids* by Susan Linn. For more information, refer to the author's source, *The American Journal of Psychiatry*, 157 (5) (200) (745-750), an article by David J. DeWit and others titled "Age at First Alcohol Use: A Risk Factor for the Development of Alcohol Disorders."

19 National Center on Addiction and Substance Abuse at Columbia University: 380-family_matters_report.pdf. See also http://www.udetc.org/Scope.html for the scope of the problem as reported by the Underage Drinking Enforcement Training Center.

20 *Tobacco: A Cultural History of How an Exotic Plant Seduced Civilization* by Iain Gately, p. 5.

21 *Historia general y natural de las Indias conquista de México* by Gonzalo Fernandez de Oviedo; published 1552.

22 Rolfe had married the Indian woman Pocahontas (whom he renamed Rebecca) in 1614, so this was a relatively safe period, allowing the crop four full years to be ready for sale, even though Rebecca died in 1617.

23 *Tobacco: A Cultural History of How an Exotic Plant Seduced Civilization* by Iain Gately, pp. 177+.

24 The 1909 Honus Wagner card from Sweet Caporal cigarettes is the most valuable sports card in the world.

25 http://money.cnn.com/2004/09/21/news/fortune500/tobacco_trial.reut/

26 NPR report, 9/21/04. For a more complete report on the beginning of the case, see http://www.usatoday.com/money/industries/2004-09-20-tobacco_x.htm

27 http://www.cdc.gov/tobacco/factsheets/HealthEffectsofCigaretteSmoking_Factsheet. htm

28 *Tobacco: A Cultural History of How an Exotic Plant Seduced Civilization* by Iain Gately.

29 *The Sunday Times*, Feb 20, 1994.

WE ARE WHAT WE EAT

We ought to be outraged.

In 1890—more than a hundred years ago—the USDA's director of research, W.O. Atwater, analyzed the American diet and published charts listing the calories, protein, carbohydrates, fat, and "mineral matters" associated with foods in the American diet. He also analyzed nutritional requirements of people doing various types of work. He found that Americans were eating too much fat, starch, and sugar. He advised men doing moderate work to take in 3,500 calories per day with 15 percent from protein, 33 percent from fat, 52 percent from carbohydrates. (His calorie count was high by about a thousand, but otherwise, proportionately similar to today's advice.)

In the 1890s, Atwater wrote, "How much harm is done to our health by our one-sided and excessive diet, no one can say. Physicians tell us that it is very great."[1]

Faced with its conflicted agenda, the USDA both encouraged Americans to eat well and, by the 1940s, introduced the idea of limiting food intake with Recommended Daily Allowances. The USDA was also responsible for the notion of seven major food groups.

Although a step in the right direction, the RDAs were not entirely successful, so the USDA tried again in 1992 with the much-maligned Food Pyramid. By attempting to capture the American imagination with an ultra-simple brand-like representation, the USDA branded our thinking about nutrition and also promoted massive grain consumption. The USDA also enraged many nutritionists who claimed the food pyramid was confusing, incomplete, misleading, and poorly designed. The foods that should be eaten most often should have been on the top, not the bottom. The pyramid did not address calories, exercise, salt, or alcohol. Some food groups were described in terms of their maximum requirements, others by the minimum, and so on.

It was easy for corporate marketers to use the pyramid to their advantage. Frito-Lay, for example, provided classrooms with a free poster picturing a large illustration of Pokemon characters and the headline, "Snack for Power, Snack for Fun." The body copy read, "Did you know Cheetos, Doritos, and other Frito-Lay snacks give you the bread/brain power that the food pyramid says you need? That means you can include Frito-Lay snacks along with toast, spaghetti, rice, and crackers as part of a nutritious diet—that's some powerful snack!" A small picture of the food pyramid was included on the poster as well.[2]

The USDA probably should have handed the revision of the pyramid project to the National Institutes of Health or the Centers for Disease Control and Prevention—both more credible in nutrition and health matters. It did not. Instead, the department forged ahead with another attempt to brand the complicated interaction of diet, nutrition, portion control, sensible eating, and fitness.

Once again, the 2005 design is a triangle. This time, a unisex figure prances up some steps along one side. The large triangle contains six colored, smaller triangles of varying sizes. Each one corresponds to a box filled with a tagline and several tips. For example, fruits are represented by a medium-sized red triangle, associated with an innocuous (and meaningless) tagline, "Focus on fruits." It suggests we eat "a variety of fruit," that we "choose fresh, frozen, canned, or dried fruit," and that we "go easy on fruit juices." Another box suggests that we eat two cups of fruit every day. With a total of nineteen information boxes and six triangles, the new design isn't much more helpful than the old one.

Perhaps nutrition is too complicated for a quick graphic representation. Maybe nutrition and fitness should be taught as full-fledged curriculum subjects in every grade of school, accompanied by ongoing, well-funded informational campaigns for all ages. If media is our most powerful educator, then we ought to put it to work in service of a healthier America with programs and promotions that evangelize proper nutrition and fitness.

Meat

On average, per person, every year, we eat more than our body weight. In a half-century, we have increased our per capita meat consumption by fifty-seven pounds. Last year, we each ate about sixty-five pounds of beef, fifty-three pounds of chicken, forty-eight pounds of pork, and just fifteen pounds of fish (most of it in fried fish sandwiches).

We love our beef, the meat product most closely linked to heart disease and cancer. Much of the beef we eat away from home is branded. We eat beef as burgers in fast-food restaurants, including McDonald's, Burger King, and Wendy's, and roast beef in Arby's. We take the family to dinner in branded steakhouses, including Outback, Lone Star, and Roadhouse Grill. On business trips, we can afford to buy better beef from a higher tier of branded beeferies: Ruth's Chris Steak House, Don Shula's, The Palm, Del Frisco's, Capital Grille, Fleming's Prime Steak House, and Morton's. All of these restaurants specialize in USDA Prime beef (itself a brand name, unique among food products). With all of these branded temptations, the message is clear: eat more beef! And so, we eat a dozen pounds more beef today than we did in the 1950s.

Quick: name a brand of chicken. Several come to mind: Tyson, Perdue, and, in fried form, KFC, Chick-fil-A, Chicken McNuggets, and maybe Popeye's or Church's. Trust Swanson, too, for their TV dinners and their chicken potpies. A healthy portion of chicken is eaten by America's children as chicken fingers, which also account for a healthy percentage of the fats in the American child's diet.

Quick: name a brand of fish. After Mrs. Paul's and maybe Groton's of Gloucester, this is a tough one. Would we all eat more fish if there were more brand names associated with these edible animals? High-end fish restaurants are slowly making a name for themselves: Boston's Legal Sea Food, for example, now operates thirty-one locations on the East Coast. They have a good tagline, too: "If it isn't fresh, it isn't legal."

Corn

If corn was a vegetable, we could all claim to eat lots of vegetables. Corn is not a vegetable, nor is it a grain. Corn is a fruit. It's the fruit of a grass called maize.[3]

A very high percentage of foods sold under brand names contain some form of corn.[4]

Mostly, our perception of branded corn is limited to cans or frozen boxes of Green Giant Extra Sweet Niblets or Jiffy Pop popcorn.

You'll find cornstarch in most baby foods. You'll also find corn or corn by-products in Hawaiian Punch, Mott's Apple Juice, root beer, French fries, graham crackers, Jell-O, marshmallows, and peanut butter.

High-fructose corn syrup (HFCS) has been a miracle worker in the food industry. HFSC is used in frozen foods to reduce freezer burn, in long-life vending machine products to make them taste fresh, and in bakery products to make them look freshly browned in the oven. Fructose now accounts for nearly 10 percent of adult calorie intake, and up to 20 percent of children's calorie intake. Like sucrose and dextrose, fructose is a sugar, but unlike these sugars, it does not break down before reaching the liver.[5] Some scientists believe this type of added sugar contributes to increased obesity. You can bet that a diet high in branded foods, or processed foods, is a diet rich in HFCS.

Even if you steer clear of branded, packaged foods, there's still no avoiding corn. There's plenty of "naturally processed" corn in our beef, chicken, milk, and butter. Corn oil is an essential ingredient in the insecticides used to treat all fruits and vegetables. We ingest corn through our skin as well: most soap contains corn, and so do many cosmetics. It is part of textile and leather processing as well, so we wear corn, too.

Like many crops, corn requires weed killers for optimum productivity. Growing corn requires the injection of nitrogen into the soil, which replenishes the nitrogen that corn zaps from the soil, and also encourages corn to grow more quickly. Unfortunately, nitrogen also causes weeds to grow, so pesticides are essential. These factors, plus the need for additional water, cause runoff rich in nitrogen and poisons. For areas where lots of corn is grown, corn is often part of an environmental mess.[6]

Fruits and Vegetables

The only vegetables eaten on any regular basis by Americans are the vegetables served in fast-food restaurants: lettuce, onions, and, if you like, tomatoes. After that, USDA research shows small numbers for true vegetables such as cabbage (used in coleslaw), carrots, celery, broccoli; for legumes that we choose to call vegetables, such as string beans; and for fruits that we call vegetables, including sweet corn, peppers, and cucumbers. In other words, we eat our veggies when they're packed into other branded products, but we don't often think to eat vegetables on our own.

Why don't we eat more vegetables? Maybe it's a bit glib, but vegetables are poor candidates for branding, and we just don't buy all that much unbranded food. If the food product lacks a brand, it's difficult to trust. Unfortunately, many of the vegetables that make it to our supermarkets are the survivors of a thousand-mile interstate journey, and, in truth, they probably weren't in great shape before they packed their bags. Assaulted by chemicals to prevent insect invasion and soil depletion, and to promote long shelf life, they don't taste garden fresh. And, because they're fading fast when they finally do arrive, they don't last long in the fridge.

It's tough for fruits, too. At least fruits have some branding that helps with their promotion. Most of us can name at least a few types of apple: Gala, Fuji, McIntosh, Empire, Rome, Granny Smith, Red Delicious, Golden Delicious. There are Chiquita and Dole bananas, and Sunkist oranges. For decades, Dole has been the smartest of fruit marketers, selling pineapples fresh in the produce section; canned as kid-friendly Pineapple Rings, Pineapple Chunks, Pineapple Tidbits, and Crushed Pineapple; or as juice; or in convenient transportable packs perfect for lunchboxes. In Hawaii, you can visit the Dole Plantation, a tourist attraction offering "Hawaii's Most Complete Pineapple Experience." Like any food company operating in less-developed countries (bananas and pineapples are produced in tropical climates), Dole has been criticized for its business practices. Question its corporate citizenship, but study Dole's branding and marketing. Dole is one of the only companies that successfully markets fruit to a national (and international) consumer marketplace.

Most adults eat about half as many fruits and vegetables as they should. Most children eat two servings of fruit per day and one vegetable (again, usually fried, formerly frozen potato). We've known that fruits and vegetables are healthy foods for more than a century.

You've probably heard about the Five-A-Day campaign,[7] which promotes five servings of fruits and five servings of vegetables every day for overall health. The campaign seems to be well known, but it is poorly funded—a few hundred thousand dollars at best, or, to put this in some perspective, about a quarter of the annual budget of Altoids mints.

Of course, the best fruits and vegetables are the ones that are grown nearby. In upstate New York, one summer highlight is the arrival of the delicious Irondequoit melon.

Still, a bit of skillful marketing couldn't hurt. When I visited a local Pennsylvania farm stand to buy some luscious local tomatoes, the woman next to me badgered the farmer for Jersey tomatoes. When he explained that his tomatoes were the same as Jersey tomatoes, that Jersey was just eight miles away, and that the whole Jersey tomato idea was really just a clever way of marketing the same tomatoes he had grown, she refused to believe him. Kudos to New Jersey for branding that worked!

Milk, Cheese, and Yogurt

Every morning, half of America starts the day with a serving of milk with a bowl of cereal, and that's not likely to change any time soon. Still, the dairy industry reminds us to drink our milk and eat dairy products via some fairly sophisticated advertising (Got Milk?). Milk is usually a local product without any significant brand; we buy what's available at the local supermarket.

Milk is one of those strange diet choices that have been with humans for centuries. Other species drink only their own milk, and then only as very young animals. Humans drink cow's milk and make cheese from the milk of cows, goats, and sheep. Nature designed cow's milk to rapidly transform a calf into a cow weighing ten times as much. Still, each year humans drink over twenty gallons of milk in liquid form, plus forty-five more in solid form as cheese (thirty pounds) and ice cream (fifteen pounds), plus butter and yogurt.

At the same time, many infants, who ought to be drinking only mother's milk, are not. For corporate marketers, there's no profit in it. Nearly all mothers are capable of breastfeeding, but the makers of baby formula have convinced us, through successful marketing, that baby formula is a reasonable alternative. That's true, but only if the mother is incapable of breastfeeding (since the 1880s, baby formula has saved a lot of young lives). The industry made its move when it convinced twentieth-century moms that the modern (processed) alternative was somehow superior to natural feeding. Once these companies got a foothold, they stubbornly refused to back off.

Their perseverance can be chilling. In the early 1980s, Guatemala adopted the WHO/UNICEF code to encourage mothers to breast feed their babies. The code prohibited products whose packaging would "idealize the use of bottle feeding." The packages were not allowed to show fat, healthy babies or other symbols suggesting outcomes. All of Guatemala's domestic and foreign suppliers complied—except Gerber, whose trademark included

> Nature designed cow's milk to rapidly transform a calf into a cow weighing ten times as much. Still, each year, humans drink more than twenty gallons of milk in liquid form, plus forty-five more in solid form as cheese (thirty pounds) and ice cream (fifteen pounds), plus butter and yogurt.

the happy, healthy, slightly chubby Gerber baby. Gerber allegedly ignored the new rules by providing free samples of Gerber formula to doctors and to new mothers in hospitals. The fight went on for years. Ultimately, Gerber won by maneuvering until it was able to threaten WTO action against the developing country. Fearing large legal bills and other trade actions, Guatemala folded.[8] As a marketer, it makes sense to fight. After all, you're selling a product that competes with something that most mothers (and babies) get for free.

We eat a lot of cheese: about thirty pounds per person per year, way up from the 1950s, when we ate just under eight pounds. We make up the difference by eating pizza and tacos and by frequenting salad bars. Most of the cheese we eat comes as part of a branded package: on a Big Mac or on a Domino's Pizza.

For cultured foodies, Kraft's Velveeta and CheezWhiz are guilty pleasures. For busy moms, Kraft's Deli Deluxe sliced cheeses are easy additions to lunch sandwiches. Once again, we've been hoodwinked, brainwashed to believe that the chemically colored orange bricks we buy in supermarkets are all we need to know about cheese.

Visit Murray's Cheese Shop in Manhattan and you'll be introduced to a new world of homestead cheese, freshly produced by cheese artisans and tasting absolutely delicious. Murray's sells 250 kinds of cheese from dozens of countries. They teach classes in cheese, which sell out a month in advance. At Murray's, learning about cheese is akin to learning about fine wine.

Taste some authentic Vermont Cheddar or Wisconsin Cheddar from a local farm in either state. Or wander into a cheese shop (or cheese restaurant) in Paris and you'll be amazed at the variety, texture, and tastes. Why spend one of your precious two to three daily servings on Kraft Deli Deluxe American when you can buy cave-aged Emmenthal instead for just a few dollars more?

In the 1970s, Dannon put yogurt on the American map with *Advertising Age* magazine's eighty-ninth-best ad campaign of all time: "Old People in Russia." [9] It made viewers wonder whether yogurt was the secret to long life. Dannon remains a dominant yogurt brand, but most yogurt sold in the United States is heavily branded (and, apart from plain yogurt, many are heavily sugared—a half-dozen teaspoons of sugar in that tiny plastic package).

Breads, Cereal, Rice, and Pasta

In short, this category has a branding bonanza, a free ticket from the FDA's 1992–2005 food pyramid, which encouraged Americans to eat more cereal, bread, rolls, grains, and pasta. All of these foods are high in carbohydrates, and most are eaten with fat or sugar [bread with butter or cheese; cereal with sugar or a sugary coating, rice with butter, pasta with a sugar-rich (sorry!) tomato sauce].

The bread you buy in supermarkets may be wrapped in a bag from a local or regional bakery, but that bakery is likely to be owned by a bakery conglomerate. IBC (Interstate Bakeries Corp.) is the largest wholesale baker and distributor of fresh baked bread and sweet goods in the United States.[10] IBC "operates fifty-seven bakeries throughout the United States and employs more than 33,000 people. From these strategically dispersed bakeries, the Company's sales force delivers baked goods to more than 200,000 food outlets. IBC brands include Wonder, Hostess, Home Pride, Drake's, Beefsteak, Bread du Jour, Dolly Madison, Butternut, Merita, Parisian, Colombo, Sunbeam, Millbrook, Eddy's, Holsum, Sweetheart, Cotton's Holsum, Di Carlo, J.J. Nissen, Marie Callender's and Mrs. Cubbison's. In addition, the Company bakes and distributes Roman Meal and Sun-Maid bread. Breads not owned by IBC may be owned by George Weston Bakeries (Brownberry, Boboli, Entenmann's, Arnold, Freihofer's, Thomas', Stroehmann); Campell's (Pepperidge Farm); Flowers Bakeries (Sunbeam, Nature's Own, Cobblestone Mill, Buttercrust, Bunny)."[11]

The fact that bagels are branded and are now the basis of franchised shops throughout the United States and the world would seem like a joke to Jews living in 1950s New York. At that time, the joke was that almost no one outside New York City even knew what a bagel was. Today, the best bagels are still found in the Big Apple (H&H Bagels or if you'd prefer to argue, Columbia or Murray's), but you could make a good case for Montreal's St-Viateur Bagel or Fairmont Bagel. "Real" New Yorkers shun the franchises, but they are popular: Einstein Bros., Noah's, Manhattan (all three owned by the same company), and the independently owned Bruegger's.

Concerned about authenticity? Don't be. Philadelphia Cream Cheese, long a favorite bagel schmear, isn't from Philly. The name was borrowed because, in 1885, the city represented top quality in food.

Even artisan bread tastes better if it comes home in a branded bag.

Whether it's from Great Harvest Bread Co. or from New York's Ecce Panis, or sourdough from Boudin Bakery in San Francisco, it's more than just the taste that's driving those purchases.

These days, mama's not rolling and drying her own pasta (she hasn't done that for generations). Instead, she's buying dry pasta by the box or bag, always the same brand because she knows and trusts it. Mama might be surprised to learn that Ronzoni, San Giorgio, Creamette, Goodman's, Prince, and many other popular brands are all made by the same company, New World Pasta the country's largest pasta maker.[12] Once again, the homemade version is a whole different thing. Fresh homemade pasta doesn't taste much like the dried, boxed, processed variety.

In the United States, rice is mostly about home cooking in a hurry. Leading brands are owned by major corporations: Minute Rice, from Kraft; Uncle Ben's, from Mars (the candy company); and Success Rice, from Ravinia (also owner of Carolina and River Rice). As with so many authentic, nonbranded products, wild rice from a Minnesota farmer is a revelation.

Whether we eat it dry or baked into a loaf, boxed with sugar and added vitamins, pressed into noodles or popped into snack foods, all of these products are made from wheat, corn, or rice. We take in about 150 pounds of wheat annually, plus about thirty pounds of corn (here, used as a grain), and about twenty pounds of rice.

From time to time most of us eat oats, either as Cheerios or as Quaker oatmeal or unbranded as an oatmeal cookie, but other grains—and there are plenty of other grains—operate on the fringe of America's brandscape.

Barley is tasty, but it's a forgotten grain because it's not part of a popular branded product. New Yorkers with Eastern European roots enjoy buckwheat, more commonly known as kasha. You'll find kasha served either in knishes (look it up) or as a side dish, *kasha varnishkes*. (When the product is homemade, the kasha is almost always poured from a box marked Wolfe's.)

Rye shows up in the increasingly popular rye whisky, but New Yorkers think in terms of rye bread. In this vein, there has been one very successful local ad campaign associated with rye: "You don't have to be Jewish to love Levy's," a New York rye bread.

America hasn't yet taken to quinoa ("keen-wa"), but the Quinoa Corp. is trying to change that. How? By selling the seed (it's not really a grain) under the Ancient Harvest brand. And if tasty, accessible quinoa's having a tough time developing a niche brand, it's hard to imagine how America will satisfy recommendations to eat more whole grains. Who among us will take on the brand necessary to cause Americans to embrace amaranth, millet, or that Ethiopian favorite, teff?

Oils and Fats

Olive oil is a sacred, righteous, generally healthy food that's been cultivated for more than six thousand years. It's used to cleanse, to bless, to cure headaches (the tree contains salicylic acid, aspirin's key ingredient), and, of course, it's used for cooking. Like wine, olive oil varies in its taste, color, aroma, and mouth feel. If you've tasted only the most widely distributed brands (Bertoli, for example), you're missing out.

The much-maligned butter is also associated with medicinal and spiritual uses (in India, ghee, a clarified butter, is the most sacred substance produced by a cow). Butter is several thousand years old. It became a commercial, branded product about a hundred years ago, but it was a local one. Even today, the butter business is regional: Keller's butter, a familiar brand in the mid-Atlantic states, now owns Breakstone's, Hotel Bar, and Texas favorite, Falfurria's Butter. For fluffier cakes and smoother sauces, chefs favor Plugrá, which has slightly more butterfat and less moisture than other butters. The one national brand that everyone seems to know and trust is Land O'Lakes, the large cooperative that is America's largest butter marketer. Most people don't think much about butter, but every household is loyal to its favorite brand. Consumers are remarkably loyal to the taste, consistency, and cooking characteristics of their preferred butter.

Butter is a commodity brand that is often added after the product has been purchased by the processor. Margarine is a manufactured product, and so it has always been sold under a brand name. You know the names Blue Bonnet, Imperial, and Country Crock because they've been advertised on television for years. In fact, margarine is not a dairy product: at first it was made from processed beef fat and became a secondary business for beef processors. As vegetable fats replaced beef fats, entrenched butter producers fought and lobbied against margarine. For years, margarine could not be colored yellow, like butter, but instead was sold white, like lard. In many countries, brand names that sounded anything like butter were prohibited. In other words, the butter industry prohibited the margarine makers from developing a brand whose attributes would appeal to consumers. By forcing margarine out of appealing brand names and appealing colors, butter producers prevented consumers from developing a set of positive beliefs about margarine. For decades, the butter bullies kept the margarine makers at bay.[13] Ultimately, margarine won the war on the basis of health concerns (and by winning the right to use the color yellow). We now buy four times as much margarine as butter.

Since the 1950s, we have multiplied our cooking, salad oil, and shortening intake by four. The culprit: endless gallons of cooking oil used in preparation of KFC, Chicken McNuggets, French fries, and the dramatic increase in the popularity of salads, which are almost always served with fat-laden salad dressings. From 1997 until 2000, our consumption of added fats globbed from sixty-four pounds to seventy-four pounds per person—a ten-pound increase in just four years!

When it comes to fats and oils, It's difficult not to conclude that we are manipulated by the food industry. While selling us branded cooking fats that are lower in cholesterol, processed foods are prepared with palm oil, a very stable fat that can remain on supermarket shelves for long periods, a product with wonderful "mouth feel" and more saturated fats than hog lard.[1]

As successful as the dairy and oils industries have been in selling us more fat every year, they're amateurs in comparison with corporations that sell us sugar.

Candy and Other Sweets

Every year, each of us eats twenty-five pounds of candy. Together, we buy $20 billion worth of candy (we only spend about $10 billion at McDonald's). In America, adults eat most of the candy.[15]

The big winner in the candy game is Mars, Inc., a secretive company whose family owners are among the world's richest. The runner up is Hershey, smaller than Mars by half. Between them, they own eighteen of the top twenty U.S. candy brands (the other two: Nestle's Butterfinger and the fiercely independent Tootsie Roll).

The most popular candy brand in the United States is M&Ms. Second on the list is the all-American Hershey bar, and third is the Hershey's Kiss. [16]

All three are chocolate candies, clearly the world's favorite sweet, and the one most dominated by brand names. As with cheese and beer, wine and olive oil, the chocolate sold in abundance by major brands isn't worth fats or calories. Belgium's Godiva chocolate (owned by Campbell's Soup since 1972) is richer in taste and more refined in texture. It is also marketed with a sense of elegance befitting Tiffany's jewelry. There are two hundred Godiva retail shops and over a thousand Godiva departments in fancy department stores and specialty stores.

Far better than Godiva chocolate is the lesser-known L.A. Burdick[17] chocolate from Walpole, New Hampshire. Arguably the finest chocolate made in America, Burdick supplies confections to New York City's most elegant restaurants. You can buy Burdick chocolates from their mail-order catalog, or from their Web site. To fully experience the brand's authentic glory, it's worth a drive to New Hampshire. Burdick doesn't spend a fortune on brand development or image, but they do have a handsome logo, a mail-order catalog, a Web site, and a signature chocolate mouse. Once you taste Burdick, or a product of similar quality, you may lose your appetite for the heavily processed, designed-for-long-haul-trucking Hershey's Kiss.

Branded Chocolate

Chocolate, it turns out, is exceedingly complex, so it's a real challenge for chemists attempting to make a synthesized version. Chocolate contains more than 1,200 chemical components, none dominant. Hundreds of chemicals give off rosy, honey, leafy, nutty, bitter, even sweaty "notes" and they all magically work together. Only about 20 percent of the chemicals found in chocolate are approved in the United States, so they cannot be legally separated or reproduced through synthesis.[18]

On our side of the world, chocolate is a two-thousand-year-old tradition, but it wasn't until the 1700s that chocolate gained popularity in Europe, and then only as a hard-to-digest, fatty beverage consumed mainly by the upper class. It wasn't until 1875 that Daniel Peter figured out how to make chocolate that could be eaten as a solid, then made a fortune selling it (and selling out to his neighbor, Henri Nestlé).

Milton Hershey bought German chocolate-making equipment in 1893 and opened a plant to make affordable chocolate for the American masses a year later. Hershey was a branding extremist. He renamed his company's hometown and renamed its main streets (Chocolate Avenue and Cocoa Avenue). He also controlled the lives of his workers, providing every conceivable form of Hershey-branded recreation, including hotels, restaurants, parks, and more. Hershey was one of many candy men whose family names became brand names: Peter Paul Halijian invented Peter Paul Mounds and Almond Joy, and L.S. Heath and his sons introduced the Heath Bar. Former Hershey employee Harry Burnett (H.B.) Reese developed the Peanut Butter Cup, which has always been made with Hershey's chocolate, and is now owned by Hershey.

In a world before air conditioning, chocolate was a product that made sense only during the cooler months. For decades, the candyman's Holy Grail was a chocolate that would not melt. Forrest Mars found his grail during the Spanish Civil War, where soldiers were eating candy-covered chocolate lentils. Based on this idea, Mars developed M&Ms in the 1940s, but they sold poorly. Mars hired the ad agency Ted Bates to figure out why. Apparently, the colored candies appealed to children, but parents controlled the money. Bates solved the marketing problem by developing a pair of cartoon characters (Mr. Plain and Mr. Peanut) to star in television commercials on two of television's most popular children's programs, *The Howdy Doody Show*, and the Disney favorite, *The Mickey Mouse Club*. Soon, kids throughout the United States knew M&Ms and knew the tagline, "Melts in Your Mouth, Not in Your Hands."[19]

By 1956, M&Ms were the top candy in America, a forty-million-dollar business.

Today, there's a four-story, 28,000-square-foot M&Ms store on the Las Vegas strip selling both M&Ms candies and M&Ms merchandise (designer jackets, jewelry, furniture).[20] With M&Ms' ColorWorks, you can mix and match M&M colors for any occasion. Elegant parties serve only black M&Ms, for example. Two companies are licensed to produce M&Ms in your company's colors. You can even order M&Ms imprinted not with M's but with your company's logo on each piece.

M&Ms are the world's most popular confection, a $2 billion business. Although we perceive M&Ms as adorable, clever, colorful, and festive, they are just mass-produced chocolate in hard sugar shells. There is better tasting chocolate available, but there is no better chocolate brand.

With just two companies dominating the candy business—and retail shelf space—it's tough for any candy brand to gain a foothold in the large commercial candy market. In recent decades, the Dove Bar is one of the few independent brands that have broken through on a national level. Since 1986, Dove Bar has been owned by Mars. Of the few remaining independents, Heide (Jujyfruits) was bought by Hershey in 1995, and Leaf North America (Jolly Roger, Whoppers, Good & Plenty, Pay Day) was acquired by Hershey's in 1996. Apart from Tootsie Rolls (advertised on *The Howdy Doody Show* as "America's Favorite Candy") or the entire Nestle product line or the British company Cadbury Schweppes, there isn't much more that Hershey or M&M Mars could acquire in the candy industry.

A Second Dessert, Perhaps a Third?

Still craving sweets? In the average supermarket, five of two dozen aisles are usually devoted to sweets: one for cookies, one for ice cream, one for cereals (mostly sweetened), one for soft drinks, and one (or half of one) for candies.

Most of us eat sixteen gallons of ice cream per year, or just over one serving per week. Among brands, it's the generic store brands that dominate the ice cream business. Among branded products, Breyer's and Dreyer's (also sold as Edy's) dominate. Also in the top ten are the upscale Häagen Dazs (made in New Jersey, and despite the silly umlaucht and the map that used to appear on the lid, unrelated to Scandinavia), and Ben & Jerry's (still authentically made in Vermont, but no longer owned by the founders).

What's the hottest (coldest?) franchise around? According to the corporate sales pitch, "You'll find it hard to resist, but why should you? Not when deep, dark, velvety chocolate is calling your name or whispering in your ear." The target audience for Cold Stone Creamery's premium ice cream is not children, but women ages eighteen to thirty-four who buy the company's frozen indulgences in three supersized portions: "Like It," "Love It," and "Gotta Have It." By 2006, there will be over one thousand Cold Stone Creamery stores.

If soda, candy, cookies, and ice cream were the only sugars we ate every day, we might stand a chance of holding the line against obesity. Unfortunately, we eat lots of sugar without even thinking about it. Sugar is a primary ingredient in Skippy Super Chunk Peanut Butter, Heinz Ketchup, Kellogg's Strawberry Nutri-Grain Bars, and Nabisco Honey Maid Graham Crackers. An eight-ounce container of low-fat yogurt often contains a half-dozen teaspoons of sugar, and if you're a female under five foot five weighing under 150 pounds, that's all the sugar you need for the day.

According to the USDA, the average American consumes 152 pounds of sugar per year—more than fifty teaspoons every day—and easily five times the amount of sugar that we ought to take in. Every day! Why? Are we stupid? In a word, yes. We're also misinformed, or partially informed. Sugars are listed on the packages of the foods we eat and drink, but the FDA has not been successful in forcing manufacturers to decode the words "fructose" or "maltose" or "sucrose" (or other such words) for what they are: sugar.

We believe and trust the brands we love, and we gain weight because they're not telling us everything we need to know. When selling cakes, pastas, cookies, and candies, full disclosure and consumer education are not high priorities. Are we addicted to sugar? If you worked in a key role in the soda, candy, or cereal business, would you encourage research to find out the answer? Or, do you already know the answer?

Processed Foods

When most of us lived on farms, we could be certain of the quality of the food we served our families. We ate whatever was in season or in storage, we suffered when crops turned out poorly, and when we needed sugar or some other commodity that wasn't available on the farm, we bought it from a barrel. Not every grocer was honest: Commodities were sold by weight, and (sigh!) dead lice carcasses look a lot like brown sugar.

Fruit? In the north, apples and pears were local and so were berries, but only during certain times of year. If you visited a northern home that served oranges, you'd be surprised and impressed, or maybe just confused because they were new to you.

In 1870, about a quarter of Americans lived in cities. Mostly, cities and towns were small: fewer than seven hundred cities or towns in the United States had populations of more than 2,500 people. By 1930, more than half of Americans lived in urban locations, and there were more than three thousand places with populations of over 2,500. As Americans moved from farms to cities, we learned to buy food from retail stores.

During the first few decades of the last century, everything seemed to change. Ethnic groups were discouraged from eating peasant foods from home and swept into the mainstream; garlic was a public embarrassment; stews and sausages were replaced by a more modern, more American meal: fried or grilled meat with a starch and a vegetable on the side. In order to be modern, "Poor Appalachian farmers shunned tasty country hams in favor of water-logged canned ones." They sold homegrown vegetables to buy the brand-named canned variety.[21]

At first, processed foods were commodities whose brand names assured at least some consistency and quality. After the Civil War, fruit merchant Joseph Campbell set up a company to produce canned tomatoes, vegetables, jellies, soups, condiments, and minced meats. In 1897, chemist John Dorrance (the general manager's nephew), figured out how to eliminate the water in canned soup. With reduced packaging, shipping, and storage costs, Campbell's Soups became a popular brand.[22] Consumers loved the product. It didn't cost much, and it provided mother with an acceptable alternative to cooking all day long. In that era, brands were built from commodities mainly by offering convenience and low prices. In 1947, Forrest Mars did the same for rice: his new Uncle Ben's Rice cooked faster than traditional rice, and it was fluffier, too. (The familiar face we recognize as Uncle Ben was a waiter in the restaurant where the idea of Uncle Ben was concocted by adman Leo Burnett, who later developed the Pillsbury Dough Boy, the Marlboro Man, Charlie the Tuna, and Tony the Tiger). Neither Campbell's soups nor Mars's rice tasted as good as their unprocessed predecessors or provided the same level of pure nutritional value, but other benefits won out. Taken in isolation, this is not much of a problem. Taken as the basis for an entirely new food industry, it turned out to be a disaster.

As processed foods gained popularity, they also attracted critics. Precisely what was in those cans and bottles? In the case of ketchup, the news was not good: tomatoes "in a high state of decomposition"—preservative helped to kill bacteria, and vinegar and spices covered taste and smell. After lots of political stonewalling, the rules were eventually changed because a factory line worker stepped forward and testified. When she did, she added that the conveyor belt was not only too fast for her to sort out rotten tomatoes, but also too fast for the mice to run off the track.

In the 1930s, several tell-all books became popular, notably *100,000,000 Guinea Pigs: Dangers in Everyday Foods, Drugs, and Cosmetics* by engineer Frederick Schlink and *Consumers' Research* Executive Secretary Arthur Kallet. Upton Sinclair's *The Jungle*, an exposé on the meat industry, and Eric Schlosser's *Fast Food Nation*, another horror story about the food we eat, bookended the twentieth century.

By the late 1950s, a typical American dinner consisted, mostly, of processed foods: Campbell's soup from a can, broiled meat, frozen French fries, a frozen vegetable, and either Jell-O or ice cream from the local supermarket.

As we've allowed major corporations to control the food chain, we've come to accept processed foods as a way of life. Pringles is a recent example of just how far we've come. For Procter & Gamble, Pringles was a breakthrough. Finally, here was a way to ship something very much like a potato chip across the country that did not shatter or go stale. Initially, Americans didn't understand the product, but P&G's clever marketers tweaked the product, the packaging, and the advertising. Today, Pringles is a top seller.[23]

Why do we eat this stuff? Chemist Michael Tordoff fed rats a sane diet, and then added foods high in sugar, fats, and carbohydrates. The rats ate the stuff that was bad for them, and within eight days they suffered from protein malnutrition. Tordoff then provided the animals with a sugar solution, which they enjoyed regularly as they gained weight. This and many similar experiments have shown that, given access to a diet high in fat, carbohydrates, and calories, humans and animals will ignore nutritional foods, gain weight, and become unhealthy.

If you are feeling as though you are living through this experiment in your own life, you are not alone.[24] And if you're feeling as though the folks running this bizarre experiment are doing so for a profit, you should consider what you eat as a snack, and the size of the operation behind that handful of Wheat Thins or Ritz Crackers. Kraft Foods sells about fifty types of cookies and crackers, from Oreos to Lorna Doones; together with the company's Post breakfast cereals business, sales exceed $2 billion in the United States alone. If you don't buy Barnum's Animals (yes, they are cute) or Cinna-Cluster Raisin Bran, you will be healthier, wealthier, and wiser. Kraft, unfortunately, will not fail to make its financial projections just because one fewer consumer will be buying sugary wads of baked flour.

Chains and Fast-Food Restaurants

From the 1930s until the 1970s, every American traveler knew Howard Johnson's. Easily recognized by their bright orange roofs, HoJos were clean family restaurants popular for a full menu that included fried clams, hot dogs, chicken pot pies, turkey dinners with mashed potatoes, and, for dessert, ice cream in a choice of twenty-eight flavors. (Before Baskin-Robbins upped the ante to thirty-one flavors, twenty-eight was a lot of flavors.)

In the 1950s, Ray Kroc improved upon the formula with restaurants that were quick, clean, inexpensive, reliable, and served just one entrée: hamburgers. By 1996, McDonald's operated or franchised more than twenty thousand restaurants worldwide. They were not alone: Burger King's name was on nine thousand more, and Wendy's added another five thousand to the total. In 1996, McDonald's opened a new restaurant every three hours—they wouldn't be opening if we weren't buying.

On its way to a trillion burgers served, McDonald's made a lot of smart business decisions. At first, each McDonald's franchisee was instructed to locate his or her store between a school and a church. The brand advertised heavily. Local franchisees got involved in their communities, developed and supported a mascot (after Santa Claus, Ronald McDonald is the world's best-known character). McDonald's franchisees focused on goals: they aimed for twenty visits per month for every fast-food eater.

They also forced the hand of headquarters to increase portion sizes.

When David Wallerstein worked in the movie theater business, he realized people did not want to buy two popcorns—but they *would* buy one larger package. Later, when Wallerstein was a member of McDonald's board of directors, he argued for larger package sizes (Ray Kroc refused because the idea smacked of discounting, which was contrary to McDonald's wholesome image). Wallerstein did his own market tests and won the argument. Sales went up, and McDonald's franchisees applied the concept to other menu items.

Responding to declining sales, former public relations executive and then-current McDonald's franchisee Max Cooper suggested what became the value-meal concept: selling the burger with fries, drink, and dessert. Once again, headquarters hated the idea because it seemed as though McDonald's was dropping prices. Once the promotion was in-market, value meals sent sales "through the roof."[25] Cooper put together his own renegade campaign, and headquarters eventually relented.

Wallerstein and Cooper recognized a business opportunity and took action. Did these men do anything wrong? Or do tens of millions of Americans have such poor impulse control that they are incapable of eating less than a full package of French fries?

Consider this: the number of calories in a package of McDonald's fries grew from 200 (1960) to 320 (late-1970s) to 450 (mid-1990s) to 540 (late-1990s) to 610 calories (now).

If the increases in McDonald's overall sales, serving sizes, and calories were isolated instances, there wouldn't be much of a problem. So many of our food choices are branded: including sandwiches (twelve thousand Subway stores), ice cream (Dairy Queen, Friendly's, Baskin-Robbins), yogurt (TCBY), breakfast foods (about five thousand Dunkin' Donuts, plus a thousand Waffle House restaurants and about five hundred IHOPs). chicken (KFC, Popeye's, Church's, Chick-fil-A, Kenny Rogers), and seafood (Red Lobster, Long John Silver's). And there's pizza (Pizza Hut, Domino's, Little Caesar's, Papa John's, Sbarro). There's Taco Bell, with nearly seven thousand units in 1996.

> **Consider this: The number of calories in a package of McDonald's fries grew from 200 (1960) to 320 (late-1970s) to 450 (mid-1990s) to 540 (late-1990s) to 610 calories (now).**

Fast-food restaurants advertise heavily, often market to children, and offer meals rich in sweets, fats, and carbohydrates—in short, foods we can't help but love to eat.

In 1970, a quarter of American meals were eaten away from home. Today, more than half of American meals are eaten away from home, half of them in fast-food restaurants. Today, one in four American meals is a fast-food meal.[26]

One study of sixteen thousand children found that the more days children ate dinner at home with the family, the more likely they were to have healthy eating patterns (more fruits, veggies, less fried food, fewer soft drinks, less far, lower sugar intake, more fiber).

In a typical day, more than 40 percent of adults eat at a restaurant, and about half of them eat fast food. Their increased intake of soft drinks, cheeseburgers, French fries, pizza, total fat, and calories is related to the frequency of visits to fast-food restaurants; similarly related to decreased intake of fruits, veggies, and milk.

The (Scary) Obesity Vortex

Approximately 25 to 40 percent of weight gain is due to genetics. The rest is due to the difference between the food we eat and the calories we burn.

More than one in five Americans is obese—sixty million Americans are, well, FAT! (Maybe more: Scientists and researchers are still counting, while we're growing fatter every day.)

The Centers for Disease Control and Prevention (CDC) labels 64.5 percent of Americans either overweight or obese. This figure was 46 percent in 1980.

In the United States, obesity is a greater contributor to chronic illness than smoking. With nearly 200 million people overweight, and 60 million obese, this is a problem that requires large-scale intervention. It's not just eating, of course, it's also exercise: Half of U.S. adults and children are not regularly active, and a quarter of us engage in no meaningful physical activity at all.

That said, a lot of the weight gain is due to (a) eating too much food; (b) eating too much sugar and too many carbohydrates; and (c) eating too much fat. If we all (a) ate less food; (b) ate (and drank) far less sugar and far fewer carbs; and (c) ate a lot less fat, we'd be in okay shape. One good way to do that would be stop eating French fries. Another would be to steer clear of anything that looks like a fast-food restaurant. Taking a walk every day would also be a step (okay, a bunch of steps) in the right direction.

Unfortunately, that's not what we're doing.

Where are we heading? Increased heart disease, increased cardio-vascular problems, and a continued increase in diabetes, which already claims one in four Medicare dollars. We're getting to know the term Obese Diabetic too well: numbness in limbs leading to gangrene and amputation; muscle tissue deterioration in legs; gallstones; increased cancer risk; excess hair; coronary artery disease, hypertension, stroke; arthritic joints; respiratory diseases; and allergic asthma.

An enormous number of people are already affected, and the numbers are steadily increasing. Rates are increasing among children throughout the world. The medical, social, and psychological impact is severe. The behaviors that cause obesity are themselves major contributors to poor health. Treatment is expensive, rarely effective, and to date, impractical on a large scale. In Italy, where Mediterranean diets and abundant sunshine have encouraged both proper eating and fitness, 36 percent of schoolchildren aged seven to eleven years are obese! This statistic is similar to the obesity statistic in the United States' hardest-hit areas. In Spain, 34 percent of children are obese. In Greece, it's 31 percent. Other European countries aren't far behind. These children are becoming fat because their diet is becoming more American—lots of sugary and salty snacks, fewer fruits and vegetables, lots of sugary sodas, and so on.[27] Obesity is a primary cause of Type 2 ("adult onset") Diabetes.

"When I was a medical student, I knew old people who got [Type 2 Diabetes]," Ivar Ekman wrote. "But kids? It's crazy. It's a catastrophic problem. They run a big risk of becoming patients for life."[28]

This is a nightmare. And it's a nightmare that we are bringing on ourselves because we are lazy, fat, and stupid with no more impulse control than one of Michael Tordent's obese rodents. (I speak from experience; I am at least 25 percent overweight.)

A $100-Billion Annual Pricetag for Treatment

Obesity kills. The AMA estimates 280,000 premature deaths per year due to obesity. (That's six times the number of traffic deaths per year. Unlike traffic deaths, which are declining, obesity related deaths are increasing, mostly because we eat too much.)

Spinning out of Control

Approximately 56 percent of the twenty thousand commercials that a child ages two to seventeen sees each year are related to food[29]—half of them candies, sweets, cereals (kids cereals are almost always sugary).

In the fifty-two weeks ending March 21, 2004, Reese's Puffs sold more than eighteen million boxes, a 10 percent increase over the previous year. The product is pitched as part of a nutritious breakfast, and sold with the tagline "The Reese's you eat with a spoon."

Nearly all breakfast cereal advertisements asserted that the cereal is part of a "balanced" or "complete" breakfast. What do those words mean, exactly, to an educated adult? What do they mean to a child? Certainly, for General Mills, a breakfast without cereal is not a "complete" breakfast and, from their perspective, it's probably unbalanced, too.

Among health professionals, there exists a high level of consensus with regard to obesity's likely causes: an excessively sedentary lifestyle related to passive forms of entertainment including television, computers and videogames; eating a high percentage of meals away from home; a steady increase in the intake of soft drinks, cheeseburgers, French fries, ice cream, and pizza; and an overall increase in portion size, daily fats, and calories, as well as less-than-desirable quantities of nutritionally rich foods, including fresh fruits and vegetables.

The Industry Perspective

The food industry claims it's not to blame. And if people really did control their diets, and if people were not easily persuaded to do the wrong thing, the industry would have a fair point when it claims:

"All foods and beverages can fit into a healthy diet." —National Soft Drink Association

"No single food is to blame." —National Confectioner's Association

Those glib statements obscure a grand plan whose components are described in far more detail in their original source by one of the most knowledgeable, articulate experts in the industry, director of the Yale Center for Eating and Weight Disorders, Kelly Brownell, PhD.[30] Here, I have built on Brownell's ideas.

Claim a commitment to public health. Visit the General Mills Web site and you'll see a healthy child showing his strong muscles with a bowl of cereal (Wheaties) and a glass of orange juice. Of nine text links at the top of the home page, one is labeled Health & Wellness, and it leads to stories about whole grain cereals, losing weight, balance, moderation, and exercise. The company funds programs related to youth nutrition and fitness, and much more. The company's most popular brands include Pillsbury (Dunkable French Toast Sticks, Toaster Strudel, Pie Crusts, Ready to Bake!

Chocolate Chip Cookies, and Grands! (supersized biscuits), Cheerios (now available in sugared form as Honey Nut Cheerios, and two types of Berry Burst cereals), Green Giant (frozen and canned vegetables, side dishes, meal starters), Yoplait (yogurt that tastes better with sugar added), Old El Paso (fried taco shells, heavily processed vegetables in jars, often with sugar and chemicals added), Betty Crocker (Bisquik, cookie and cake mixes, Potato Buds, Suddenly Pasta Salad, Hamburger Helper), Häagen-Dazs (truly excellent ice creams), plus Wheaties and Chex. Shouldn't a company with a strong commitment to public health sell mostly products that are nutritionally rich and generally free of sugars and fats?

Claim there are no "good" or "bad" foods. It's dismaying to find the statement "There are no 'bad' foods, just bad eating habits" on the Web site[31] for USDA/ARS Children's Nutrition Research Center at Baylor College of Medicine.

Play the "choice" and "freedom" cards. For decades, this worked beautifully for the tobacco industry. Disregard or discount the scientific experiments demonstrating the tendencies of humans and animals to select unhealthy food choices.

Wave the flag and warn Americans of the slippery slope. You know the old argument: first, they'll be telling us what we can and cannot eat, and then they'll be telling us what we can and cannot do in every aspect of our lives.

Gently blame the parents. Don't take responsibility for making sugared cereals or Coca-Cola, or for advertising them heavily. Pretend you're not marketing to children. Explain that responsible parenting always involves choices. Responsible marketing always involves choices, too, and those choices are most often guided by quarterly profits.

Shift attention to the need for physical activity. Our food choices would matter less if we exercised more. In truth, if we exercised more and ate properly, we'd be in better shape.

Reinforce the confusion surrounding nutritional information. Pretend to be playing a role by publishing nutritional information as necessary, but make no effort to explain what the terms and numbers mean, or to place them in a meaningful context.

Intimidate critics. If the critics become too vocal, find a way to either discredit their findings or credentials, or fight back with a convincing counter-claim that threatens their livelihood.

Claim to be the real victim. It's not the obese citizens who are hurting, it's the companies that do so much to put the best foods on our tables. If this demonization continues, these companies just won't be able to do that anymore.

Directly influence public policy. Whether it's campaign contributions or op-ed pieces, stories placed by front groups or campaigns to discredit scientists take advantage of every opportunity to influence the perception of the media, the government, and the public.

Lobby like crazy, and, if you can, write the laws. According to the *New York Times,* twenty states have passed "common sense consumption" laws that "prevent lawsuits seeking personal injury damages related to obesity from ever being tried in their courts." As of June 2005, another eleven states had legislation pending. The *Times* explains, "Adoption of common sense consumption laws by almost half the states reveals how an organized and impassioned lobbying effort, combined with a receptive legislative climate, can quickly alter the legal framework on a major public health issue like obesity." In Colorado, Pete Meersman, president of the Colorado Restaurant Assocation, apparently drafted language in the bill,[32] which passed the Colorado legislature with just a handful of nay votes in May 2004.

The Eater's Perspective

In the 2001 study conducted at Penn State: men and women volunteers, all reporting the same level of hunger, were served lunch on four separate occasions. As portions increased, participants ate larger amounts. Result: Human hunger could be expanded by offering more and bigger options.

It would be fair to estimate that half of all commercials seen on television encourage us to buy processed food of some sort. Almost none of these commercials promote fruits, vegetables, or other healthy (nonprocessed) foods.

Foods offered in large portions tend to be higher-calorie foods. And higher-calorie foods taste better, which also leads to increased consumption.

On average, Americans eat enough grain servings (eleven per day) required for a man engaged in heavy physical activities or a busy teenaged boy. We do that every day.

For heavy Taco Bell users, it was value and price, not food or presentation, that matters. They said, loud and clear, "We want more food for less money."

We are *purchasing* obesity. Nobody is forcing us, or our children, to eat Reese's Puffs in place of fruit. When one-fourth of our national vegetable consumption turns out to be French fries, it's tough to criticize the evil corporations.

Is Food the New Tobacco?

Although eerie in its similarity to the tobacco debacle, the food story is more complicated.

It's been forty years since the first Surgeon General's report on tobacco, but tobacco sales remain robust. It's been just a few years since the first Surgeon General's report on obesity—so we could be facing decades of discussion before much of anything is done, and a *century* before the problem is solved.

Cigarettes are a single product that can be tested and controlled; minors, for example, can be excluded from legal cigarette sales. It's difficult to conceive of a similar, practical solution to reduce access to unhealthy foods.

Also, tobacco has a well-defined addictive substance in nicotine. The relationships between food, diet, and exercise make analysis more complicated and results more difficult to explain. (This difficulty provides food companies, lobbyists and front groups with all they need to disparage scientists and their results for many decades.)

When someone regularly smokes cigarettes, they apparently straddle the line between industry-encouraged addiction and personal choice. When someone is overweight, the problem is considered personal—not an issue where government intervention is suitable or required. There is a widespread belief that obese people are responsible for their own condition— not physicians, insurance companies, corporations grinding out high-calorie, high-sugar foods, or the nation.

Scientists are still forming opinions, and some are contrary. Dr. Jeffrey Friedman, an obesity researcher at Rockefeller University, studied national data and found that Americans are not growing uniformly fatter. Instead he found that little has changed among thinner people, and that in the middle range, we're only about six or seven pounds heavier than we were in 1991. The increase in obesity comes at the top of the weight range, where there's been a 30 percent increase in the number of obese people since 1991.

For those charged with setting our national agenda, the bombardment of varying scientific opinions, strong marketing and political pressure from the food companies, and the American consumer's dubious habits and behaviors make the job exceedingly difficult. Taxes on unhealthy foods, for example, require acknowledgment that particular foods are indeed unhealthy, and then evoke images of Big Brother telling people what they can and cannot eat. So what can be done? This book's final chapter describes numerous ways of taking action.

Endnotes

1   *Food Politics* by Marion Nestle, p. 33.

2   *Consuming Kids* by Susan Linn, p. 89.

3   A fruit is fleshy covering for seeds. Tomatoes and green peppers are fruits, too. So are eggplants and cucumbers, and so are all legumes, such as string beans.

4   *Much Depends Upon Dinner* by Margaret Vesser, p. 22.

5   *Fat Land: How Americans Became the Fattest People in the World* by Greg Critser, p. 10.

6   *Much Depends Upon Dinner* by Margaret Vesser, p. 49.

7   "National 5 a Day Program for Better Health" a joint National Cancer Institute (NCI, part of NIH), and industry-funded Better Health Foundation (PBH) program.

8   Story from *WTO: Whose Trade Organization* by Lori Wallach and Patrick Woodall, pp. 92+.

9   The top-five campaigns included the Marlboro Man, McDonald's "You Deserve a Break Today," and Nike's "Just Do It." See them all at: http://www.adage.com/century/campaigns.html

10   In 2004, IBC filed for bankruptcy protection.

11   http://www.corporate-ir.net/ireye/ir_site.zhtml?ticker=IBC&script=2100

12   In 2004, IBC filed for bankruptcy protection. Why did our largest bakery and our largest pasta maker file for bankruptcy in the same year? The 2004 popularity of the branded Atkins diet may have been a contributing factor.

13   *Much Depends Upon Dinner*, p. 102.

14   *Fat Land*, p. 14.

15   Per capita, the average child probably eats more candy than the average adults. The fact you don't see here is the ratio of children to adults. There are 71 million children and 209 million adults. The total amount of candy eaten by the adult majority exceeds the total amount eaten by the minor minority.

16   Here's the rest of the list, according to a 2002 industry survey that included mostly large stores and supermarkets. Number four was Starburst, five was Reese's Peanut Butter Cups, six was Snickers, seven was Skittles, eight and nine were Wrigley's gums, and ten was York Peppermint Patty.

17   http://www.burdickchocolate.com/

18   *The Emperors of Chocolate: Inside the Secret World of Hershey's and Mars* by Joël Glenn Brenner, p. 64.

19   *The Emperors of Chocolate: Inside the Secret World of Hershey's and Mars* by Joël Glenn Brenner, p. 47.

20   http://uk.mms.com/mms/uk/about/history/default.htm

21   *Paradox of Plenty* by Harvey Lowenstein, chapter 1.

22   http://www.campbellsoupcompany.com/history.asp?cpovisq=

23   *Paradox of Plenty* by Harvey Lowenstein, p. 197.

24   *Food Fight: The Inside Story of the Food Industry, America's Obesity Crisis, and What We Can Do About It* by Kelly D. Brownell, PhD, p.25.

25   *Fat Land: How Americans Became the Fattest People in the Land* by Greg Critser, p. 23.

26   Economic Research Service / USDA, "Demand for Food Away from Home" AER-29.

27   "The Italian Blob," by Ivar Ekman, *Financial Times* magazine, April 15, 2005.

28   "The Italian Blob," by Ivar Ekman, *Financial Times* magazine, April 15, 2005.

29   All of this is based upon: "Impact of Television Viewing Patterns on Fruit and Vegetable Consumption Among Adolescents" by Reneé Boynton-Jarrett, SM; Tracy N. Thomas, MPH; Karen E. Peterson, ScD, RD; Jean Wiecha, PhD; Arthur M. Sobol, MA; Steven L. Gortmaker, PhD; American Academy of Pediatrics, 2003: 112, 1321-1326 or online: http://pediatrics.aappublications.org/cgi/reprint/112/6/1321

30   *Food Fight: The Inside Story of the Food Industry, America's Obesity Crisis, and What We Can Do About It* by Kelly Brownell, PhD, pp. 18+.

31   http://www.kidsnutrition.org/consumer/archives/nobadfoods.htm

32   "The Food Empire Strikes Back," *The New York Times*, July 7, 2005.

BRANDS EVERYWHERE

Today, a woman told me she had lost one hundred pounds. I asked her how she did it. She told me that she had eliminated sugar, soda, cake, cookies, cereal, and most bread from her diet. She carried a "before" picture with her, but almost nobody believed she had ever looked that way. If we eliminate most branded food from our diets, can we banish most of our obesity?

Robert Greenway studies both psychology and ecology (he is, in fact, an "ecopsychologist"). Greenway collected feedback from more than one thousand people who had recently participated in wilderness trips. A full 90 percent of the respondents said they felt "an increased sense of being alive, well, full of energy" and an equal number broke an addiction after the trip. When they returned, 77 percent experienced a major life change in their personal relationships, employment, lifestyle, or living arrangements.[1] What had changed for them? Like the woman who lost one hundred pounds by eliminating sugar, they had removed themselves, their very beings, from the world they had been living in. If we live in a brand-free, media-free, natural environment, can we eliminate stress and depression, and live happier lives?

Author Bill McKibben describes a parallel phenomenon in his book, *The Age of Misinformation*. In it, McKibben compares the experience of watching 1,700 hours of cable TV programming with a brief camping and hiking trip in the Adirondacks. The on-screen experiences were vapid, out of context, not useful, and often silly. The experience on a mountaintop was filled with useful, interesting, fulfilling information. If we live free from commercial media, can we learn to focus our considerable mental powers to make the world a better place?

Kalle Lasn, founder of the anticommercial *Ad Busters* magazine, writes, "We can barely remember the last time we drank from a stream, smelled wild skunk cabbage, saw the stars from a dark remove well away from the city. We can't identify three kinds of tree or explain why the sky is blue."

Affluenza authors John DeGraaf, David Wann, and Thomas Naylor explain, "We buy plantation-grown coffee, not realizing that each cup exposes another migratory songbird to potentially lethal pesticides on coffee plantations. The songbirds no longer fly thousands of miles from Central to South America because they're dead. And if they do survive to return home, chances are good that their northern habitats will be covered with roads, homes … and parking lots."[2]

Screens

Today, when we think of a "star," we immediately jump to Julia Roberts or Tom Cruise. That's a recent phenomenon. Before we lived our lives on screens, a star was a miracle in the heavens

The last time you used the word "stream," were you discussing the way the Internet distributes audio or video programming, or were you talking about a place that's wet, where you can fish or muddy your feet?

Increasingly, we live our lives through screens, not in reality. We might have this conversation with our children at home:

Son: "I'm talking to my friends."

Dad: "No, you're typing to your friends."

Science writer James Gleick noted that the world is beginning to run out of names. We've made up so many phony names for businesses and brands, there aren't enough for a worldwide digital economy. Cybersquatters anticipate future trends, buy up URLs, and resell them while trying to stay out of court. The FDA is growing concerned because similar-sounding names of pharmaceuticals sometimes confuse patients who may take the wrong medicine. Maybe we've taken this whole branding thing too far?

"Quiet feels foreign now, but quiet may be just what we need."[3]

Ethnic Branding

When I was a child, our neighbor Fay was "my second mother;" her apartment was my second home. One summer, I asked Fay why she had a number tattooed on her arm. Later, I came to understand that Fay was branded as a Jew, branded to die in the Nazi concentration camps.

To the Nazis, the Jews were evil subhumans who deserved to die. During the same war, to Allied forces, the Japanese were evil subhumans who deserved to die. To Americans in the 1800s, Indians were not people, they were dangerous savages whose lives were worth less than the land they occupied. Social scientists describe this dark shadow of branding as "racist ideology." It works like this: The enemy is reduced to a stereotype, based upon "a few simple, vivid, memorable, easily grasped and widely recognizable characteristics." The promoter then "reduce[s] everything about the person to those traits, exaggerate[s] and simplify[ies] them, and fix[es] them without change or development to eternity."[4] The stereotyped group becomes the evil "other"—a Godless abomination. Soldiers cannot be trained to kill real people. Instead, they kill the evil other.

Blackface and Garlic

"By exaggerating the physical features of African-American men and women, making them laughable and useable in everyday items, items reinforced beliefs about the place of Blacks in American society (salt and pepper shakers, trading cards, sheet music with pictures of happy Sambo and plump mammies and wide-eyed pickaninnies)."[5] Although updated, some remain. Aunt Jemima, based upon a popular song[6]; Uncle Ben (rice), and Uncle Rastus (Cream of Wheat).

A century ago, minstrel shows were mainstream entertainment. Built from the comedy of bigotry and stereotype, they featured white and black performers in blackface, making jokes, and "performing songs and skits that sentimentalized the nightmare of slave life on Southern plantations. Blacks were shown as naive buffoons who sang and danced the days away, gobbling "chitlins," stealing the occasional watermelon, and expressing their inexplicable love for "ol' massuh."[7]

In the 1930s, NBC radio's biggest hit show, *Amos 'n' Andy*, was piped into movie theaters on Monday nights because moviegoers refused to miss even a single episode (without the in-theater broadcasts, people stayed home to listen to the radio show). The program was also popular on CBS television, a valuable property that CBS Films syndicated everywhere, including Africa. The NAACP managed to get the show off the air in the early 1950s. Why? Some answers from a 1951 NAACP Bulletin:[8] "Every character in this one and only TV show with an all Negro cast is either a clown or a crook ... Negro Women are shown as cackling, screaming shrews in big mounted close-ups, using street slang just short of vulgarity ... All Negroes are shown as dodging work of any kind ..." (and so on).

In 1939, *LIFE Magazine* reflected the national attitude when it wrote of promising Yankee outfielder Joe DiMaggio: "He never reeks of garlic," and he speaks English "without an accent."[9]

For decades, comedy derived from ethnic identity was mainstream comedy. Watch a rerun of I Love Lucy; some of Desi's funnier moments are when he capitalizes on his Cuban heritage. Our long-time fascination with the Mafia continues to provide comedians with material based upon Italian stereotypes. Where would Lucky Charms be without their carefree little leprechaun? Certainly, we're seeing and hearing far fewer jokes about black Americans as watermelon eaters, but we're also seeing Chris Rock and other black comedians making fun of their own cultural stereotypes for financial gain. Through our newly acquired cultural sensitivity filter, we wince when we see old movies with stereotypical Irish cops or greedy Jewish merchants, but for the better part of American history, this was the basis of our humor. Other countries are not so sensitive; the Danes still tell jokes about the Swedes, perhaps not on television but to one another. And every Dane seems to understand why the joke is funny.

Brand Nippon

In our more enlightened world, we no longer rely upon branded stereotypes for humor. Instead, our principal interaction with other cultures is through restaurants.

In the 1960s, when the Kennedy White House and Julia Child popularized French cuisine, people said, "You can't get a bad meal in France." French restaurants became known as the epitome of sophistication, status, and impeccable taste.

In the 1970s, the spotlight moved to, of all places, Japan. Here was a country that was our enemy in the 1940s—a country whose cheap toys and crappy manufacturing were the butt of 1950s jokes that ended with the punch line, "Made in Japan."

On New Year's Day, 1970, Craig Claiborne wrote, "The public seemed to take to sushi and sashimi ... [with] what could be regarded as passion." Suddenly, New York City had fifty new Japanese restaurants, and Americans were filling their tummies with tiny morsels of raw fish.

We respected the simplicity of the food, pretentiously ordered the fish with Japanese names, and compartmentalized a fifteen-thousand-year-old culture into a cultural bento filled with raw fish, origami, Panasonic VCRs, a Sony Walkman, a vague sense of Japanese baseball, a white flag with a red circle, a flimsy understanding of Japanese religion and, in a large compartment, we might place a sumo match. For children, this would be a successful introduction to another culture. For adults, it's the equivalent of eating and running, accepting the icons and flavors at face value, developing an understanding of another country by eating its food and buying a souvenir. While preferable to stereotyping for humor or hatred, we continue to brand a country by its branded essence.

Perhaps this tirade was pointed more at me than at you. I've loved Japan since I was a child, and when I was an adult, I visited several times. What I didn't realize was that what I was visiting was a picture postcard, not a real place. I began to understand the difference when I was sitting cross-legged on the floor in a ryokan (old Japanese inn). That evening, I promised to send a young Japanese girl a *Sesame Street* toy. I also listened to her father describe the morning of August 6, 1945, when Americans killed his father with a bomb nicknamed "Little Boy." The man had not met many Americans. None had apologized. When I did, we became friends for the evening. Sitting in our yukata on tatami in our minshuku,[10] we shared tea.

"Have You Ever Seen a Real Indian?"

That line was the basis of a public education campaign whose advertisements appeared in *Rolling Stone* and several other magazines. The campaign promoted the American Indian College Fund.

What traits do you associate with today's American Indians? What do you know about them? If you met one, what questions would you ask? Would you ask about casinos or alcoholism, poverty or living on reservations, the environment or restitution, or maybe the Crazy Horse monument? Maybe the new museum in Washington, D.C.? Maybe you'd discuss a book you had read about Indians, maybe a movie like *Dances with Wolves*?

Feel as though you're talking to a real-live Negro and asking him about basketball?

Despite our newfound social awareness, we're still struggling with the problem of American Indians, or Native Americans. Neither label is okay: Indian was the result of mistaken identity (explorers believed they were in India, not the New World), and American is a variation on the name of European explorer Amerigo Vespucci, whose maps and exploration helped to remove the native people from their homeland.

Children still sing "Ten Little Indians" and still play "cowboys and Indians."[11] *Amos n' Andy* episodes are no longer shown on TV, but there's no such ban on cinematic representations of Indians: bloodthirsty, lawless savage, tragic, inevitable, lazy, shiftless, drunk, oil rich, illiterate, educated

Mòn

half-breed, unable to live in either white or Indian world. We continue to envision the American Indian as noble hero, stoic, unemotional, first conservationist.

You can still buy a Jeep Cherokee (imagine buying a Chrysler Jew or a Ford Puerto Rican!), or a Pontiac, or travel in style in a Winnebago. You can buy a T-shirt with a grinning Cleveland Indian, or chew Red Man tobacco, or delight in the natural purity of Land O' Lakes butter, whose Indian maiden logo recalls the innocence of Hiawatha. Tomahawk missiles were deployed during the Gulf War.

Nearly 30 percent of our native people live below the poverty line. Their numbers are few (4.3 million people, or 1.5 percent of the population—slightly less than all Americans claiming Norwegian ancestry). They are neither valuable to marketers nor are they powerful forces for change. (Tribal casinos are changing the situation, but not for all.)

Crazy Horse malt liquor is one of the few brands that has apologized for its branded exploitation and made reparations. John Stroh III, chairman of SBC Holdings, read a letter of apology to descendents of Crazy Horse and other Indians at the Rosebud Reservation, roughly 250 miles southwest of Sioux Falls: "We understand your deep and sincere feeling that the marketing of malt liquor beverage ... disparaged his spirit and caused you and your and his other descendents emotional distress." The corporation then honored the memory of the man who was known to his people not as Crazy Horse, but as Tasunke Witko, by providing thirty-two Pendleton blankets, thirty-two blades of sweet grass, and seven thoroughbred race horses, all culturally significant to the estate.[12]

U.S. History: Branded Myths

The goal of history textbooks is to convey a 'cherished mythology'[13]—a consensus view of history full of inaccuracies and misrepresentation. This approach is consistent with our chosen style of classroom education, in which broad coverage is valued, and in-depth knowledge is not. Students are exposed to a spectacular landscape that includes polynomials, mitochondria, Charlemagne, Pavlov, centripetal force, Manifest Destiny, congruence, and spheres of influence. But every topic must be covered quickly and efficiently because the overall list of topics is so very long. As a result, every story must be reduced to its essence—simplified, reduced, limited in terms of context, and delivered by teachers and textbook publishers in a memorable way. Often, nasty details are left out or polished over, leaving children with generally positive impressions of American life and a clear sense of good guys and bad guys. In other words, many of the principles that apply to branding also apply to the way that we educate students—especially with regard to history.

Brand: Columbus

When the story of Christopher Columbus is taught to young American children, they inevitably hear the ditty, "In fourteen hundred and ninety-two, Columbus sailed the ocean blue." They learn that Columbus discovered America, and that he proved the world was not flat. The U.S. Embassy's official Web site[14] confirms this information. As ambassador to the world, the site whitewashes the story, never mentioning the negative consequences of Columbus's invasions.

Columbus was hardly the man who discovered the New World, the Americas, or what became the United States. For one thing, Columbus never set foot on any of the fifty states, nor did he sail by them (he did visit Puerto Rico, a grand reason to offer the island statehood). What's more, Columbus was hardly the first to visit the region. Nearly thirty thousand years ago, North America was first populated by Asians who came via a land bridge; apparently, these people did not survive. The land bridge reopened around eleven thousand years ago, and that's how our "Indians" migrated from Asia. In 986, Bjarni Herólsson was driven off course from Greenland and found himself in the area of the present-day Labrador or Newfoundland. Leif Ericson ended up with Herólsson's ship and maps and visited the area, too. Then, there's the Chinese Admiral Zheng He, who visited what became the middle Atlantic states around 1405–1433 (he sailed to lots of other places around the world as well). Then came Columbus, who came no closer than Puerto Rico or Cuba. Of the European explorers, it was Ponce De Leon who first set foot on what would become a U.S. state. He did so in April 1513 while visiting Saint Augustine, Florida.

The facts about Columbus and his adventure probably aren't appropriate for the youngest children. High school students can probably handle the truth about America's difficult origins.

Columbus was an educated man from Genoa who meticulously prepared for his trip to the Orient. He did not discover nor did he set out to prove that the world was round; this was old news, well accepted centuries earlier. Columbus made a deal with Queen Isabella and King Ferdinand: he would establish a land route to the spices and riches of the Orient.

Unfortunately, Columbus was confused about where in the world he was voyaging; two weeks after he made landfall in this hemisphere, he convinced himself that the island we now call Cuba was, in fact, the Cipangu (most likely, Japan), which traveler Marco Polo had described in his writings.

Columbus's crew called the natives either Caribs or Arawak. Regardless of what they called them, Columbus and his crew put the natives through the 1490s version of a holocaust. When it became clear that natives would not provide riches for the king and queen, that they were unfamiliar with weaponry or the concept of property, there was no stopping the European visitors. Between 1494 and 1496, one-third of the 300,000 original natives died or were killed. A decade later, only 60,000 were still alive. The dead may have been the fortunate ones.

In his log, Columbus wrote of the natives, "They are very simple and honest and exceedingly liberal with all they have, none of them refusing anything he may possess when asked for it. They exhibit great love toward all others in preference for themselves." It continues, "They would make fine servants. With fifty men, we could subjugate them all and make them do whatever we want."[15]

Columbus's men severely abused the Indians, frequently for sport. "Those who fled to the mountains were hunted with hounds, and those who escaped, starvation and disease took toll, while thousands of the poor creatures in desperation took cassava poison to end their miseries."[16]

Columbus was under enormous pressure to bring back gold (he mentions the word seventy-five times in the first two weeks of his journal) and to convert natives to Christianity. Columbus could not send back gold, so he sent slaves instead: five hundred were sent, but only three hundred arrived alive. [17]

Columbus's legacy, confirmed by a variety of sources,[18] also includes the stabbing of natives for sport; the hunting of natives with vicious dogs and rifles; beheading; smashing babies' heads on rocks; throwing children to the dogs to be eaten; throwing newborns into the jungle; widespread rape of native women; and most devastating, European diseases to which the natives had no immunity (typhoid, typhus, diphtheria, smallpox).

Samuel Eliot Morison wrote, in the 1954 biography *Christopher Columbus: Mariner*, "The cruel policy initiated by Columbus and pursued by his successors resulted in complete genocide."[19]

After reading this—and there's certainly more that's gone undocu-mented—it's easy to understand why the story of Columbus has been simplified and transformed into a discovery myth. Worse, Columbus sets up a cycle in which natives are routinely killed by European visitors, a cycle that comprises all but a century of our nation's history. At best, to celebrate an annual holiday rather than a national day of mourning is insensitive. To elevate the man's name both as a national holiday and as our nation's capital seems inexcusable.

Brand: MLK

Martin Luther King Jr. used nonviolence to get black Americans the civil rights they clearly deserved. The facts about Dr. King tell a more complicated, nuanced story. Although he is considered one of the century's greatest heroes, a leader at a time when leadership was desperately needed, not much is told about his life beyond 1963's Lincoln Memorial speech ("I Have a Dream") and his high-profile civil rights appearances.

Dr. King's story is not without blemishes. These are rarely mentioned to generations of children who learn about the good that he did, as they may cast doubt upon an American hero and disparage one of most significant positive role models to emerge in the past century.

Still, there are disconcerting stories about plagiarism, particularly with regard to Dr. King's doctoral dissertation; connections between Dr. King and the Communist movement; and reports of Dr. King's aggressive sexual treatment of women[20] (any or all of these could have been magnified by the FBI, which was frequently antagonistic toward Dr. King).[21]

By 1967, civil rights advocate King had begun to expand his domain to include human rights and economic rights. The turning point was a well-publicized April 4, 1967, speech at New York City's Riverside Church. In that speech, he spoke directly to those who asked, "Why are you speaking about the war, Dr. King?" He explained, "Such questions mean that the inquirers have not really known me or the commitment of my calling." He then articulated, in considerable detail, the history of U.S. involvement in Vietnam, the devastating impact of the war on the people of Vietnam, and the reasons why the war should be ended immediately. In the same speech, he railed against international exploitation in the name of capitalism ("… individual capitalists of the West investing huge sums of money in Asia, Africa, and South America, only to take the profits out with no concern for the social betterment of the countries …"). Dr. King called the United States: "The greatest purveyor of violence in the world today. …"[22] This speech was denounced by *LIFE Magazine*:[23] "demagogic slander that sounded like a script for Radio Hanoi."

In his last months, King was organizing a militant Poor People's Campaign. His plan was to crisscross the country, assembling a "multi-racial army of the poor" that would descend on Washington, D.C., engaging in nonviolent civil disobedience at the Capitol, or if need be, until Congress enacted a poor people's bill of rights. *Reader's Digest* warned of an "insurrection."

In the case of King, whose brand is often represented not by his full name or by the respectful Reverend King or Dr. King, but by the initials MLK, the issue is that the MLK brand reduces a man's lifetime accomplishments to civil rights, and essentially erases his other accomplishments: his role in the antiwar movement, his activism on behalf of those who suffered in other countries, and on behalf of our own poor.

Religion professor (and former King associate) Vincent Harding[24] rejected the notion that the King holiday commemorates merely "a kind, gentle and easily managed religious leader of a friendly crusade for racial integration." Such an understanding would "demean and trivialize Dr. King's meaning." With regard to the Poor People's Campaign, Harding wrote, "Martin Luther King was calling for a radical redistribution of wealth and political power in American society as a way to provide food, clothing, shelter, medical care, jobs, education, and hope for all of our country's people."

Once again, we have a national holiday celebrating the life and accomplishments of a branded persona whose story is only partially told. When we're explaining the story to children, this is reasonable. When we succumb to the legend as adults, we are victims of the brand monster. In time, the real story fades away and we are left only with the legend, the essence of the brand. One can't help but wonder what else we haven't been told.

Historical Figures in the Classroom

This brand essence is the bread and butter of a new kind of educational company, one that provides historical figures to classrooms. Mobile Ed Productions[25] of Redford, Michigan, employs twenty-eight full-time performers, including seven Martin Luther Kings, five Abe Lincolns, and two Thomas Edisons.[26]

Although King looks real to the children, you know the actor isn't discussing his ideas on a redistribution of wealth and political power.

Education Builds Strong Brands

For generations, *Sesame Street* has been America's pre-eminent preschool educator. Built on the assumption that television's commercial style could

> **While acknowledging the many good lessons taught to children via the television series, it would be fair to say that Sesame Street also teaches parents to buy products for their very young children based upon television characters.**

be used to teach ("brought to you by the letter A ..."), the series has been popular for nearly three decades. The project is funded, in large measure, by revenues from toys and other licensed products based upon *Sesame Street's* Elmo, Cookie Monster, Big Bird, and other well-known characters. While acknowledging the many good lessons taught to children via the television series, it would be fair to say that *Sesame Street* also teaches parents to buy products for their very young children based upon television characters. For fiscal year 2003, Sesame Workshop (formerly Children's Television Workshop) received two-thirds of its ninety-million-dollar revenue line from product licenses and merchandising.

Learning to count? From 1998 until 2000, more than a million families bought Cheerios counting books in just a few years. If you'd prefer, there's the *Oreo Cookie Counting Book* (shaped like a giant Oreo Cookie), or the *Froot Loops Counting Book*, or the *Hershey's Kisses Counting Board Book*, or the *M&M's Brand Chocolate Candies Counting Book*, or the *Pepperidge Farm Goldfish Counting Fun Book*, or the *Reese's Pieces Peanut Butter Counting Board Book*. For variations on the counting theme, look for books from Twizzlers (shapes and patterns), Skittles (math), and Home Depot (tools).

In time, children are taught to buy all sorts of products based upon familiar brands. As children graduate from *Sesame Street* to Nickelodeon, then to MTV and ESPN, they learn consumer behavior.

Much of our learning occurs outside the classroom. That's why Petco, Sports Authority, Saturn dealerships, and Krispy Kreme stores offer—what else?—school field trips. Says Dan Fuller, director of federal programs for the National School Boards Association: "In a perfect world, schools would have the funds they need to send kids where they feel is most educationally appropriate." In the real world, a trip to Petco costs less than a trip to the zoo. In both cases, the kids learn about animals.[27]

Here's the pitch from Lifetime Learning Systems (a division of the company that publishes trusted classroom magazine *Weekly Reader*): "Having created more than two thousand programs, Lifetime Learning

Systems knows how to link a sponsor's message to curriculum standards and create a powerful presence for your message in America's classrooms with informative and engaging materials."[28]

Some of these "curriculum materials" may be familiar to your children, or to you (this is hardly a new practice):

- *The Incredible Journey from Egg to Home* (American Egg Board)
- *Prego Thickness Experiment*
- *Encounter Math (Count on Domino's)*—(Domino's pizza)
- *100 Percent Energy to Go* (Mars, Inc.)
- *Count Your Chips* (National Potato Board)
- *Grade A Donuts* (Dunkin' Donuts)
- *Project Learning Tree*—a K–8 favorite for more than twenty years—"investigate environmental decisions and encourages them to make informed decisions"
- *The Council for Wildlife Conservation and Education* (affiliate of the National Shooting Sports Association): film—*Wildlife for Tomorrow: The Story of Our Un-Endangered Species*
- *Caretakers All*—Beef Industry Council
- Twenty thousand free kits for teachers
- "Pure one-sided image-building for farmers and ranchers, disguised as lessons in land conservation"[29]

One of the strongest educational campaigns is brilliantly disguised as a means for schools and school districts to raise money and to partner with corporate America: soda vending machines. The marketing plan is brilliant: split the profits with the schools, gain free advertising and logo exposure, and sell soft drinks directly to children. Despite the occasional community outrage, nearly half the schools in the country take part in these programs because they need the money. Kids understand the message: If the school sells them, then it must be okay to buy and drink these beverages. As further inducement, many schools have gotten free sports scoreboards (with soft drink company logos). Shame on us: Rather than paying the bills to educate our children, we have provided commercial brands to infiltrate and gain the endorsement of our schools and our educators.

Rick Nichols, a writer for *Philadelphia* magazine, sent a twenty-five-dollar check to suburban Doylestown's school district to cover its one-year profit on soft drinks from one student. His point: He'd rather pay the difference than provide the beverage companies with this level of access to children in an educational environment.

The Branded Curriculum

Did you ever stop to wonder about the curriculum, the subjects taught at school? These, too, are affected by our branded ways of thinking. For the most part, the school curriculum of today is based upon ideas established more than a century ago, when factory workers were taught to behave in a regimented, standardized manner.

Modern educators have brought about significant change, but most students still slog through year after year of math, English, social studies, science, and gym as if these were the only topics worth knowing. These are legacy brands of American education, supported by a rigid belief system whose original purposes may no longer apply.

With few exceptions (some high school seniors among them), every student spends more than an hour each day either learning, studying, or doing homework related to mathematics. For at least ten years, every pupil has studied the basics of arithmetic, algebra, geometry, and trigonometry. In defense of the math brand, there is ample evidence that the rigors, facts, and thinking styles involved in learning math can be useful in learning other subjects. Still, there is little in the current math curriculum (apart from basic arithmetic) that is used by the majority of the adult population, in part because the processes are generally irrelevant to the real needs of everyday life, and in part because spreadsheet software can do much of the work in an instant. Let's not eliminate math from the curriculum, but let's reconsider the reasons why every student spends about 20 percent of their time in school studying math. The concentration upon math is certainly useful for future engineers and scientists, but for other students, probably the majority of students, more time should be allotted to other endeavors that may be more closely related to their own interests, skills, career directions, and citizenship. Other legacy curriculum brands should be questioned, too.

Just as McDonald's assures the same hamburger will be available in each of its restaurants, an educational system based upon standards assures that every child will learn what he or she needs to know in order to function in modern society. McDonald's does not serve the best burgers, not does it serve an especially wide variety of other foods, but the burgers are consistent; they meet but never exceed the standards. Schools provide consistent educations to students who will become consistent workers. Teachers are paid to educate but they are not graded. Instead, student performance is measured without regard to the quality of the education provided to them.

Branded education is not for everybody. Steve Jobs fell out of the system by dropping out of Reed College in Portland, Oregon. He credits a few calligraphy courses with his focus on meticulous design, a key component in the success of Apple Computer. Bill Gates lasted less than two years at Harvard because he was more excited about the infant computer software industry than he was about the coursework offered by one of America's top universities.

In our schools, the most important lessons are often unrelated to math, social studies, or other academic subjects. More important are the standardized beliefs the system impresses on every student who spends a third of his or her life in this managed environment. This assessment of American education is based on the work of long-time public school teacher John Taylor Gatto:[30]

Learn the basic facts and figures and you will be rewarded with good grades. Don't bother to think about how this information fits into a larger context. You will not be rewarded for big-picture thinking. And don't offer contrary points of view.

Just because you think you understand something doesn't mean you have actually learned. You cannot evaluate whether you've learned something; this can be done only by a teacher or by a written test.

The purpose of grades is to teach kids that they are at the mercy of authorities who have nearly absolute power to judge them on their worthiness.

There is always a hierarchy. You are not the one in control. Authority figures decide who may speak, when people may go to the bathroom. Learn this lesson well; you are always going to be emotionally dependent upon the person in charge.

If you're interested in something other than what is being taught in class, school is rarely the place to explore that interest. Do it on your own time.

No task is so important that it must be completed. When the bell rings after forty minutes, time's up; the task can be discarded, or at least forgotten until tomorrow.

You are where you belong. If the system groups you with kids who aren't very bright, they you probably aren't very bright, either.

Competition is good. If you work hard, and you nurture your teacher's interest in you, and you aren't too upset by the rigors of testing, you will succeed.

You cannot hide, and you cannot keep secrets. Students have no private time or space. If there is a problem, students are encouraged to report the problem to the teacher, regardless of personal consequences.

When these ideas are considered with the context of branded behavior that corporations design and government endorses, the real purpose of school becomes clear. It is to teach Americans how to behave, work, and think.

School Names and Mascots

If you were the parent of an African-American child in the South, would you be uncomfortable if your child attended a school named for Robert E. Lee?

Former NAACP chairman Julian Bond said, "If it had been up to Robert E. Lee, these kids wouldn't be going to school as they are today. ... They can't help but wonder about a man who wanted to keep them in servitude."[31]

Many students attend schools named for their towns or locales. Others attend schools named for local or national heroes. The United States[32] has forty public schools named for George Washington, plus ten more named for George Washington Carver. There are eighty-nine named for John Kennedy, forty-seven for Martin Luther King, none for Richard Nixon or John Steinbeck, fifteen for John Glenn, six for Malcolm X, none for Jimi Hendrix or Bill Gates, and one for Ronald Reagan. Among Confederate heroes, there are sixteen Robert E. Lee public schools, four schools named for Jefferson Davis, and nine for Confederate General Stonewall Jackson.

Colleges and universities have adopted brands and marketing—and not just in their athletic programs.

Colleges have long promoted "school colors." Among the many examples: Princeton (orange); Rutgers (scarlet); Harvard (crimson); Michigan (blue and gold) among them. Many colleges and universities are represented by symbols, but few are better brand marketers than Penn State University, whose Nittany Lion pawprints are magnetically attached to thousands of minivans throughout Pennsylvania.

At Penn State, students, faculty, and alumni can choose from thousands of items, including hats, shirts, blankets, neckties, aprons, bed sheets, watches, baby towels, children's dinner sets, stained glass floor lamps, door mats, golf bags, and breakfast cereal. Penn State Crunch cereal is a joint venture with Ralston.

Often, a sports mascot becomes central to the institution's brand. In 1970, more than three thousand athletic programs (both high school and college) referred to American Indians in their nicknames, logos, or mascots, according to Morning Star Institute, a Native American organization. Today there are about one thousand, but the usage is still common among professional sports teams, notably the Cleveland Indians, Atlanta Braves (complete with a tomahawk cheer), and in our nation's capital, the Washington Redskins.

For nearly eighty years, Chief Illiniwek has been the University of Illinois's mascot. (In fact, there was a confederation of tribes in the central Mississippi valley that the French called the Illini or Illiniwek). While trying to get the throwback chief "honorably retired," Marge Sodemann, a new college board member and daughter of an American Indian, said, "The chief stands for the values, trust, and honor of everything that went on in the past." Local attorney John Gadaut, who spent more than five thousand dollars on keep-the-chief billboards and buttons, said "I'm Native American ... I was born and bred in Illinois. The chief means something to me, too. People keep saying we have a mascot. Now, we have a symbol." And there we have it, a brand wrapped up in a belief system. About eight hundred faculty members who signed a petition believe the chief's time as come. So, too, does Genevieve Tenoso, seventh-generation descendent of Sitting Bull, who had hoped to remain out of the fray, but now calls herself a 'reluctant activist': "I wanted to ignore it ... but I saw the chief head on a cushion. Then, I went online and noticed one of the new items for sale is a chief bathroom scale and a little two-piece toddler set that said 'Love Me and Love My Chief.'"[33]

Places as Brands

Cities and countries have been marketing themselves as brands for decades, and in some cases, for more than a century.

Few destinations share the cachet of Paris, San Francisco, or Rome—these places are among the world's best tourism brands. The same can be said for London and New York City. In recent years, Sydney, Prague, Venice, Hong Kong, and Las Vegas have successfully invented or refurbished their brands.

Many cities, countries, and regions have hired advertising and public relations agencies to develop not only images and strategies but also commercials and print advertising campaigns to support the imagery. This approach has worked well for Jamaica and the Bahamas. Some countries have developed logos, or symbols, to associate with their brands. For its tourism logo, Denmark reshaped its flag into the shape of a friendly heart. Ireland reinforces its lucky stereotype and rural purity with a shamrock and the slogan, "Live a Different Life." The tiny European country of Estonia transformed its economy through intelligent branding and tourism marketing. Japan has publicly set a goal of doubling the number of foreign visitors by 2010. Its campaign, simply called Visit Japan (or, *Yosoko Japan*), is focused on five countries with the highest potential for tourists: the United States, Korea, China, Taiwan, and Hong Kong. One feature of the campaign is the *Lost in Translation* package, in which visitors can stay at the Park Hyatt hotel, where much of the Bill Murray film was shot, or at a local Oakwood Apartments complex, where the crew was housed. In Salzburg, Austria, the *Sound of Music* tour remains a popular attraction. You, too, can sing "Do-Re-Mi" in the Mirabell Garden or visit the Nonnberg Abbey, where Julie Andrews' Maria was a novice nun. Cities like Salzburg have a great deal to offer, but many visitors opt for the familiar, the Hollywood version, often instead of concentrating on local attractions. (Sure, it's fun to see a place where a favorite movie was shot, but it's also a strange way to spend your limited time in one of the world's most beautiful cities.) Not all branding is intended for tourists. Korea, Taiwan, and other Asian nations have successfully invested in branding for industrial development. Pittsburgh is no longer perceived as a steel mill town; now, it's a progressive technology and education center that's home to seven Fortune 500 companies and several top universities.

> Just as local public schools have looked to the sale of branded products to close budget gaps, so, too, have municipalities and nonprofit organizations.

A new seven-county initiative is sorting out the Philadelphia region's many educational, scientific, and technical strengths so they can be developed and shaped into a coherent offering. Caught between the tourist magnets of New York City and Washington, D.C., Philadelphia has lacked the coherent branding that Baltimore has successfully exploited with its Inner Harbor shopping and recreation area. Philadelphia's advertising campaign features adults in pajamas and slippers, as an announcer encourages visitors to stay in the city overnight. Sure enough, advertising works: tourism is up in Philadelphia, in part due to the campaign.

When Procter & Gamble markets Febreze or Crest or Bounty, a brand manager establishes a plan, gets a budget approved, and implements the plan. The manager controls the messaging: what is said, why it is said, and where the messages appear. Apart from corporate politics or the occasional marketplace surprise, life is relatively simple. When a city or a country markets a brand, the situation is more complicated. Potential visitors form opinions from many sources: friends and neighbors, an old movie that happened to pop up on TV, the current ad campaign, a news story about a social issue in the region, a cousin who visited, and more. Places involved in brand marketing quickly learn that perception is reality, and today's perception is far more powerful than a one-million-dollar ad campaign or two thousand years of history.

Perception of place drives real estate values. A neighborhood with strong brand equity will be filled with houses that sell for higher prices, and spend less time on the market, than other neighborhoods. In 2001, the safe, 77.4 percent white community of West Hempstead, New York, wanted to differentiate its image from its neighbor, Hempstead, New York, whose population had a darker skin. The West Hempstead Civic Association promoted the altogether delightful name Mayfair Park, but its confused citizens never settled the matter with a vote. In fact, Hempstead's crime rate was higher than West Hempstead's, but the difference in black and Hispanic population was just 10 percent.

Naming Rights to Public Places

"The moment you slap any sort of trademark on a public institution, you're reducing the sense of public investment," wrote Siva Vaidhyanathan, New York University Assistant Professor of Culture and Communication.

At first, you might not think of urinals in New York City's Penn Station as public places, but that's just the point. One Internet startup helped establish its name by placing advertisements as unconventional splashguards. The same company convinced the town of Halfway, Oregon, to rename itself half. com, Oregon—a move that got national attention, including an interview of the founder on *The Today Show*, which led to the company's ultimate acquisition by eBay.

Just as local public schools have looked to the sale of branded products to close budget gaps, so, too, have municipalities and nonprofit organizations. For example, Nextel paid Las Vegas fifty million dollars to plaster its name on the monorail station at the Las Vegas Convention Center and on one of the nine trains. Briefly, San Diego experimented with Chevy as the city's official beach patrol vehicle.

New York City Mayor Michael Bloomberg has repeatedly suggested the sale of naming rights to city parks. Facing what could be a budget gap of more than one billion dollars in coming years, the city's transportation authority, known as the MTA, quietly issued requests for proposals from marketing firms that would arrange sponsorships and the sale of naming rights to its subways stations, bus stations, bus lines, bridges, and tunnels. MTA officials said they could easily imagine: Delta Times Square Shuttle, or the IBM adoption of Tarrytown (Metro North) train station. Those on the sales side point out that Times Square is the busiest subway station in America.

Since 1996, New York City has been more resourceful and doubled its advertising revenues, allowing companies to monopolize entire subway stations, subway cars, and buses. In 2003, New York City took in $73 million in ad revenues, mainly for unorthodox concepts. Would New Yorkers be happier with branded subway stations or with higher fares and tolls? Opinions are mixed. Commercial Alert's executive director asks, "How low will New York sink?"[34]

Before you're quick to express an opinion, think about baseball, where half the teams play in ballparks whose names have been sold to Ameriquest, Comerica, Kauffman, Network Associates, Safeco, U.S. Cellular, and Tropicana, Bank One, Coors, Miller, Minute Maid, Petco, SBC, PNC, Citizens Bank, and Pro Player. In the National League, the calls are tougher: Busch, Turner, and Wrigley share names with corporate giants, but its unclear whether the man or the corporation are being celebrated. After a while, we become desensitized, and a name is just a name. Maybe that's just the point. Ruskin notes: "This is part of the decline of American values. We used to name things after people who were heroes. Now we name things after the corporation with the deepest pockets." *No Logo* author Naomi Klein agrees: "Our intellectual lives and public spaces have been overtaken by marketing—and that has real implications for citizenship."

Prior to the NFL opener at FedEx Field in September 2003, ABC televised *NFL Kick Off Live* from The National Mall presented by Pepsi Vanilla, and starring Britney Spears, Aerosmith, and Aretha Franklin. The $35 million event irritated some D.C. residents, who believed that the Mall was meant for noncommercial endeavors. (The 2002 event was held in Times Square; the 2004 event in a private venue.)

Is there a difference between the Mall and Times Square? (The answer is "yes." The National Mall is a national park.)

If ExxonMobil wanted to buy an association with the clean natural environment of Yosemite National Park (3.5 million annual visitors), how much should it pay for a small ExxonMobil sign at every entrance? How does this differ from the sale of naming rights to a publicly owned baseball

stadium or to a city bridge or to corporate underwriting of public television programs?

Regardless of your opinion, the Supreme Court has made it clear that the river flows in only one direction. When private groups distributed leaflets in shopping malls (Lloyd Center, Portland, Oregon, and Valley Plaza, Altoona, Pennsylvania), claiming they were the new Main Street, the court sided with the owners of the private shopping centers.

Branding in Politics, Spin in Government

What an odd, foolish choice: mixing the work of governing the people with a marketing process; requiring potential public leaders to become brands and to immerse themselves in highly competitive marketing campaigns before earning the right to govern. The inevitable result: marketing and spin become part of governing.

Fundamentally, it's probably a good idea for political parties to resemble brands, each with a logo (donkeys and elephants wouldn't have been a contemporary brand wizard's first choices, but tradition dies hard). In theory, attributes of each party are clearly defined, so voters can make decisions based upon their brand attributes, brand associations, brand equity, and so forth. Unfortunately, neither party's brand is bathed in trust. Instead, Republicans claim fiscal responsibility while sending the country into its largest all-time deficit, and Democrats often turn their backs on the average people whom they supposedly represent.

Watching the 2004 presidential candidates was an embarrassment. In this race for the top governing position in the free world, the candidates and their parties were reduced to name-calling. Each attempted to stereotype the other, minimizing the opponent's accomplishments, reducing each to a stereotype. This is remarkably crappy behavior for a man who had been a state governor and the son of a U.S. president, and for a four-term U.S. senator. Kindergarteners are taught better behavior, but these men are caught in a strange parallel universe, where promises are forgotten or spun, and campaigns are managed by political consultants whose goal is not social good, but just winning the race.

The result: every major political race exhibits the worst aspects of brand management: pandering, lying, distorting the truth, relying upon polls and market research before making any decision, keeping messages so brief that people cannot make intelligent choices, arguing endlessly about minor details of televising debates, organizing negative testimonials but claiming no responsibility for what was said or who said it ... the list goes on. If corporate marketers engaged in this behavior, they would be skewered by the media, by consumer groups, and by the FDA, FTC, and FCC. Candidates who engage in this behavior become national leaders, setting the example for others who run for political office.

Lessons are not easily unlearned. A ruthlessly branded candidate is not easily transformed into a model public servant. Once in power, our government leaders tend to manage every situation in sight—offering incomplete or misleading information and making decisions for their own political gain. Americans desperately want to trust, to believe that their elected officials are guided by public interest, but we have been disappointed time and again. Every political science student is more than familiar with the term, "the masses are asses."

Children as Brands

Do you know why your parents decided to name you Dorothy or William or Teresa or Juan-Carlos? Do you remember why you named your children Sabrina or Chloe or Stephen? Why are so many young girls these days named Madison, Alexis, or Emily? When parents name a child, the name carries positive associations and hope for the child's life.

In our modern society, raising children has always been about defining the child's identity: teaching her to become a productive community member; supporting some personal interests and relationships while discouraging others; encouraging successes with potential for self-discovery or career building. If parts of the physical presentation are imperfect, plastic surgery has become a popular solution, a way to improve the presentation of the person/brand to the outside world.

Would you sell the right to name your unborn child? When I wrote the proposal to sell this book to a publisher in December 2003, I included a story about a magazine editor who was auctioning the rights to name his child. The publisher and I wondered whether this was too crazy to be included in the manuscript. From the transcript of his CNN interview:[35]

"And we started thinking, well, maybe there would be a way so that we could create an actual financial benefit for our girls, our daughters, and for our soon-to-be-born son ... my mother, the girls' grandmother, is actually rooting for Microsoft right now. That's been her top choice as we've been talking about this. ... This is really a serious marketing opportunity that we're helping to create right now. ... There are going to be (recurring) opportunities throughout his life as he's growing up where people are going to take an interest in this child and they're going to want to know, how is he doing? How is he progressing? Did he graduate? When did he hit his first home run in Little League?" He had no takers.

By May 2004, the story was no longer unlikely. A Ruffles Potato Chips advertisement in *USA Today* read, "Would You Name Your Baby Horton? If so, Ruffles wants to pay for your baby's college education!" Beginning at noon on May 13, 2004, the first family to do so was promised a fifty-thousand-dollar college tuition fund in child's name. Sure enough, forty-nine parents applied, and on May 16, 2004, Horton Chesleigh was born. His parents, Sean and Donna Chesleigh, appeared on CNN to receive the fifty-thousand-dollar tuition award, plus an additional fifteen thousand dollars to cover taxes. His mom said, "I'd be crazy not to ... my son has his college education paid for now. It was a way for us to give him a head start." (It's unclear whether this particular campaign caused a blip in the $338 million in sales that Ruffles claims in the $2.7 billion potato chip category.)

People as Brands

Lizzie Simon, author of *Detour: My Bipolar Trip in 4D* explained[36] that she could label herself "bipolar," but that that label is far down on the list, well below other labels that she chooses or other choose for her, labels like friend, lover, ex-lover, daughter, writer, public speaker, and so on. The brand you choose for yourself is the brand that defines you, and defines yourself for others.

Despite its stunning popularity, I'm not sure *Queer Eye for the Straight Guy* probably was the best thing that ever happened to gay America. For millions of Americans, the fab five defines gay culture in extraordinarily narrow terms: grooming (Kyan), food/wine (Ted), fashion (Carson), culture (Jai), and design (Thom). Do gay men work in other professions? Is it being gay all about making a nice presentation for yourself and your home? When a life choice is branded, it must be simplified to its essence—and that essence becomes the story that people remember, and believe.

Tom Peters' August 1997 *Fast Company* cover story ("The Brand Called You") taught workers to manage themselves as brands. The cover resembled a box of Tide laundry detergent. Peters struck a nerve. In the dot.com marketplace, job change had become commonplace, and job security was becoming a memory, so individuals needed to take control of their careers. They needed to manage their careers as if they were brand managers, coordinating and promoting their own particular attributes and assets, carefully selecting their associations with particular companies, nurturing and networking business relationships. The resume became a personal advertisement. The job interview was revealed to be nothing more than a sales call.

Many people were struck by the cynicism of Peters's approach. In fact, he probably didn't take the concept far enough. Many of the same brand management activities that apply to the job search also apply to dating, for example: very careful selection of clothing; elevated consciousness of messages sent and received; a presentation that may or may not reflect actual day-to-day involvement.

In some ways, celebrities have it easier. They are *expected* to create a persona, a brand they employ for public and commercial purposes. When the celebrity is involved in a skirmish, it only adds to his street-smart image, to her bad-girl image. When a highly publicized romance doesn't work out, and the media covers the breakup, the coverage only helps to define the brand. Sometimes—probably more often than most celebrities would like to admit—the more famous branded persona overtakes the former self. Imagine changing your name and becoming someone else, a some-one whom you invent, based partly on who you really are and partly on who you want to be.

All of these people did exactly that. All of them are familiar to you, but under different names. Take a moment and see whether you can decode these people's brand names: As with names of commercial products, names of people may be valuable assets. You may remember when Spike Lee sued Viacom over the naming of the Spike television network. Deroy Murdock wrote in the *National Review*,[37] "A Spike Lee victory could expose Viacom to fresh lawsuits. Actor Nick Nolte could demand a share of the ad revenue from Viacom's Nick at Nite classic TV ... What if the Fox News Channel actually is named after Michael J. Fox? ... Judge Walter Tolub should do the right thing: Reject this monument to Spike Lee's monomania and fine him and Johnnie Cochran $1 million each for wasting the people's time with such breathtakingly infantile nonsense."

Some corporations have found that a person can embody the power of the brand. In the 1980s, Lee Iacocca was the face of Chrysler. Martha Stewart was and is once again both the face of her own "omnimedia" em-

REAL NAME	BRAND NAME
Allen Konigsberg	Woody Allen
Alphonso D'Abruzzo	Alan Alda
Tom Mapothes	Tom Cruise
Margaret Hyra	Meg Ryan
Issur Danielovitch	Kirk Douglas
Walter Matuschapshay	Walter Matthau
Donald Drumpf	Donald Trump (name may have been changed by his father)
Alice Rosenbaum	Ayn Rand
Michael Douglas	Michael Keaton, taken by another actor (SAG: no duplications)
Marvin Lee Adair	Meat Loaf
Marshall Bruce Mathers III	Eminem
Abigail Tomalin	Susan Sarandon
Annie Mae Bullock	Tina Turner
Reginald Dwight	Elton John
Christina Ciminella	Wynona Judd
Trevor Tahiem Smith	Busta Rhymes
Robert James Ritchie	Kid Rock
Caryn Johnson	Whoopi Goldberg
Calvin Broadus	Snoop Doggy Dog
Carlos Estevez	Charlie Sheen
Jason Greenspan	Jason Alexander (Alexander was his middle name)
Steveland Hardaway	Stevie Wonder
Liu Yuan Kam	Bruce Lee
Ramon Estevez	Martin Sheen
Diane Belmont	Lucille Ball
Krishna Bhanji	Ben Kingsley
Marie Rosich	Vanna White
Eric Blair	George Orwell
Samuel Clemens	Mark Twain
Norma Jean Mortenson	Marilyn Monroe
Frederik Austerlitz	Fred Astaire
Maurice Micklewhite	Michael Caine
Dana Owens	Queen Latifah
Declan Mcmanus	Elvis Costello

pire and a television celebrity. Clever Richard Branson seems to embody the equally clever Virgin industries. When he hosted a Sunday evening Disney anthology series on ABC, Michael Eisner tried to conjure the ghost of

Walt Disney, whose signature remains the company logo. When I think of Ben & Jerry's, I can picture the founders. Their authenticity endows the brand.

Nonprofit Brands

Brand development and brand marketing has also become important to the development and success of nonprofit organizations.

When a consumer interacts with the marketplace, he or she behaves based upon beliefs and trusts in brands. A brand is the public face, the way that an organization describes what it's all about. A brand is more than a logo, but a logo quickly and efficiently describes the brand.

The American Red Cross possesses a good, solid brand, one that has survived some negative media attention in recent years. The American Red Cross logo is one of the most easily recognized in the world. What's more, the symbol and the organization's name are identical: a red cross. When we see the logo, we know help will be provided to people in need. When there's a disaster, we know to contact the Red Cross to offer help or money. We know that the Red Cross acts locally, and that it's part of an international movement. Details about Red Cross activities are wholly consistent with the brand's image, identity, and purpose. Everything makes sense, everything ties together as a single idea: "community services that help the needy; support and comfort for military members and their families; the collection, processing and distribution of life-saving blood and blood products; educational programs that promote health and safety; and international relief and development programs."[38] There aren't many better examples of nonprofit brands in action.

When a loved one dies, and you donate to the American Cancer Society or the American Heart Association, you send the money with the trust and belief that these organizations will somehow help other people, probably through research. In comparison with the Red Cross, I'm a little hazy on who these organizations are, what they do. I'm pretty sure the cancer society uses a caduceus and the heart association uses a heart as a logo, but I can't easily visualize the logos. When I get to the American Lung Association, I'm even hazier.[39] Despite the number of AIDS deaths, I cannot easily name the charitable organization associated with the disease. I know that Elton John started a foundation, but the details are hazy. We trust familiar names, and we give them money. If there's no familiar brand name associated with AIDS, that's a problem.[40]

I can easily picture the logos used by the Boy Scouts of America and the Girl Scouts of America. The images may be clear, but the brands are no longer as appealing as they once were. Many teenaged boys keep their membership a secret and avoid wearing the uniform in public. The Girl Scouts of America recently launched a new organization called Studio 2B because their system rarely appeals to girls older than eleven.

Branded Holidays

Each year, there are ten official national holidays in the Untied States, plus several more associated with religions or special events. In many cases, the original intent of the celebration or memorial has been obscured by the commercial activities. In other cases, the holiday exists primarily as a means to sell products. Is it necessary to demonstrate respect and affection with the purchase of a gift or a meal? (Ask Hallmark.)

New Year's Eve provides the champagne industry with a high percentage of its annual sales; most people celebrate with a reasonably priced brand such as Champagne Mumm or Moët Chandon, but the richest among us go for the Dom Perignon.

February is the traditional month for furniture discounting (in order to clear the sales floors for the new product lines), so furniture stores have abducted two well-known historical brands—George Washington and Abraham Lincoln—to hawk their wares. These two national heroes get more television airtime selling furniture than they do for any other reason.

According to the National Hot Dog and Sausage Council,[41] Americans buy 150 million hot dogs for the Fourth of July. Each year's celebration of our nation's independence provides the meat industry with an opportunity to connect its brand with the American flag, fireworks, and patriotism. Ralph Nader called "fat-furters" "… America's deadliest missiles."

Thanksgiving Day begins with a national tradition, The Macy's Thanksgiving Day Parade on NBC, whose biggest stars are giant inflated versions of media and marketing brand icons. The 2004 parade featured: Barney (the purple dinosaur), Jeeves (from the Web site Ask Jeeves), Big Bird, Garfield the Cat, Spongebob SquarePants, *Monopoly* icon Mr. Moneybags, Clifford the Big Red Dog, Super Grover, Kermit the Frog, and The Red and Yellow Brighten the Holidays M&Ms Chocolate Candies. The other big brand on Thanksgiving is the subject of a news story on just about every news outlet in the country: Butterball, America's number-one turkey brand.[42] Butterball's free advice about cooking turkeys on Thanksgiving

Day is a brilliant way to keep the brand in front of consumers on the one day of the year when that branded relationship matters most.

Christmas

Anchored by the Christmas holiday, the fourth quarter of the year provides retailers with about 40 percent of their annual revenues. In order to drive consumers to the stores, the television networks generate high interest in new and returning programs in September and October. It's a cycle based upon commercial need, and it works. Christmas has become an annual marketing festival in which Jesus Christ's birth sometimes seems secondary to Santa Claus, candy canes, and Christmas sales.

There is no evidence that Jesus Christ was born on, or near, the end of December. Instead, the connection between the birth date of Christ and the date call Christmas Day was a matter of convenience. The winter solstice (start of winter) has long been a time of celebration. Saturnalia, one of the most popular Roman holiday festivals, was held in late December. It was a wild party involving cross dressing, the reversal of master and slave roles, and inevitably, orgies and debauchery. Unable to fix the date of Christ's birth, his followers established the date just after the winter solstice. Over the centuries, the holiday has been celebrated with varying degrees of enthusiasm.

In the early days of the United States, the Puritans had more or less convinced their neighbors that Sundays were holiday enough. By the 1840s, though, retailers began to take an interest, as the exchange of gifts was becoming popular—though mostly on New Year's Day. When the Civil War separated families, thirteen of thirty-three states made Christmas a legal holiday, and slowly the Protestants accepted what had been mainly a Catholic holiday. By 1875, Christmas gift giving was commonplace, and in 1900, the *Jewish Daily Forward* quoted an immigrant who said, "The purchase of Christmas gifts is of the first things that proves one is no longer a greenhorn."[43] With department stores now central to downtown areas, windows were filled with enticing Christmas scenes, and stores stayed open late to making shopping easier for families. Manufacturers learned to package products specifically for the holiday season: cartons of cigarettes were packaged in foil paper and embossed with wreaths, for example. In time, Santa Claus became the dominant personality associated with Christmas, a jolly soul invented and perfected through the joint efforts of media, marketers, and parents who continue to adore the mythology.

Many of our images and beliefs related to Christmas were defined by the media. Thomas Nast developed Santa Claus for Civil War readers of the illustrated newspaper, *Harper's Weekly*. Every few months, Nast created an illustration featuring Santa Claus. In January 1863, for example, Santa visited the Union troops while holding a small puppet figure of Confederate leader Jefferson Davis with a noose around his tiny neck.[44] In December, 1863, Nast added Santa's big bag of gifts to the imagery. Over the next few decades, downtown department stores began to make use of vivid Christmas images, including people dressed as Nast's Santa Claus, wintertime displays in store windows, elves, and more. The modern version of Christmas took shape about a century ago. By 1941, when Bing Crosby introduced the song "White Christmas" on his Kraft Music Hall radio show, traditions were well established. Nine-year-old Natalie Wood learned to believe in Santa Claus in 1947's *Miracle on 34th Street*. The next two decades were a Christmas bonanza, with LPs from Elvis Presley to the Beach Boys; a 1960s barrage of star-studded Christmas television specials; and *A Christmas Story*, in which little Ralphy Parker copes with a crazy dad, neighborhood bullies, and his dreams of owning a Red Ryder Carbine Action 200-Shot, Range Model Air Rifle.

We fantasize about an old-fashioned Christmas and buy Department 56's tabletop Christmas villages to remember the days gone by. This publicly traded company sells more than seventy million dollars worth of these villages every year.

Apparently, the first Christmas trees were tabletop models in Germany and England, with tiny lightweight gifts hanging from their branches. In the modest number of households that participated, each child in the seventeenth or eighteenth century had his or her own small tree. When the idea of a tree migrated to the United States, it was an admission-only attraction to see a much larger tree (everything in the United States is large, including our Christmas trees). Social reformer Jacob Riis encouraged Americans to associate the tree with the fellowship of dinner with the poor at a settlement house, and caroling as a symbol of light in a city filled with forgotten poor and lonesome rich. Riis also managed to get a tree into New York City's Madison Square Park that could be enjoyed by all, rich or poor, without an admission charge.

By the 1920s, The Society of Electrical Development was encouraging President Coolidge to demonstrate the power and beauty of electricity with a tree on the White House lawn. Reports disagree on details, but Potomac Electric Power Co. erected a sixty-foot tree on the Ellipse (near the White

House lawn). The White House tree lighting is now an annual media event, paralleled by the one in New York City's Rockefeller Center; both provide television advertisers with commercial avails in star-studded television specials to kick off the retail season.

Kwanzaa was created in 1966 by Maulana Karenga, the founder of a black nationalist organization and now a professor of the Department of Black Studies at California State University, Long Beach. The concept of a black Christmas has been around since the mid-1800s, but Karenga packaged a festival of light with indigenous cooking and added black to the traditional red-green color mix associated with the holiday season. The Jews have reshaped Chanukah, once a minor festival, so that it now offers children eight nights of gift giving (far better than one Christmas morning, at least in some households). Some put up a Christmas tree but call it a Chanukah bush.

Branded Religion

A few years ago, while I was traveling in Japan with my friend Nick (son of a Greek Orthodox priest), he wondered aloud: "The Buddhists are represented by a fat, happy guy who is always laughing. The Christians are represented by a man who is deathly thin with spikes through his hands. Who would *you* rather have on your side?"

Acknowledging the blasphemy, Nick and I giggled when, like children, we concocted the stereotypical brand icon for my (Jewish) religion: a wise white-bearded man named Max, dressed in black and saying "oy" between bites of a bagel. (In fact, the Jews do not believe that God can be understood as a visual image. The Muslims take the concept a step further by prohibiting imagery related to God or His creations.)

Still, the Roman Catholics are thriving: Sixty million people share common beliefs. Roman Catholics comprise the largest U.S. religion; only Brazil and Mexico are home to more Catholics, with 134 million and 86 million, respectively. Catholic imagery is rich and varied. There are two very popular holidays: Christmas (a national holiday in many countries), and Easter, plus New Year's Day, if you accept the Anno Domini (A.D.) approach to counting the years since Christ's birth.[45] Half of America's most popular boys' names are based upon the names of saints. At least fifty saintly names would be instantly familiar to most Americans. This is remarkable "unaided recognition." If the Roman Catholic religion was a corporation, it would rank at the center of the Fortune 500, near Kellogg's and Texas

Instruments, with vast real estate holdings, plenty of cash on hand, and an impressive annual revenues figure in the $10 billion range.

When comparing religion and marketing, the subject of missionaries as religious marketers is difficult to dismiss. Missionaries are true believers who spread the word of their religion (typically, a Christian religion), attempting to change the behavior of others. Television has provided an opportunity for some of Christianity's entrepreneurial evangelists and preachers to reach out across the North American continent and across the world to ask for money so they can continue to do God's work. Approximately one in ten U.S. broadcast television stations are religious broadcasters. The best-known preachers raise between $50 million and $100 million per year. And that's the key: to be a personality that people know and trust. Some of the best-known preachers are household names: T.D. Jakes, Dr. Robert Schuller, Dr. Charles Stanley, and several dozen others would be instantly familiar in faith-based households.

Like Christianity, Judaism is well known throughout the Western world. The religion is several thousand years older than Christianity (the Jews are currently celebrating year 5766). There's a rich heritage here including many lessons and stories in the Old Testament that are regularly taught today and are the basis for both Judaism and Christianity. The iconography is mainly related to study (Torah) and reverent celebration (candles).

Judaism

Modern Jewish leaders are concerned because their market share is shrinking. Only half of Jewish men marry Jewish women, so each generation has half as many Jewish children as the one before. This, plus the devastating impact of the Holocaust in the 1940s, has reduced the total number of Jews to about fourteen million.

Judaism possesses a rich heritage, an admirable emphasis on learning and childhood education, a sense of permanence despite hardship, and centuries of common tradition. Jewish households have produced a large number of people notable for extraordinary accomplishments; the long list includes Viacom leader Sumner Redstone and NBC leader David Sarnoff, Stephen Spielberg, Steve Ballmer (Microsoft CEO, who calls himself "the richest Jew in the world"), Albert Einstein, musicians George Gershwin, Rodgers & Hammerstein, Stephen Sondheim, Bob Dylan, Neil Simon, Isaac Asimov, Arthur Miller, Marcel Proust, Woody Allen, and, probably, Leonardo DaVinci.[46] Jewish families who are steeped in tradition also enjoy their own old-world language, Yiddish, whose words and humor helped to invent the Broadway theater.[47]

Still, Judaism has struggled with centuries of devastating cultural stereotyping (merchant, lender, etc.). Many Jews possess strong emotional connections with Israel, which makes the religion admirable (for some) and controversial (for others). To varying degrees, depending upon each individual congregation's traditions, Jews pray in a combination of English and Hebrew. In many congregations, Hebrew is a language that at least half of congregants don't completely comprehend, and many do not understand at all.

In order to flourish, Judaism must encourage loyalty and insure positive associations within its constituency. Strengthen the modern version of the religion and relevant elements for today's society and make the most of its rich history, its sense of permanence, and its emphasis on family values. (None of this is new; some of these discussions are centuries old.)

Is it appropriate for Jewish leaders to meet regularly to discuss their issues in terms of marketing? Will the religion continue to survive without attending to the religion as if it was a brand? On a local level, where congregational leadership must cope with declining membership and raising the funds necessary to support synagogues, Hebrew schools, and community activities, the conversation often goes to programs likely to capture the imagination of families who are unaffiliated with congregations, some of these programs include Texas Hold 'Em Poker parties; gambling nights; karaoke; and free trial memberships (first year of membership is free).[48]

Islam

Islam is America's fastest-growing religion. As is so often the case, the facts about Muslims are quite different from media snapshots of the Muslim brand (as seen on TV). For example, most Muslims live not in the Middle East, but in South Asia. Nearly one in four Muslims who live in the United States were born here. Muslims tend to be high income, to be very involved in family and education, and to vote in U.S. elections at a greater rate than the rest of the U.S. population.

Religious Marketing

The terms are rarely used in the same sentence, but the similarities are profound. The goals of religion are related to the sharing beliefs, and often, shared lifestyles within a community. Many religions evangelize, or "spread the Word" through techniques that are remarkably similar to marketing. Still, marketing and religion ought to be different. Religion should be focused on a connection with the spiritual world, a sense of unity with fellow humans and with the broader world/universe, faith in a vision that is deeper and longer than human life, and a means to cope with evil, sadness, and tragedy. For an increasing number of people, branded products have come to serve similar purposes.

Endnotes

1   *Affluenza: The All-Consuming Epidemic* by John DeGraaf, David Wann, and Thomas Naylor, p. 188.

2   *Affluenza: The All-Consuming Epidemic* by John DeGraaf, David Wann, and Thomas Naylor, p. 88.

3   Kalle Lasn, *Culture Jam: The Uncooling of America*, p. 14.

4   "Winnebagos, Cherokees, Apaches, and Dakotas: The Persistence of Stereotyping of American Indians in American Advertising Brands," by Debra Merskin, *Howard Journal of Communications*, 12:159-169, 2001.

5   Merskin, "Winnebagos, Cherokees …"

6   From http://www.prmuseum.com/kendrix/trinity.html: Aunt Jemima was created at the end of the 1880s in Missouri, when Chris L. Rutt and Charles G. Underwood invented an instant pancake flour. Rutt created the trademark after a visit to the theater in 1889, where he saw minstrels in black face, aprons, and red bandannas performing a tune called "Old Aunt Jemima." The song, very popular in its day, inspired Rutt to use the same image as the company logo.

7   http://www.musicals101.com/minstrel.htm

8   http://www.amosandy.com/Review%20Articles/naacp.htm

9   *LIFE*, May 1, 1939.

10   Cotton robe; floor mat; small Japanese inn

11   Long a popular association, cowboys didn't have as much interaction with Indians as we might think. Instead, it was the settlers of the American wilderness (for example, people who traveled via wagon trains) and the U.S. Army soldiers who were most affected by the Indians. Most of their interaction was as far east as Pennsylvania and not much further west than Missouri. For the most part, cowboys worked the Great Plains and into the foothills of the Rockies, and then, for only about thirty years in large numbers, roughly the 1860s to 1890s.

12   "Crazy Horse Malt Liquor Apologizes," by Dennis Gale, AP, April 27, 2001.

13   From "School Textbooks: Unpopular History or Cherished Mythology," by Earl Lee, on pages 73-81 of *You Are Being Lied To*, edited by Russ Kick.

14   For example, http://beijing.usembassy.gov/columbus_day.html

15   *A People's History of the United States* by Howard Zinn, p.1.

16   The quote appears in an essay by Howard Zinn titled "Columbus and Western Civilization," in which Zinn quotes Columbus biographer Samuel Eliot Morison. One of numerous copies on the Internet can be found at: http://www.zmag.org/CrisesCurEvts/columbus_western.html

17   Zinn, "Columbus and Western Civilization."

18   Bartolome de las Casas, a Dominican priest, came to the New World a few years after Columbus arrived and spent forty years on Hispaniola and nearby islands. There were witnesses: A group of Pompeian friars addressed Spanish monarchy to intercede and corroborated las Casas's testimony.

19   *A People's History of the United States* by Howard Zinn, p. 7.

20   http://en.wikipedia.org/wiki/Martin_Luther_King,_Jr.#King_and_the_FBI.

21   One graphic example was reported in *Newsweek*, January 19, 1968, p. 62.

22   "Lord of the Doves," *Newsweek*, April 17, 1967.

23   "Dr. King's Disservice to His Cause," *LIFE*, April 21, 1967, p. 4.

24   Professor of Religion and Social Transformation at the Iliff School of Theology in Denver, writing in *The New York Times* (1/18/88). http://www.martinlutherking.org/thebeast.html

25   http://www.mobileedproductions.com/aboutus.htm

26   "The Smell of the Greasepaint, the Roar of Those Third Graders," *The New York Times*, by Claire Hoffman, December 3, 2003.

27   "Brand Name Field Trips," by Lisa Takeuchi Cullen, *TIME*, June 28, 2004.

28   http://www.llsweb.com/about.html

29   *Food Fight: The Inside Story of the Food Industry, America's Obesity Crisis, and What We Can Do About It* by Kelly D. Brownell, PhD, p. 137.

30   *Dumbing Us Down: The Hidden Curriculum of Compulsory Schooling* by John Taylor Gatto (a New York City schoolteacher for twenty-six years).

31   "Schools debate slave-era names," by Steve Szkotak, Associated Press, December 21, 2003, http://washingtontimes.com/metro/20031220-113215-4024r.htm

32   National Center for Education Statistics: http://nces.ed.gov/ccd/schoolsearch/

33   "The Squabbling Illini: Rallying Cries Lead to Rift," *The New York Times*, December 16, 2003, and *FAQ About the Chief* from The Chief Illiniwek Educational Foundation and the Honor the Chief Society.

34   "Now a Message from a Sponsor of the Subway: Transit Agency Weighs Sale of Naming Rights," *The New York Times*, July 27, 2004.

35 http://www.cnn.com/2001/US/07/27/black.cnna/

36 On *Voices in the Family*, WHYY Radio, Philadelphia, October 4, 2004.

37 "Got Spike?" by Deroy Murdock, *National Review*, June 26, 2004.

38 http://www.redcross.org/aboutus/

39 Having just checked the Web, the logos are a red heart with a torch, and a sword with a serpentine handle. The lung association uses a doubled cross.

40 I did a Google search on "AIDS charity" and came up with the United Kingdom's AVERT and Children with AIDS, as well as a few sites filled with links to organizations with AIDS in their names. Nothing was especially familiar.

41 http://www.hot-dog.org/pr/pressroom.htm

42 Butterball is owned by ConAgra, home to Chun King, Chef Boyardee, Crunch n' Munch, Slim Jim, Manwich, Reddi-wip, Hebrew National, Jiffy Pop, and other popular food brands.

43 As late as the 1960s, immigrant Jews were openly concerned about appearing to be a greenhorn—an inexperienced or unsophisticated person from the "old country"— so they actively adopted the slang, lifestyles, and values of their adopted America.

44 http://www.sonofthesouth.net/Original_Santa_Claus.htm

45 For non-Christians, the term "A.D." simply is not used, and B.C. (Before Christ) is replaced by B.C.E. (before current era).

46 For DaVinci, at least on his mother's side, which is the side that determines religion for Jewish families. Other notable Jewish men and women include scientists Niels Bohr, and Richard Feynmann; thinkers Baruch Spinoza and Ludwig Wittgenstein; musicians Billy Joel and Carole King; writers Judy Blume, Franz Kafka, Marcel Proust, and Isaac Asimov; many of Broadway's legendary composers and lyricists; artists Franco Modigliani and Frida Kahlo; and, in the "oy" category, Jack Ruby and Monica Lewinsky.

47 In New York City, the Yiddish Theater was an invention of the immigrants, who established the New York City theatrical tradition and trained many of its composers and performers.

48 Last night, I attended a meeting of Jewish community leaders, and each of these approaches was suggested by a leader of local congregations.

WHAT WE SHOULD DO

It's not a hopeless situation. In the game whose prize is control over our time, our money, and our behavior, we can control the way we spend our time, the way we spend our money, and the way we behave. In fact, brands are just figments of someone's imagination. Like Tinkerbelle, brands exist only if we believe in them.

Trust

Ultimately, we are asking to trust the companies whose products and services we buy and use every day. We are asking that they be honest with us regarding issues of product safety, potential dangers, side effects, or predictable patterns of troubling behavior.

When L.L. Bean's boots fell apart and his company almost went out of business, Bean refunded his customers' money and built a better company. We are asking that every company provide its customers with a similar motivation for trust.

Every citizen should understand the personal and societal cost of owning, operating, and disposing of a car. We should hold the car and fuel industry responsible for providing safe transportation that does not wreck the environment. We should require the car and fuel industry to develop cars that (a) last longer than previous models; (b) offer improved gas mileage every year; (c) are less likely to be involved in personal or property injury; (d) cannot be operated by a driver who is intoxicated or otherwise unable to legally drive a car; (e) make efficient, cost-effective use of the latest available technologies to reduce environmental impact of all kinds; and (f) whose parts are safely manufactured and disposed of with minimal environment impact. Faulty cars should be 100 percent returnable, with full refunds. Used cars should be bought and sold at fixed prices that are fully disclosed and fair to both the retailer and the consumer.

In 2005, General Motors developed a clever—and very successful—promotion. GM offered consumers the same discount as the one enjoyed by company employees. Personally, I'd be happier to pay General Motors a fair profit on their cars, provided the company abides by the spirit and letter of the list in the previous paragraph. General Motors has framed the story so that it's about price. In fact, the game should not be played on the basis of price. It should be played on the basis of a trusting relationship between a responsible manufacturer of quality products and a consumer who is willing to pay a fair price for those products. We need to change the way we think. In the long run, we will save money, save lives, and do less damage to the environment.

Playing by the Rules

Corporations whose motivations are profits and asset protection, and government agencies whose actions often promote commerce, have perfected the rules of the game.

As currently written, the rules of the game allow brands to exist and to prosper, sometimes to the detriment of the public good.

In order to affect any meaningful change in individual behavior, we need to look carefully at the rules of the game and determine how best to level the playing field.

It's important to understand that rules are *often* changed. Frequently, changes are due to active involvement by citizens, either through formal organizations such as MADD or through direct contact with legislators. The people who make our laws are not only accessible, they are responsive to requests for personal appearances, in-person meetings in their government or local offices, and, in particular, to well-organized members of their constituencies who persevere in public campaigns dedicated to specific issues. Campaigns that tie up their phone lines and jam their e-mail boxes also tend to get their attention, but persistent, in-person influence is always the best way to affect change. Influence is most likely to cause change when it's coordinated with an ongoing television, radio, and Web media coverage.

Which rules should be changed? In general, the rules that should be changed are the ones that provide brands and the corporations behind those brands with large amounts of unfair or unbalanced control over our time, our money, and our behavior.

Media Rules

Over time, we've allowed large media companies to establish policies and ownership that run contrary to our public interest. It is time to roll back these policies and operate our media in ways that primarily serve the public.

Media companies should not be owned by corporations with interests in other industries. Neither General Electric nor Altria nor Dow Chemical should own a television network, a newspaper, or a radio station. When it comes to Microsoft, Verizon, or Wal-Mart, the situation becomes stickier; Microsoft already owns part of MSNBC, and operates MSN and other popular Web sites; Verizon is heading into the business of distributing television channels to compete with cable operators; and Wal-Mart has probably considered a home shopping channel to compete with QVC. Acknowledging the potential complexities, particularly as they apply to rapidly changing definitions of media due to digital technologies, better rules are possible and should be devised.

The size of media operations should be set at more reasonable limits. In any one market, no single company should own more than two AM, two FM, and one broadcast television station. The same company should not own any large local newspaper or local cable systems in the market. Similarly, no one company should own more than two of the top twenty or five of the top fifty national cable networks or Web sites. Broadcast and cable television networks should not own or control more than 25 percent of the programs on their schedules. By avoiding concentrations of major power, media companies are more likely to (a) make a broader range of independent decisions, and (b) innovate in order to attract larger audiences and more advertising dollars.

A new tax on revenues from commercial television and radio should be used to completely fund two public television and two public radio networks, along with associated local stations. Funds should be collected and distributed by an independent authority operating without any government involvement.

The programming shown on television in any market should accurately reflect the economic, language, and ethnic mix found in that market. A quota system, similar to EEO, should require a fair and reasonable depiction of race and ethnicity throughout the program schedule (and on all commercials and public service announcements).

Children should be encouraged to watch television for no more than two hours per day. Commercials and public service announcements on television and in other media should reinforce this discouragement.

One thought from media mogul Ted Turner: "At this late stage, media companies have grown so large and powerful and their dominance has become so detrimental to the survival of small, emerging companies, that there remains only one alternative: bust up the big conglomerates. ... Big media itself was cut down to size in the 1970s, and a period of staggering innovation and growth followed."[1]

Advertising Rules

Neither alcohol nor tobacco should be advertised or promoted in any medium, sports venue, or any other place where messages may be seen or heard by children.

Every commercial or advertisement for soda, soft drinks, candy, sugary cereal, or fast food should be accompanied by a public service announcement of equal quality and identical running time. Advertisers should bear the cost of production and airtime. Noncommercial messages should encourage proper nutrition, appropriate portion sizing, choice of healthy foods, and discourage buying or eating foods with excess fat, sugar, and those lacking in nutritional value.

Every food advertisement in any medium should contain a clear, candid disclosure of significant nutritional concerns associated with the advertised food (for example, every Coca-Cola commercial should explain that a twelve-ounce can of Coca-Cola contains the equivalent of twelve teaspoonfuls of sugar). Within reason, the same rule should apply to all consumer products and services.

If a sponsor is paying for media exposure, this should be disclosed to the viewer (not hidden within a storyline as a product placement).

Stories provided by public relations agencies or front groups should be clearly identified as such, with complete disclosures regarding clients and intent.

Rules Governing Corporations

Corporations should be required to pay no less federal tax on U.S. revenues than their salaried (nonhourly) employees.

Corporations with U.S. revenues exceeding $1 billion per year should be required to adopt (build, improve, maintain) a public school in need. For each $1 billion more, another school gets help.

If a single company controls more than one-third of the market for any given product or service, it should be subject to increasingly rich public service requirements, progressively higher taxes, and increasingly transparent disclosures.

If a single company controls more than two-thirds of the market for any given product or service, its public responsibility should be expanded in a like manner. It should be annually reviewed by an independent agency for status as a potential monopoly. If monopoly status exists, then a special Monopoly Court should decide upon appropriate action.

In order to be effective, these rules must be developed, adopted, and enforced by the United States and by other major nations.

While we're changing things, we ought to rethink the rules and regulations regarding lobbyists and their access to lawmakers.

Tax and Lending Rules

Every federal tax form should be provided with an easy-to-understand explanation of the federal budget, along with a meaningful mechanism for citizens to express their opinions about the ways in which the government spends tax money and, within reason, to vote on certain allocations.

In clear, large type, every credit card should be imprinted with every cost associated with using the card, along with appropriate warnings regarding debt.

Credit card companies should be required to provide substantial, ongoing consumer education with regard to borrowing and debt management. Interest rates should be no higher than other forms of consumer borrowing.

Election Rules

No candidate for public office should be allowed to advertise on television or radio.

Every television and radio station and network should be required to produce and broadcast a substantial series of half-hour and hour-long programs for and with each candidate, including one-on-one interviews, town hall meetings, biographies, and more. At the local level, cable systems should be required to provide similar coverage.

Every media outlet should be required to actively and aggressively promote voting until it becomes a national obsession.

Every president, governor, mayor, senator, congressman, and judge should be elected by popular vote. It is the job of every citizen to learn about the candidates and the issues, and to vote. Some citizens may not do their jobs; decisions will be made by citizens who do.

Government Organization

No government agency should be charged with the conflicting responsibilities of business promotion and consumer protection. Every decade or so, the roles of the USDA, FCC, and other government organizations should be reviewed and reconsidered.

We may need only one department or agency to promote America's business interests. The Department of Commerce is a candidate; there are others.

We may need only one department or agency to make and enforce rules and monitor America's businesses. The FDA is one candidate; there are others.

Agencies and departments charged with consumer protection should be provided with more resources, larger staffs, and should be operated with minimal opportunity for influence from lobbyists, legislators, or other politicians. The FTC, FDA, SEC, and other such organizations should be provided with sufficient resources to do their jobs without undue delay.

Rules Regarding Intellectual Property

In China, you can buy a DVD copy of a popular motion picture for less than one dollar. This drives the U.S. motion picture industry insane, but for China, the protection of U.S. intellectual property is, in a word, unimportant.

The result is that there are unofficial Hard Rock Café restaurants— along with the compulsory T-shirts and caps—in places where the owners of the Hard Rock license never granted permission. The question is whether Hard Rock's ownership of its trademark in the United States and in other countries gives the corporation global control over its own trademark.

In the United States, the record industry has responded to unauthorized distribution of recorded music by suing twelve-year-olds, making an example of them. Clearly, this sort of legal action suggests that something is profoundly wrong with the system.

How will all of this affect, say, Mickey Mouse? For corporations reliant upon legal protection of their intellectual property assets, the answer is pure fear. Disney lobbied Congress in 1998 and won another twenty years of copyright protection for its valuable rodent. In time, though, globalization and massive digital distribution will nibble away at Disney's control over Mickey, *Bambi*, and other valuable media brands—and Disney will respond by pressuring governments to provide more and more legal protection over its valuable assets.

A movement toward free culture and the loosening of copyright restrictions is well under way. You can find out more about it by either reading Stanford law professor Lawrence Lessig's book, *Free Culture*, or by visiting http://creativecommons.org.

More Changes

While we're in the midst of changing the world to avoid being brainwashed by brands, let's add a few more items to the rant.

Cars

If you're convicted of driving drunk, you should lose your license for a year. If you're convicted twice, you lose your license for a decade. If you're caught a third time, you may no longer drive a car in the United States. No exceptions.

As soon as possible, we need a device that's standard in every car and truck. This device should test the alcohol level of the driver, and should not permit the vehicle to start or to be operated by anyone whose alcohol level exceeds the local DUI limit.

> It's time to set the gas-powered vehicle on a timeline for extinction. It's also time to aggressively fund the development and promotion of alternative transportation systems and lifestyle changes. The next generation should no longer see a Fortune 500 whose top slots are devoted to cars and gasoline.

And while we're designing cars, let's install a system that eliminates the need to handhold a cell phone while driving. (These systems existed in the early days of car phones, but they have been forgotten.)

Cars and trucks were an interesting twentieth century innovation, but they are too costly, too dangerous, and too taxing on the environment. It's time to set the gas-powered vehicle on a timeline for extinction. It's also time to aggressively fund the development and promotion of alternative transportation systems and lifestyle changes. The next generation should no longer see a Fortune 500 whose top slots are devoted to cars and gasoline.

Food

We need a national policy to permit only healthy foods in schools.

We need schools to adopt nutritional education and fitness as standard curriculum for every grade level. We need to stop feeding schoolchildren candy, pizza, cookies, potato chips, French fries, and soda—especially in school cafeterias. We need to provide every student with well-prepared, fresh, varied, nutritionally smart foods that will encourage them to make informed choices throughout their lives. We need to use the cafeteria as a classroom to teach them how to make smart decisions to control their weight.

We must teach all Americans how to eat sensibly, how to measure portion sizes, how to plan meals effectively. The food industry must change its packaging, portion sizing, and promotion to support these efforts.

Fresh fruits and vegetables from local growers should be very low priced (supported by subsidies if they are grown nearby), and made as easily available in workplaces as coffee. In schools, fresh fruits and vegetables should be available, appealing, and free (or as nearly free as possible).

Complete nutritional information should be part of every restaurant menu. For smaller restaurants, where this work may be a hardship, quick and easy scientific measurement tools should be devised and implemented, perhaps with tax relief for smaller businesses.

Sin taxes should apply to alcohol, tobacco, and all foods that are rich in fat, sugar, and calories. Junk food should *always* cost more than healthy food.

Making Exercise Easy

Each of us needs an easy way to measure ten thousand steps per day, and we need encouragement to fulfill this obligation through media promotion (and, perhaps, a brand with an accompanying campaign).

We need easily accessible parks and walking paths near every workplace. We need facilities that accommodate for weather and provide safe rights of way. The government needs to adopt this as a national priority and provide tax incentives so that every community makes this happen for their people.

A high percentage of our population should be able to walk, bicycle, or, if necessary, take comfortable, reliable, reasonably priced public transportation to school, work, shopping, and to community events. A small percentage of us should feel the need to drive cars to work and to other routine destinations. The entire system, and its underlying philosophy, needs to change. We need fewer cars, and we need to drive them less. How might government and industry make that happen?

Conspiracy?

Strictly speaking, there is no conspiracy. For a conspiracy to exist, individuals or companies must work together on a plan whose result would be illegal.

Strictly speaking, there is no "tort" because two conditions must be met: existing law that establishes civil liability, plus the injury of a third party.

Corporate attorneys make certain that consumer brands operate within the bounds of the law. Lobbyists working for corporations and for industry groups work full time to change those laws to allow corporations and their brands to earn more money. Public relations firms and front groups working for those corporations and industry groups support the work of the lobbyists.

There is, however, another tricky concept at work here: time.

Many laws are made to address offenses that can be measured within fairly narrow time frames. When potentially troublesome behavior occurs over a very long period of years—and the damage is gradual—our system of lawmaking and enforcement may be somewhat ineffective. Despite the presence of abundant medical, scientific, ethical, and social science evidence, it has been difficult for anti-tobacco interests to transform behavior through law. The same may ultimately be true with regard to some drug side effects and food-related public health issues, such as obesity.

Still, the marketing and ultimate success of many brands has exploited our worst impulses. These activities have:

- Placed many consumers hopelessly in debt
- Encouraged us to spend our money foolishly
- Fed us a steady diet of fear-inducing, titillating, high-gloss stories that distract us from considering more meaningful issues
- Encouraged us to become sedentary and obese
- Encouraged us to eat foods rich in sugar, salt, and fat—all harmful substances directly linked to widespread diseases and causes of mortality
- Discouraged us from eating foods that are healthy
- Connected alcohol with spectator sports in a massive, ongoing national campaign
- Killed millions of people through dangerous drugs, such as tobacco
- Destroyed or damaged environmental assets

- Encouraged global warming, deforestation, soil depletion, and poisoned water
- Encouraged larger homes, and suburbs and sprawl while sacrificing safe neighborhoods and towns, leaving many urban centers in a shambles

There is no conspiracy, no single group of people who get together on a regular basis to discuss how best to destroy the environment or how to cause children to become obese. Instead—and this may be even more dangerous—the entire system is set up to reward individual brand managers and marketing managers who sell more Budweiser beer, to pay commissions to network advertising executives who increase the size of Budweiser's annual ad buys, to increase the value of stocked owned by Altria shareholders when Philip Morris succeeds in selling more cigarettes.

Over time, we become desensitized to the real issues. At the most basic level, on the streets of New York City, it's not unusual to hear the jingle, "The creamiest dreamiest soft ice cream you get from Mister Softee." In neighborhoods with lots of kids, this jingle is played loud, and it's played many times each spring and summer day. Most people ignore the incessant ditty, but it drives other people nuts. Mister Softee instructs drivers to use music judiciously, but, as one driver told *The New York Times,*[2] "To be honest with you ... when you spent five to six days a week, nine to ten hours a day, on a Mister Softee truck, you become desensitized."

Feeding the Children

The average child in the United Stated sees at least fifteen thousand food commercials per year. This is the equivalent of spending twenty school days per year doing nothing but watching television commercials. The vast majority of these commercials promote sweet or salty snacks, candy, soft drinks, fast food, and sugared cereals. If we are going to continue to allow this type of advertising (though it's difficult to understand why that would be a good idea), then an equal amount of advertising time and money should be spent on the cultivation of proper nutrition.

Each year, $30 billion is spent on food advertising. Roughly $10 billion is used to advertise to children.[3] The money is spent for two reasons. First, companies must advertise to sell current products. American children (ages five to fourteen years) control the spending of $20 billion per year and influence the spending of up to several hundred billion dollars annually. Second, brands must develop the next generation's consumer spending habit.

"Recognizing that children are not yet fully mature, we control the promotion of alcohol, firearms, and tobacco. Yet we routinely assume that children can rationally decide about food choices that have important health consequences, and we expose them to intense marketing of products that are largely devoid of nutritional value but replete with calories" (and sugar and fat).[4]

Let's reconsider the whole idea of marketing to children. What would happen if no advertisements were allowed on television programs whose viewership was, say, children ages two to sixteen? What if restaurants were not allowed to sell or give toys to children? Would our society perish, or would the television networks find some other way to capture the lost revenue?

The hits just keep on coming ...

Ask a busy commuter about E-ZPass, and he or she will likely focus on the brand's key attribute: saving time at busy toll plazas. Ask a busy marketer about E-ZPass, and you'll hear about targeting consumers based upon their driving patterns. E-ZPass is a means to gather information about consumer behavior—a system funded by consumers. Every time you drive a toll highway, or travel over a bridge or into a tunnel, E-ZPass improves your database profile.

Cell phones also sell convenience, but they also come with a personal privacy cost. Cell phone calls are more easily monitored than landline calls. As more cell towers are posted, your current position (and your historical positions) can be plotted. Cell phone data is also collected in a database.

New technologies save time and make our lives easier. We don't want them to go away. We do, however, want full disclosure. What do E-ZPass and Verizon do with the data they collect? We ought to know.

Changing Schools and Education

For most children, beliefs are initially developed as a result of interaction with parents and other family members. The media encourages certain beliefs and discourages others. However, for sheer hours spent pounding information into young minds, nothing beats the persistent daily curriculum of a dozen years of public school.

School provides new generations with cues about how people are supposed to behave, how to gain attention and recognition, what is important to know, and how to think about yourself and others. Brands, corporations, and government rely upon a standardized education for all Americans.

Standardized education has been widely criticized, and some schools have responded by modernizing their curriculums to allow students to learn in a more individualized manner. Our reliance upon standardized test scores, for example, has been widely criticized because education based upon these tests tends to discourage original thinking and encourage the belief that questions have only one correct answer.

In fact, the world is complex. Questions may have more than one correct answer. Answers are, often, subjective. Stories are rarely simple. In order to make the right decisions, we must learn how to think more effectively.

In order to prepare the next generation of citizens to make informed, intelligent decisions, several new or enhanced curriculum areas should be added to *every* grade level, from kindergarten to senior year in high school. Some examples (feel free to edit mine, or to add your own):

• *Media Literacy and Critical Thinking*—Increasingly, we need our schools to produce people who understand how to think about a wide range of topics. For example, the media environment is now far wider than books and magazines, but our literacy curriculum is still known as "English" and still emphasizes reading and writing in an era when television, the Internet, e-mail, instant messaging, motion pictures, and other forms of communication have overtaken both the writing of essays and the reading of books. It's time to reconsider the deeply entrenched brands called English and math, and to broaden their mission to embrace, and perhaps replace, these old-style educational brands with new ones called, for example, media literacy and critical thinking. Media literacy should encompass language, linguistics, images, persuasion, cinema, books, public speaking, and other forms of communications. Critical thinking should embrace logic, problem solving, statistics and analysis, economics, philosophy, social science, and numeracy (the numerical form of literacy).

• *Human Relations*—Every student should develop a deep understanding of the ways in which humans relate to one another. These lessons should incorporate communications, psychology, sociology, conflict assessment and resolution, anger management, friendship and love, prejudice and hatred, and the interaction of humans within institutional and corporate environments. This is a new curriculum brand, one that's a part of life in every company of any size, but rarely more than a side effort in most schools.

• *Health and Nutrition*—Through an integrated health, fitness, and nutrition curriculum, students should gain an increasingly broad and deep understanding of how the human body works. This curriculum should combine science, fitness, food preparation, and some practical aspects of mathematics. Each student should emerge from thirteen years of public or private school with the capability to select food ingredients, prepare a range of nutritious meals, and evaluate the results of diet, exercise, and lifestyle decisions. Gym should not be the lead subject: health should be (fitness is part of health, not the other way around.) Students should be required to exercise daily by (at least) walking one mile indoors or out, in safe facilities provided by the school and/or the community.

Let's stop pretending that the cafeteria is anything but a classroom—and let's take the opportunity to teach children to eat in ways that discourage obesity.

• *Nature and Environment*—Every student should gain a deep and wide understanding of how the earth works and what must be done in order to maintain its long-term health. This curriculum should include a robust curriculum that encourages students to learn about nature and to spend considerable time outdoors in the real world where little to nothing is man-made.

• *Global Community*—Every American student should be able to speak English and Spanish,[5] and should have basic familiarity with Chinese,[6] Hindustani, Arabic, Russian, and French. Students should know the location and something about every country on earth (just over two hundred). For each of the world's most newsworthy countries and regions, school students should possess a nuanced understanding of key issues related to public health, communications, economy, politics, climate, major industries, and concerns of average citizens.

Why Make These Changes?

If Americans are to interact with the powerful, well-funded future of brands and the companies that own them, we must understand how the media operate and we must become smart enough to evaluate messages through critical thinking. We must understand how we are wired, how we behave, how our minds work. We must understand how our bodies work, and how to manage nutrition and fitness activities in order to keep our bodies healthy. We must understand how our world operates so that we can evaluate potential impact. We must stop thinking about America as a superior world power and start understanding how our country fits into the global community. If we do not reshape our educational curriculum—and yes, this means tossing out a fair amount of what we currently teach—we will continue to turn out beer-guzzling, SUV-driving, cigarette-smoking citizens whose adult fate is working at a super-sized retail store because it's the only job in town, and whose health diagnosis is littered with symptoms related to obesity, diabetes, heart disease, and cancer. We can do better.

It's Our Money

In 2004, The Coca-Cola Co., which sells syrup and promotes the Coca-Cola brand, earned over $20 billion in revenues. The same year, Coca-Cola counted about $22 billion in revenues. Coca-Cola Enterprises ("The World Largest Bottler"), the world's largest marketer, producer, and distributor of products of The Coca-Cola Co., earned $20 billion more. Imagine: $42 billion spent on soda. Who buys it? You, me, and people like us around the world.

> If Americans are to interact with the powerful, well-funded future of brands and the companies that own them, we must understand how the media operate.

McDonald's did not become a $20 billion company by secretly selling arms to a third-world country, or through obscure government contracts. McDonald's got there by selling nearly a trillion hamburgers to consumers who were too busy to prepare lunch or dinner, traveling without taking the time to eat properly, keeping the kids entertained, or just felt like eating a burger and fries.

Wal-Mart is now a larger economic power than Belgium and may well overtake Germany in the next twenty years. Wal-Mart (and other discounters) didn't force shoppers to shun their local stores. Individual Americans made the decision to spend less money in stores that offered more products for less money. Cognizant of Wal-Mart's business practices, but wooed by Always Low Prices, Americans made Wal-Mart the richest company in the world.

It's interesting to browse through the Fortune 50 companies, just to see how many corporations have grown rich with money from our wallets. How many consumer products companies are in Fortune's list of top fifty companies? In the superstar range, there's Wal-Mart Stores, Exxon Mobil, General Motors, Ford Motor, ChevronTexaco, and ConocoPhillips—most sell either cars or gasoline, and all top the charts with about $100 billion in revenues. Also in the top fifty, there's Home Depot, Verizon Communications, State Farm Insurance, Kroger (supermarkets), Pfizer, Procter & Gamble, Target, Dell, Costco Wholesale, Johnson & Johnson, Marathon Oil, Time Warner, SBS Communications, Albertson's (supermarkets), MetLife,

Walgreens, Lowe's, Sears Roebuck, and Safeway (supermarkets). At least half of America's top companies are consumer products manufacturers, marketers, or retailers. [More, if you include the consumer side of IBM,[7] Hewlett-Packard, Dell, and Intel, or the corn sweeteners and other ingredients provided by agri-giant Archer Daniels Midland (ADM), whose tag line was "supermarket to the world."]

All of the corporations on this list—along with hundreds more—are funded by money that we earned and then gave to them. When Harrah's Entertainment asks us, annually, for about $5 billion to play in their casinos and stay at their hotels, we respond, annually, with an enthusiastic "yes!" When Apple Computer asks us to buy millions of iPods and clever computers so they can take in over $8 billion in revenues, we transform their idea into our lifestyle statement. When BJ's Wholesale Club asks us for over $7 billion, we give them our money.

Every year, we pay about $4,000,000,000,000 ($4 trillion) to Fortune 500 consumer businesses—about one-third of the U.S. gross domestic product relies upon our consumer economy. If every American decided to hold back and save even 5 percent of the money that we currently spend (that's five cents less spending per dollar), we would keep $200,000,000,000 ($200 billion) in our pockets, or about $667 per person per year. That may not seem like much, but $404 per year, at 2.5 percent interest, over a working lifetime of forty years, would yield nearly $28,000—enough to pay for a year or two of college. If we all put our money together for just a year, we could buy the entire Coca-Cola Co. (and shut it down, if we like). That's the power you have and I have, the power that we choose to exercise by investing in the convenient twelve-pack of Coca-Cola cans that fit so nicely into a refrigerator shelf.

Activism

Activism can be effective. It gets results. It's a ton of work, and generally unpaid work at that, but consumer activists have caused an enormous amount of societal and legal change. In the 1960s, when we were still learning the craft, activists were directly responsible for the Federal Hazardous Substances Act (1960); the Color Additive Amendment (1960); The Child Protection Act (1966); the Air Quality Act (1966); the Flammable Fabrics Act (1967); the Fire Research and Safety Act (1967); the Consumer Credit Protection Act (1968); the Child Protection and Toy Safety Act (1969) and more.[8]

MADD: Branded Activism

In 1979, Laura Lamb and her mother were hit by a drunk driver, a repeat offender traveling at 120 miles per hour. Laura was not yet a year old. She became a quadriplegic. In California, thirteen-year-old Cari Lightner was killed by a drunk driver who had been released on bail after two prior convictions; after Cari's death, the driver still had his California driver's license. By 1981, Lamb and Lightner joined forces with a clear mission—to reduce and ultimately eliminate deaths and injuries due to drunk driving. They called their organization MADD: Mothers Against Drunk Driving, a brand with instant recognition. By 1982, there were seventy MADD chapters, mostly begun by victims in search of answers. By the early 1990s, MADD had more than four hundred chapters, plus more than fifty community action teams, and now there are more than six hundred chapters in all fifty states, plus more outside the United States.

In truth, MADD got off to a powerful start with the help of NBC (what a difference big media can make!). In March 1983, NBC aired a made-for-TV movie, *The Candy Lightner Story*. By the end of the month, 122 new MADD chapters were open. At the same time, a poll revealed that 84 percent of people in the United States had heard about MADD, and that 55 percent believed that MADD was accomplishing its mission.

MADD gets things done:

In the 1980s, MADD popularized the idea of "designated drivers." (The term's meaning is clear and distinct. It is immediately actionable. It is tied directly into beliefs, and into a desire to remain alive. It is easily remembered and easily communicated. In short, it is a terrific brand name.)

In the 1990s, MADD worked with federal legislators to essentially force every state to increase the drinking age to twenty-one (the states' alternative: loss of federal highway construction funds).

MADD has reduced drunk driving offenses by more than 20 percent—and that was the result of just one campaign, whose goal was reached three years early. Since MADD's inception, alcohol related fatalities have declined 43 percent. Due to MADD's good work, more than 138,000 people are alive today and an untold number have received comfort, support, and assistance.

At any given time, MADD is hard at work at over a hundred different issues, all related to drunk driving. Unlike many of the corporations, lobby groups, and government organizations it must move, MADD makes its objectives extremely clear and posts them on its Web site. You'll find them by clicking on the "Activism" link on www.madd.org. One example: the end of happy hours in bars and restaurants, if not voluntarily by the industry, then by law.

"MADD will not close its doors until drunk drivers stop taking innocent lives."[9]

What Is Progress?

For a corporation, progress is equated with growth, increased market share, increased profitability and efficiency, and often, wider distribution.

For a community, progress means none of those things. Instead, progress means a safer, more pleasant place to live, with more recreational, educational, and social options for more of its citizens—along with a stable tax base that allows people to live within their means.

As brands have taken over our lives, the corporate version of progress has become more important than the community version of progress. Our priorities have been reversed. We need to rethink our definition of a healthy economy and a healthy community.

"If an eight-year-old girl can walk safely to a public library six blocks away, that's one good indicator of a healthy community. For one thing, you have a public library worth walking to, and a sidewalk to walk on. But more importantly, you have neighbors who watch out for each other. You have social capital in the neighborhood—relationships, commitments, and networks that create an underlying sense of trust."[10]

Ultimately, we need to think differently.

As Donella Meadows wrote in *Beyond the Limits*, "People don't need enormous cars, they need respect. They don't need closets full of clothes, they need excitement and variety and beauty. People don't need electronic equipment, they need something worthwhile to do with their lives. People need identity, community, challenge, acknowledgment, love, and joy. To try to fill these needs with material things is to set up an unquenchable appetite for false solutions to real and never-satisfied problems. The resulting psychological emptiness is one of the major forces behind the desire for material growth."

The Corporate Version of Progress: Nutraceuticals

According to Novartis Consumer Health, the U.S. market for "functional foods" is estimated to be $10 billion to $20 billion a year, with 10 percent annual growth. Apparently, functional foods are foods that serve a purpose beyond the one that nature provided. When you eat a French fry that's be-come a healthy product because the potatoes have been genetically enhanced and the oil has been chemically treated, you're enjoying a functional food, part of the next wave of processed food. Monsanto has developed an improved solids potato that absorbs less moisture, so it takes in less oil. Monsanto has also devoted its substantial scientific resources to the development of a low-calorie, low-saturated fat oil to cook the new-fangled super-fries. Johnson & Johnson, a company whose products we don't typically eat, now sells Benecol, a concoction that promises to "reduce 'bad' cholesterol levels while maintaining 'good' cholesterol levels" when used in place of spreads like margarine (three servings a day recommended).

New York University Professor and nutrition expert Marion Nestle asks, "With all of this progress, is it only a matter of time before fortified ice cream nudges broccoli completely off the plate?" She continues, "Food, drugs, and supplements should be separate. This is really not a good idea, except for marketing purposes. The assumption is the more vitamins the better, but I'm not sure that's true."[11] Professor Nestle—one of the more sensible thinkers in the food field—suggests substituting a chocolate bar and a vitamin pill for the nutraceutical power bar because power bars are often loaded with sugar and calories. Better that you know what you are eating.

Smaller Solutions

After reading most of the book, you're probably wondering what, exactly, *you* can do. No matter how much you reduce your "average ticket" at Home Depot or reduce your Coca-Cola consumption, it's not going to mean much to those companies. If you tell every one of your friends and relatives and co-workers to do the same thing, your impact will be negligible. You can write letters, express opinions on the editorial page and on Web sites, but you're not going to change Wal-Mart's business model and you're not going to dismantle NBC Universal.

Still, there is a lot that you and I can do. It's reasonable to expect that our changes will affect other people, and they'll change, too. This spread of memes—mind viruses, or ideas—operates in an odd, sometimes inexplicable way. Ideas take on a life of their own, and given a nurturing environment, some memes tend to grow, to gain momentum, to capture the imagination.

Start with your own life. Start with the food you eat.

If it's prepared in a fast-food restaurant; cooked in a microwave oven; stored in a freezer; or bought in a bag or can, odds are the product contains an abundance of sugar, fat, or calories, or its nutritional value is disappointing, or it won't taste too good. Instead of buying these foods, buy foods that are fresh. You will spend more time buying and preparing food; you will need to evaluate your life to find an additional half-hour a day to do what's right for your body.

You don't need a food pyramid.

You know that you must minimize your consumption of burgers and fries, chicken nuggets, chicken fingers, beef, fried foods, snack foods, sugary cereals, and heavily processed foods.

You know that you must increase your consumption of fruits, vegetables, fresh fish, whole grains, and water. Most likely, you need to increase the variety of these foods as well.

When you indulge in chocolate, pizza, coffee, tea, cake, pie, red meat, or French fries, it makes no sense to just buy what's available nearby. Instead, find the very best burger or chocolate or ice cream, and enjoy it thoroughly. The experience will be special, memorable, and if you possess a normal adult's capacity for self-control, this is not the sort of thing you'll do every day.

You know that you need to exercise for about an hour, every day.

Walk. Anywhere you can. Or bike. If you need to use the car, group your errands to save gas (and to make better use of your time). In the middle of the workday, go out for a fifteen-minute walk. Take a coworker or two. Combine routine meetings with walks. Make walking a habit. Keep moving! It's healthy and you'll find yourself to be less of a target.

Encourage your friends and family to do the same. Walk with them.

If you're driving to a discount retailer to save a few bucks, take a closer look at independent retailers. Avoid the temptation to save a few bucks at Lowe's. You'll improve the local economy, get personal attention, and you might even make a friend.

Buy a house. It's the best investment you will ever make. Don't delay buying a house because the brand monster's captured your attention with a plasma screen or a fancy car. Save your money. Buy the house.

Get involved in your community. The world belongs to people who pay attention and show up. Visit a neighbor (visiting neighbors is down from 50-plus percent in the 1950s to under 30 percent today). Rather than spending the evening watching television, spend the evening with people who live nearby.

Think twice about settling in a place where more than about fifty thousand people live—unless you're cultivating an urban lifestyle. Think twice about living in a place without a central Main Street or a downtown designed for walking.

For every ten minutes of additional commuting time, there's 10 percent less community involvement. People who are likely to move within the next five years are less likely to become involved in church, clubs, or community projects. Don't add to congestion and lack of involvement by moving far away.[12]

When it's time to sell, don't immediately head for branded help from Century 21 or RE/MAX; a small local Realtor may possess more experience and a wider network of local contacts. All Realtors have access to the same multiple listings; you need not work with a nationally branded broker.

At least once a year, spend a full week someplace you've never been, someplace that will help you see the world through different eyes. (Resorts and cruises don't count.) If you're confident, travel solo. You will spend more time exploring and less time in tourist attractions.

In addition to online activism, get together with real people who share your interests. You'll find the offline version of people to be multifaceted, and you'll rarely feel the need to apologize for an off-topic comment. Face-to-face conversations are *always* richer and more satisfying than conversations typed into a computer.

Make noise if you sense something is wrong.

Get involved with a good fight. Choose an environmental group (as do four per one hundred adults). Help get a candidate elected. Participate in a protest and help to change a bad law or to establish a new one.

When you sense the government is making the wrong decision, visit your local legislator, in person, in his or her office. Make sure you know how he or she is voting. Share what you've learned with others who live nearby (e-mail and the web are ideal for this type of informational activism). If the legislator does something good, let everyone know. If you don't understand, ask questions and share the answers.

If you can pay for it with cash (and you're not sacrificing valuable buyer's protection), do so. Use your (one) credit card when it makes practical or financial sense to do so.

Find a more productive way to occupy your time than shopping. Volunteer to help others; they can use your help. Helping will cost you less money and will make you happier in the long run.

Consciously move toward nonmaterialistic satisfaction. Teach yourself to relate happiness with something more meaningful than product purchases. Consider the balance between earning progressively more money and owning progressively more of your time and sanity.

Give part of what you earn to a charity or two. Learn about them. Participate. Care. You'll feel great. Right now, about a nickel out of every one hundred dollars earned goes to charity. In 1932, during the depths of the Depression, it was fifteen cents.

Before you watch television, decide what you want to watch, and for how long you will watch. Limit yourself to two hours of television per day. Don't just watch TV because you have nothing better to do. (Find something better to do.)

Celebrate Small Victories

You can reward yourself for each of these achievements, but you might want to simply enjoy them for the sake of having achieved them. Once again, feel free to customize the list:

• Saved fifty dollars because I didn't buy soda or cigarettes this week.

• Instead of going to Burger King, I prepared a meal of fresh vegetables and fresh bakery bread.

• Instead of driving a mile today, I walked a mile.

• Instead of watching TV for an hour tonight, I read a book.

• Instead of watching TV for an hour tonight, I started writing a book (even better!).

• By replacing breakfast cereal with fresh fruit, I lost four pounds this month.

Why Bother?

Is any of this really worth the time?

All of life is not a marketplace; this is not a one-for-one trade.

If you do these things, you will probably lose weight and keep it off; you will feel physically better; you will save money; you will help the local economy; you will be exposed to fewer media and marketing messages; you will cause less damage to the environment; you will know your neighbors better, and they will know you; you will know people who make decisions, and affect them; you will make friends and deepen relationships, and you will help others. And you will break the pattern of addiction to the brand monsters.

In short, it's worth the *time* to drive (or bike) to the next town to a small bookstore. Your modest action will help to keep that bookstore in business.

It's worth the *trouble* to prepare a fresh meal with nutritious ingredients; your family will be healthier and your children will learn the right lessons. It's worth the *expense* to help pay for a new football scoreboard, rather than allowing Pepsi to build market penetration among your high school students. What's more:

You may surprise yourself with your impact and your interest.

You will likely affect other people.

If you don't say or do something, who will?

Please Be Straight with Us

Scott Bruce and Bill Crawford, authors of *Cerealizing America: The Unsweetened Story of American Breakfast Cereal,* tell a funny story you may have heard before. An adman takes two coins out of his pocket. The coins are identical. He explains that his job is to convince you that one coin is better than the other.

Same authors, same book: "General Mills opened sales meetings in the 1940s with a blind taste test. Unmarked bowls of Wheaties and other rival whole-wheat cereals ... were placed in front of every salesman. ... Time after time, year after year, they couldn't tell the difference. ... Wheaties was a child of advertising."

Same idea, different experts: Suspecting there was no meaningful difference between cola drinks, a thirteen-year-old researcher asked peers to first state a taste preference for either Coke, Pepsi, or a nonadvertised store brand. She then conducted a blind test to see whether her peers could identify their favorites. No surprise: 73 percent could not identify their favorite sodas.

If one product is no better than another, then it's all just hocus-pocus. Since our health and our money are at stake, it would be comforting to believe that someone is keeping an eye on all of this, that we are not being bamboozled into buying products based upon hype alone. If nobody is watching out for us, then we need to watch out for ourselves. Sadly, it has become clear that, much of the time, nobody is watching out for us.

If pharmaceutical companies are going to advertise directly to consumers, then they should be required to educate consumers and to tell the truth about the relative effectiveness of the advertised drugs. If an expensive, heavily advertised drug doesn't dramatically improve upon the effectiveness of less costly alternatives, or upon treatments not based upon drugs at all, they ought to be required to tell us so.

As the branded television judge Judy Sheindlin reminds us, "Don't Pee on My Leg and Tell Me It's Raining."

Working Together

To make significant changes, we need to work together. We need to speak out and make our opinions clear to the legislators who are paid to represent our interests. We need to use the Internet to build communities that stop unfair practices or unethical behavior.

Can an individual's bake sale alter the results of a presidential election? Ask Moveon.org, a Web-enabled organization that started in 2001 with nothing but a petition. It has emphasized local community activities like bake sales to bring people together, and it has also learned to use the Web to keep its growing community informed. When the House of Representatives considered a major cutback in public television and radio funding, moveon. org mustered a million petition signatures in less than two weeks!

We need to lead corporations toward better solutions, as company managers and executives, as employees, as customers, and as forward-thinking entrepreneurs who understand that there's often a better way.

Keeping in Touch with Legislators

When you send an e-mail to a legislator, it may or may not be opened, logged, or read. When you send paper mail to a legislator, it is more likely to be logged and placed in a folder of mail that nobody besides an assistant finds the time to read. When you visit a legislator in his or her office in the capitol, you may get only five or ten minutes, but you will get your time and you will be able to state your case directly to the person who makes the laws. You can, in fact, visit any legislator at any time, and you can maintain constant contact with their staff members. They are paid to serve you. When you visit a legislator with a group of concerned citizens, you do so repeatedly, and you make sure to visit other influential legislators, your voice will be heard. Reinforce your ideas with petitions, a Web site, and some news coverage, and impact will be multiplied. Most individuals don't take the time to do any of this. Most large corporations employ a staff of people (often former legislators) to do nothing but this, day after day after day. To add spice, the corporate lobbyists have other resources at their disposal: money, favors, campaign finance, influence, and so on. Who wins? We can, but only if we become activists.

One way to spark this activism is to keep track of every vote by every legislator. Imagine how the re-election process would change if every candidate's voting record was published, and explained with context, online.

Imagine how this impact might be magnified if the news media could be trained to rely upon this database for information about voting records, campaign contributors, business relationships, and personal history. Since reporters are busy people, and this approach can make their jobs easier, this type of "database activism" could become a standard news source.

Distributing Information via Technology

Corporations have never been larger or more powerful, but we've never had so much information available, and we've never before possessed the technology to instantly compare notes on a massive, global scale.

The Web is one of the worst things that could have happened to automotive retailing. Now, thanks to www.edmunds.com and similar sites, when a customer visits a dealership, he or she knows that most people paid about $19,300 for the 2004 Honda CR-V LX AWD four-door SUV with side airbags. When there's a potential repair or safety issue, the customer knows this, too. If a car's a clunker, a connected community will soon have the power to force the company to either fix the problem or pull the car off the market.

We've only begun to understand the power of a totally connected consumer society. If you're taking a particular medication and experiencing headaches or loss of memory, and I am, too, then we can ask other people whether they're experiencing similar symptoms. Wouldn't it be great to have a message board for every prescription drug, just to compare notes with others? (And wouldn't it be nice to know how much they paid, and where in the world they live?) Maybe pharmaceutical companies should be required to provide this service, and to publish their research reports so that everyone involved knows all there is to know?

And more ...

In the bewildering maze of global conglomerates, opaque government agencies, multibillion-dollar marketing budgets, and impenetrable corporate hierarchies, it's tough to believe that even groups of individuals can make a difference. Are we really going to be capable of causing computer hardware manufacturers to safely dispose of their exhausted equipment? (Ask Dell or HP, both of which now demonstrate corporate responsibility by doing just that; for more, visit www.computertakeback.com/.) Can we get the car companies to do the same thing?

We must acknowledge scale of the obesity problem. We must teach people to understand the human suffering and to recognize the enormous current and future costs associated with obesity. We must learn to resist the seductive argument that people do this to themselves.[13] How can the Web be used to teach people about obesity? Can we create a massive database that contains easily accessible information about every food we eat? Have a look at Wikipedia, an online encyclopedia with articles on every conceivable topic. It's written not by scholars, but by users. Can elementary and high school education help to educate the next generation eliminate obesity? In an era where MADD has made such a difference in changing our perception of drunk driving, the answer may be "yes."

One of the big concerns today is the growth of global corporations and the lack of coordinated international rules to guide their behavior. Once again, it may be the Internet that plays a role in connecting interested, concerned citizens. Right now, it's difficult to understand just how quickly Wal-Mart or McDonald's or Starbucks or Home Depot is growing. A coordinated global map could easily track each company's progress. Each company's local practices, pricing, and policies can be tracked locally, and communicated globally. As global citizens see trends that are discomforting, the evidence can and should be used to prompt coordinated multigovernment action. If employees of global companies are encouraged to communicate, perhaps with a promise of confidentiality and anonymity (with or without company permission), international regulators would gain insight into an often opaque corporate world.

A Simple Plan to Save the World

One especially well-informed citizen is economist Jeffrey Sachs. After I read his May 2004 *Esquire* magazine article, I was inspired to republish some of his ideas and to add some of my own.[14]

- Beyond any single religion, we will need global ethics.
- Telling the truth is wiser than lying or hiding the truth.
- The real struggle is living together on an increasingly crowded planet.
- Our natural bounty is vast, but we are wrecking it nevertheless.
- We should demand much more from corporations and from the super-rich.
- If we lead, Washington and the world will follow.

(Or Not)

When my wife's father died from causes related to tobacco addiction, we grieved. We assembled in his memory, but not in protest of the products that were sold to him or a government that knew the products to be deadly but allowed them to be sold anyway. We did not reach out to the press. We did not contact our congressman and tell him to put an end to cigarette companies. We let his memory pass in silence.

I think we made a mistake.

And when I read this final page to my wife, she said, "My father would be *appalled* if he knew you wrote that!" Right before he died, she asked him whether he had any regrets about smoking. He said, "No, if I had it to do all over again, I would have done exactly the same thing."

Endnotes

1   "My Beef with Big Media," by Ted Turner, *Washington Monthly*, July/August 2004.

2   "As Jingle Plays, Resistance Is Futile," *The New York Times*, June 23, 2004.

3   In Sweden, Norway, and Finland, advertising to children under age twelve is not permitted, but these laws are unusual. Most countries do not protect their children in this manner.

4   *Food Fight: The Inside Story of the Food Industry, America's Obesity Crisis, and What We Can Do About It* by Kelly Brownell, PhD, p. 97.

5   Currently, one in five American households is Hispanic. The growth of the U.S. Hispanic population is three times the growth of the general U.S. population. (http://www.census.gov/Press-Release/www/releases/archives/population/005164.html)

6   I'll leave it to language experts to determine whether students should learn Mandarin or another Chinese dialect.

7   Now owned by Lenovo, a Chinese firm.

8   *A Consumer's Republic: The Politics of Mass Consumption in Postwar America* by Lizabeth Cohen, p. 360.

9   http://www.madd.org/aboutus/0,1056,1686,00.html

10   *Affluenza: The All-Consuming Epidemic* by John De Graaf, David Wann, and Thomas Naylor, p. 64.

11   "The French Fry That Will Save Your Life," by Ann Patchett, *The New York Times*, June 11, 2000.

12   *Bowling Alone: The Collapse and Revival of American Community* by Robert Putnam, p. 213.

13   *Food Fight: The Inside Story of the Food Industry, America's Obesity Crisis, and What We Can Do About It* by Kelly D. Brownell, PhD, p. 18+.

14   In fact, this should be the intent of copyright law: to provide reasonable protection of intellectual property while encouraging others to add their own ideas.

FINAL THOUGHTS

It's a sunny late summer day in September. Apart from a few fact checks, I finished the manuscript today. I woke up early and followed my wife and younger son to a parade celebrating the success of our town's Little League teams. Hundreds of people showed up, including our congressman and our governor. The governor made a short speech, then spent more than an hour autographing free baseballs for anybody who wanted one. He listened to concerns about relief for Hurricane Katrina victims, but mostly he was there to celebrate our hometown team's near-win of the Little League World Series.

On that perfect morning, nobody was obese or smoking heavily. Nobody was racing off to shop for a new SUV or the latest Sony Playstation. We were there for the kids, and for each other. Two local financial institutions helped make the event a success: UBS, which provided a hospitality tent, and Commerce Bank, which provided hundreds of free baseballs. Both contributed money to local baseball. The focus was on the kids, who tried not to look bored during the local politicians' speeches and seemed to take the newfound fame in stride.

In the afternoon, my son played his first solo on euphonium with a full band behind him. He got through it without mishap and was proud. A hundred people whom he had never met applauded. That made his parents proud enough to produce tears.

That night, we were invited to an American Legion installation dinner. A good-hearted community member was taking charge as the new post commander. Fresh from my writing of this book, I counted the number of American cars in the parking lot, and found only a handful of cars with European or Japanese badges. My wife warned me to keep my research to myself. Inside, there were people who loved their country, who had fought for their country, who had seen friends die for their country. There were American flags, and it felt good to be around them. There were veterans who had dedicated many hours to finding and honoring POWs and MIAs, and it felt good to be around them, too.

It was a special day, and not just because I had finished a tough manuscript. It felt good because it was a day spent in the real world, the place where people matter more than brands, where kids make parents proud, where people believe in their country, with all of its blemishes. And maybe that's the whole point: What we've got going here is pretty great, and it drives me crazy to see it so roundly abused.

BIBLIOGRAPHY/
RECOMMENDED READING

The following books and articles were used in the development of *Branded for Life*. The author is grateful to the many writers, scientists, economists, social critics, and others who provided useful background information, ideas, ways of thinking, examples, and illumination.

Books

A Branded World by Michael Levine.

A Consumer's Republic: The Politics of Mass Consumption in Post-War America by Lizabeth Cohen.

Admiral of the Ocean Sea: A Life of Christopher Columbus by Samuel Eliot Morrison.

Affluenza: The All-Consuming Epidemic by John DeGraaf, David Wann, and Thomas Naylor.

Ashes to Ashes: America's Hundred Year Cigarette War by Richard Kluger.

Asphalt Nation: How the Automobile Took Over America and How We Can Take It Back by Jane Holtz Kay.

Bowling Alone: The Collapse and Revival of American Community by Robert Putnam.

Breaking the News: How the Media Undermines American Democracy by James Fallows.

Buy Now Pay Later by Hillel Black.

Chain Stores in America 1859–1962, Godfrey M. Lebher, editor.

Consuming Kids: Protecting Our Children from the Onslaught of Marketing & Advertising by Susan Linn.

Culture Jam: The Uncooling of America by Kalle Lasn.

Downtown: Its Rise and Fall by Robert Fogelson.

Drink: A Social History of America by Andrew Bass.

Drinking in America: A History by Mark Edward.

Fat Land: How Americans Became the Fattest People in the World by Greg Critser.

Financing the American Dream: A Cultural History of Consumer Credit by Lendol Calder.

Food and Drink in America by Richard J. Hooker.

Food Fight: The Inside Story of the Food Industry, America's Obesity Crisis, and What We Can Do About It by Kelly D. Brownell, PhD.

Food Politics: How the Food Industry Influences Nutrition and Health by Marion Nestle.

Global Spin: The Corporate Assault on Environmentalism by Sharon Beder.

I Want That!: How We All Became Shoppers by Thomas Hine.

Let the Trumpets Sound: The Life of Martin Luther King by Stephen B. Oates.

Merry Christmas: Celebrating America's Greatest Holiday by Karal Ann Marling.

Much Depends on Dinner by Margaret Visser.

No Foreign Food: The American Diet in Time and Place by Richard Pillsbury.

Not Like Us: How Europeans Loved, Hated, and Transformed American Culture Since World War II by Richard Pells.

On Target: How the World's Hottest Retailer Hit a Bull's Eye by Laura Rowley.

Overdosed America: The Broken Promise of American Medicine by John Abramson.

Paradox of Plenty: A Social History of Eating in Modern America by Harvey Lowenstein.

Pour Your Heart into It: How Starbucks Built a Company One Cup at a Time by Howard Schultz.

Profit Over People by Noam Chomsky.

Protecting America's Health: The FDA, Business, and One Hundred Years of Regulation by Philip Hilts.

Revolution at the Table by Harvey Levenstein.

Snake Oil, Hustlers and Hambones: The Great American Medicine Show by Ann Anderson.

Soap Opera: The Inside Story of Procter & Gamble by Alecia Swasy.

Spoiled: The Dangerous Truth About a Food Chain Gone Wild by Nicols Fox.

Sundae Best: A History of Soda Fountains by Anne Cooper Funderburg.

Tastes of Paradise by Wolfgang Schivelbusch.

The Age of Missing Information by Bill McKibben.

The All-Consuming Century: Why Commercialism Won in Modern America by Gary Cross.

The Consumer's Guide to Effective Environmental Choices by Michael Brower and Warren Leon.

The Credit Card Industry: A History by Lewis Mandell.

The Culting of Brands by Douglas Allen.

The Emperors of Chocolate: Inside the Secret World of Hershey's and Mars by Joël Glenn Brenner.

The Empire of Tea: The Remarkable History of the Plant That Took Over the World by Alan and Iris MacFarlane.

The Fall of Advertising and the Rise of PR by Al Ries and Laura Ries.

The Real State of the Union: From the Best Minds in America, Bold Solutions to the Problems Politicians Dare Not Address Todd Halstead, editor.

The Real Thing: Truth and Power at the Coca-Cola Company by Constance L. Hayes.

The Truth About the Drug Companies: How They Deceive Us and What to Do About It by Marcia Angell.

Tobacco: A Cultural History of How an Exotic Plant Seduced Civilization by Iain Gately.

Whose America?: Culture Wars in the Public Schools by Jonathan Zimmerman.

Why We Buy: The Science of Shopping by Paco Underhill.

Why We Shop: Emotional Rewards and Retail Strategies by Jim Poder.

WTO: Whose Trade Organization by Lori Wallach and Patrick Woodall.

You Are Being Lied To, Russ Kick, editor.

Pamphlets, Presentations, Papers

US International Travel and Transportation Trends, U.S. Department of Transportation, Bureau of Transportation Statistics, 2002.

"America, the World, and the New Challenges for Global Brands," NOP World (PowerPoint presentation).

"Hidden Cost of Wal-Mart Jobs: Use of Safety Net Programs," UC Berkeley Center Briefing Paper Series, by Arindrajit Dube and Ken Jacobs, 2004.

Articles

"2 PC Makers Favor Bigger Recycling Roles," *The New York Times,* May 19, 2004.

"A Brand New You," by W. Eric Martin, *Psychology Today,* September-October, 2003.

"A Is for Alpha, C Is for Christ," *Brand Strategy,* October, 2003.

"A Simple Plan to Save the World," by Jeffrey Sachs, *Esquire,* May, 2004.

"Also Starring (your product name here)," *USA Today,* August 12, 2004.

"Are Brands a Force for Good?" *Brand Strategy,* June 2004.

"Are Countries Brands?" by Chris Powell, *Advertising Age Global,* December 2001.

"As Jingle Plays, Resistance Is Futile," *The New York Times,* June 23, 2004.

"At $2 a Gallon, Gas Is Still Worth Guzzling," *The New York Times,* May 16, 2004.

"Big and Bad—How the SUV Ran Over Automotive Safety," *New Yorker,* January 12, 2004.

"Brand America," by Janet Guyon, *Fortune,* October 27, 2003.

"Brand Name Field Trips," by Lisa Takeuchi Cullen, *Time,* June 28, 2004.

"Brand Synthesis: The Multidimensionality of Brand Knowledge," by Kevin Lane Keller,

Journal of Consumer Research, March 2003.

"Branding Stereotypes," *Brand Strategies*, November 2003.

"Building Brand America," *Business Week*, December 10, 2001.

"California on Path to Becoming Nation's Gambling Capital," *The Los Angeles Times*, August 25, 2004.

"Coherence or Confusion: The Future of the Global Anti-Trust Conversation," by John Shenefield, *Anti-Trust Bulletin*, Spring–Summer 2004.

"Coke's Sinful World," by Paul Klebnikov, *Forbes*, December 22, 2003.

"Consumers and Their Brands: Developing Relationship Theory in Consumer Research," by Susan Fournier, *Journal of Consumer Research*, March 1998.

"Corporate Sponsorship of Philanthropic Activities: When Do They Impact Perception of Consumer Brands?" by Satya Menon, *Journal of Consumer Psychology*, Vol. 13, Issue 3.

"Country of Origin: Does It Matter?" *Total Quality Management*, March 2001.

"Crazy Horse Liquor Apologizes," Associated Press, April 27, 2001.

"Credit Cards Entice Users with More Cash," *USA Today*, August 12, 2004.

"Damn Americans," by Jim Edwards, *Brandweek*, May 17, 2004.

"Does Brand Name Imprinting in Memory Increase Brand Information Retention?" by William E. Baker, *Psychology and Marketing*, Vol. 120 (12), December 2003.

"Effects of Brand Local and Nonlocal Origin on Consumer Attitudes in Developing Countries," Rajeev Batra, Venkatram Ramaswamy, Jan-Benedict Steenkamp, S. Ramachander, *Journal of Consumer Psychology*, 2000, Vol. 9, Issue 2, p. 83.

"Faith of Our Fathers," by Jay Tolson, *U.S. News & World Report*, June 28, 2004.

"Finding Strategic Corporate Citizenship: A New Game Theoretic View," *Harvard Law Review*, Vol. 117, Issue 6, pp. 1957–1980.

"Flunking Lunch," *The New York Times*, March 7, 2003.

"Get out of My Namespace," by James Gleick, *The New York Times Magazine*, March 21, 2004.

"Girls Gone Wild: Milking It," by Abram Sauer, *Brandchannel*, May 3, 2004 (http://www.brandchannel.com/features_profile.asp?pr_id=178).

"Goodies in Small Packages Prove to Be Big Hit," *The New York Times*, May 30, 2005.

"How Advertising Affects Consumers," by William M. Weilbacher, *Journal of Advertising Research*, June 2003, Vol. 43, Issue 2.

"How Brand Names Are Special: Brands, Words, and Hemispheres," by Possidonia Gontijo, *Brain and Language*, September 2002.

"Impact of Television Viewing Patterns on Fruit and Vegetable Consumption Among Adolescents," by Renee Boynton-Jarrett and others, *American Academy of Pediatrics*, 2003: 112.

"Impressionable Minds, Indelible Images," by Robin Kramer, *Clearing House,* July–August 2003.

"Kidnapping," *Fortune,* February 2, 2004.

"Kids' Likes and Dislikes," *Brand Strategy*, July–August 2004.

"Listening to the Climate Models and Trying to Wake up the World," *The New York Times,* December 16, 2003.

"Mad Cow Overshadowing Other Food-Borne Illnesses," by Allison Young, *Philadelphia Inquirer,* January 5, 2004.

"Miracle in a Bottle," *New Yorker,* February 2, 2004.

"My Beef with Big Media," by Ted Turner, *Washington Monthly*, July–August 2004.

"Nalgene Outdoor Venturing," by Jared Salter, *Brandchannel,* February 21, 2005.

"New Sports Trend: The Team Doctors Now Play the Team," *The New York Times*, May 18, 2004.

"Now a Message from a Sponsor of the Subway: Transit Agency Weighs Sale of Naming Rights," *The New York Times*, July 27, 2004.

"Nutrition Policy in the 1990s," by Stephen R. Crutchfield and Jon Weimer, *Food Review,* September 2000.

"Personality & Values-Based Materialism: Their Relationship and Origins," by Aaron C. Ahuvia and Nancy Wong, *Journal of Consumer Psychology*, 12 (4).

"Predictors of Behavioral Loyalty Among Hikers on the Appalachian Trail," Gerard Kyle, Alan Graefe, Robert Manning, James Bacon; *Leisure Sciences*, Volume 26, Number 1 / January–March 2004.

"Public Gives Ideas to Update Food Pyramid," *The New York Times,* July 31, 2004.

"Really MADD: Looking Back at 20 Years," *Driven,* Spring 2000.

"Ronald Reagan's Role of a Lifetime," *Television Week,* June 14, 2004.

"Ruffles Award Parents Who Find Baby a Chip off the Old Block," *Brandweek,* March 22, 2004.

"Schools Debate Slave-Era Names," by Steve Szkotak, *Associated Press,* December 21, 2003.

"Seeing the World on Ten Coffees a Day," by Daniel Roth, *Fortune*, July 12, 2004.

"Should We Admire Wal-Mart?" by Jerry Useem, *Fortune*, March 8, 2004.

"Sin: Category TV Ads on the Rise," *Television Week,* June, 2004.

"Study: Low Wal-Mart Wages Cost California $86 Million," *Reuters*, August 3, 2004.

"Teva: Making Tracks," by Diane O'Brien, *Brandchannel,* September 1, 2003 (http://www.brandchannel.com/features_profile.asp?pr_id=142).

"The Corporation: The Pathological Pursuit of Profit and Power," *Future Survey,* June 2004.

"The Cow Jumped over the U.S.D.A." by Eric Schlosser, *The New York Times*, January 2, 2004.

"The Dangers of Media Mergers," *Business Week*, July 12, 2004.

"The Ethicist: The Prosecution Rests," *The New York Times Magazine*, May 23, 2004.

"The French Fry That Will Save Your Life," by Ann Patchett, *The New York Times Magazine*, June 11, 2000.

"The Italian Blob," *Financial Times Magazine*, April 15, 2005.

"The Land of the Bland," by Michael Houston, *Canadian Business*, June 7, 2004.

"The Meaning of Brand Names to Children: An Developmental Investigation," by Gwen Bachman Achenreiner, *Journal of Consumer Psychology*, Vol. 13, Issue 3, 2003.

"The One and Only M. Night Shyamalan," *Philadelphia Inquirer*, July 25, 2004.

"The Squabbling Illini: Rallying Cries Lead to Rift," *The New York Times*, December 16, 2003.

"The Tug of the Newfangled Slot Machines," *The New York Times Magazine*, May 9, 2004.

"The Tyranny of Copyright," by Robert S. Boynton, *The New York Times Magazine*, January 25, 2004.

"Tobacco Regulation: It's No Pipe Dream," by John Carey, *Business Week*, January 12, 2004.

"Trademarking Senses and Sensibility," by Randall Frost, *Brandchannel*, April 26, 2004 (http://www.brandchannel.com/features_effect.asp?pf_id=207).

"Turning Sour Grapes into a Silk Purse," *The New York Times Magazine*, June 6, 2004.

"TV's Toll on Young Minds and Bodies," by Jane Brody, *The New York Times*, August 3, 2004.

"Winnebagos, Cherokees, Apaches, and Dakotas: The Persistence of Stereotyping of American Indians in American Advertising Brands," by Debra Merskin, *Howard Journal of Communications*, 2001, Volume 12.

Other

Fortune magazine, 2003, 2004, and 2005 *Fortune 500* special issues.

Books of Interest

The Creative Professional:
A Survival Guide for the Business World
By Howard J. Blumenthal

Finally, a business book to help right-brained people survive in a left-brained world.

Your unconventional approach makes you a valuable player at work, but sometimes the very traits that give you that creative edge can cause turbulence in a corporate atmosphere. *The Creative Professional: A Survival Guide for the Business World* shows you how to recognize opportunities to excel *and* get the system to reward you and respect your work.

The Creative Professional covers all the important issues:
- How you can best manage your time, space, tools, and life
- The pros and cons of freelancing versus working for a company
- Ways to successfully collaborate with different work styles and philosophies
- Intellectual property and copyright law, and other laws affecting creative work
- Strategies for getting ahead and being happy in the corporate world

The Creative Professional will help you navigate the professional world, deal with corporate drones, and get paid—all while maintaining your individuality and doing satisfying work. Believe it or not, it's possible to succeed in business without sacrificing your mojo!

ISBN: 1-57860-245-9
Price: $14.95 Paperback

Available at local and online booksellers, or at www.emmisbooks.com
Emmis Books, 1700 Madison Road, Cincinnati, OH 45230